Local Government
and Politics in
UGANDA

Local Government and Politics in

U G A N D A

FRED G. BURKE

Syracuse University Press   1964

967.61
B959L

141585

Manufactured in the United States of America.

Composition and press work by The Heffernan Press
of Worcester, Massachusetts; binding by Vail-Ballou
Press of Binghamton, New York.

To Fritzi
An Unanticipated Bonus

Foreword

Social scientists concerned with the study and analysis of sociopolitical phenomena in rapidly changing tropical Africa are faced with the dilemma of interrelating and contrasting radically different institutions and behavior.

Lloyd Fallers, one-time director of the East African Institute of Social Research, was among the first to wrestle with this problem. He spoke for many when he asked ("Africa: Scholarship and Policy," in *World Politics,* January, 1957):

> What, in this situation, is to be the unit of study? What, indeed, is the "real" unit, the unit which "matters"? Is it the tribe, because the colonial territory is simply an artificial boundary enclosing a congeries of people who feel no mutual loyalty or kinship, held together only by the superior force of a European power? Or is it in fact the colonial territory, because the tribes are too small and their institutions too foreign to the nation-state pattern to have a future. . . .

This study is the product of a long interest in Africa combined with an even longer concern with the study of local government and politics. It would appear that there is under way a quickening interest in the study of political behavior and institutions in a context both less and more extensive than the nation-state. On the one hand the obvious trend toward transnational association in our time requires that increased attention be directed toward the study and analysis of international organization and politics. It is also possible to discern a revived concern with the locality and community, which in part is a product of the social scientist's contemporary emphasis on "behavior." But of major importance to this work is the renaissance of interest in the locality resulting from a quickening of interest in non-Western social and political institutions and behavior.

A classical approach to the study of local government and politics in Uganda likely would have emphasized the legal aspects of local government institutions within an over-all context of the politics and government of the nation-state system. On the other hand, a primary concern with tribal and other segmental associations to the relative exclusion of modern local political and governmental organization would have failed to take into account the extraordinary significance of social and political transition. It was with this dilemma in mind that I have attempted, through the use of a structural functional comparative method, logically to encompass traditional transitional and

modern institutions and behavior. The method developed for this purpose—because it is regarded primarily as a device and aid to research
and analysis—is not described in detail in the body of this work; but
for those who, like myself, regard methodology as critical to social
science inquiry, it is included in an abbreviated form in the Appendix.

My interest in local government and in the development of a relative comparative methodology was stimulated in 1954 while working
with Professor John Sly as a research associate in the Princeton Surveys. His initial encouragement, assistance, and sustained interest in
the research underlying this study have contributed far more than he
possibly realizes. Much of the material and supporting methodology
were developed at Oxford University in 1955 and in Uganda in 1956
and 1957. Opportunity was had to return to Uganda in 1961 and
most recently in 1962-63.

Over this seven-year period thousands of Ugandans have contributed (albeit upon occasion unwittingly) to this work. A debt of
gratitude is owed to these people not only for permitting an inquiring foreigner to observe the extraordinary changes under way in their
country, but also for a willingness to take time to talk about these
events.

I am particularly indebted to the people of Bunyoro, Bukedi and
Teso who, because this inquiry focused on them, were asked more
questions and visited for more extended periods. More than five hundred chiefs, councillors and local government officials in these three
districts took time and cared enough to supply me with detailed data—
and to them a great deal is owed.

The caliber and obvious dedication of ministers and officials—at
first British and more recently Ugandan, particularly impressed me.
Their patient willingness to direct the inquiring scholar to source
materials and to give freely and frequently of their knowledge and
experience, has changed little since independence.

The East African Institute of Social Research not only graciously
made available necessary amenities, such as housing and research
equipment, but also provided an academic environment wherein ideas
and techniques were stimulated and freely exchanged. The guidance
and encouragement given by Dr. Lloyd Fallers and Dr. Aidan Southall,
past directors of the East African Institute of Social Research during
the initial stages of research, were invaluable.

Responsibility for the initial development of local government in
Uganda, in the last analysis, rests upon the shoulders of the District
Officers (African and expatriate). It was they who welcomed the
author into their districts, opened their files and permitted him to
accompany them on numerous safaris. Three District Officers, John

Kaboha, Frank Kalimuzo and Edward Cunningham took an extraordinary interest in the research and in the process of assisting the author, sometimes complicating their own schedules.

The staff of Teso College graciously provided both encouragement and housing, while the enthusiastic assistance of the students made possible the village surveys.

Warden D. N. Chester, Professor K. Robinson and Mr. B. Keith-Lucas at Nuffield College, Oxford University, made numerous worthwhile suggestions on the research design and were kind enough to read and comment upon this manuscript. The Institute of Colonial (subsequently Commonwealth) Studies at Oxford, in addition to providing office space, provided library and staff resources. Both Mrs. S. Chilvers and Mrs. M. Holdsworth of the Institute of Colonial Studies were particularly helpful.

Lastly, I should like gratefully to acknowledge the assistance of my wife, Daphne, because she invariably had the last word, not only as to punctuation and spelling, but often on what was and was not relevant as well.

The most recent research in Uganda and assistance in the preparation of this book were made possible by the Cross Cultural Analysis Project of Syracuse University's Maxwell Graduate School of Citizenship and Public Affairs. Two Deans of the Maxwell School, Harlan Cleveland and more recently his successor, Stephen K. Bailey, provided encouragement, assistance and advice.

Although it is in no way responsible for the substance of this study, this opportunity is taken to acknowledge the assistance of the Ford Foundation without whose aid the first stages of the supporting research would not have been possible. The errors in fact, which it is hoped are few, are of course solely my responsibility. Errors in judgment are something about which reasonable men are entitled to differ. Even so, let us hope the differences are few and minor.

FRED G. BURKE

Syracuse, New York
December, 1963

Contents

Tables

Figures

CHAPTER ONE

Introduction

Great Britain sought, particularly after World War II, to develop in its African territories a democratic system of local government based upon the English model. In Uganda, this program was seen as requisite to a viable independent and democratic nation-state. However, Uganda is not one nation but rather is composed of a complex of tribal nations, each possessed of its own peculiar culture and form of traditional political organization.

In most instances the modern local government areas coincide with tribal segments which, for historical and social reasons, are not always regarded by the people as "local authorities" according to the English model. In other areas of Uganda, however, the local government unit encompasses a number of small and antagonistic tribal groups. Although the English system of local government is being developed uniformly throughout Uganda, the problems encountered in implementing the system vary from one district to another.

Struggles for independence, negotiations leading up to self-government, as well as the subsequent emphasis upon nation-building and international relations, have tended to focus scholarly attention upon the capital city, central government institutions, and leading national personalities of the new African states. It is not necessary to denigrate this focus to draw attention to the relatively few studies dealing directly with the critical relationship of the transition and development of local political institutions to the emergence of viable nation-states in Africa.

The men most familiar with the problems of local political development in Africa—the colonial service officers and local government officials in the field (both African and expatriate)—long appreciated the vital role that local political institutions would be required to play in preparation for independence and self-government. In 1947 the Secretary of State for the Colonies dispatched to the Governors of the British African territories a policy statement, the implications of which provide the major theme for this study.

> The key to success . . . of our achievements in the program of political, social and economic advances on which we have now embarked . . . lies in the development of an effective and democratic system of local government.[1]

The purpose of this work is to analyze the evolution of local political systems in Uganda, with particular emphasis upon the relationship of the process to the development of a Uganda nation. Aware of the immensity of the continent and of its extreme diversity, some might question the value, at this stage of knowledge of Africa, of a microscopic approach.[2]

Why should one concentrate on local institutions and behavior in a delimited region of Africa when ignorance is of continental proportions? In the long run, stable, viable, and more or less democratic African states will depend, in large measure, upon the effective employment of organizational forms and principles in hundreds and thousands of African localities. And it is to the locality that one first must look if he is to analyze and evaluate a people's capacity for or inclination toward democratic decision making. As events have indicated, a super-imposed replica of the American or British constitution does not guarantee political democracy.

Uganda's modern local governments are not evolving in the same social system as existed even a few decades ago, for the institutions and people of this new nation are undergoing rapid and differential alteration. New problems of locality order and integration are arising at a bewildering pace and though some old problems are disappearing, many still persist. It will be seen that some structures of some local political systems fail to provide channels capable of coping with the complexities of both modern and traditional problems. Such failures or dislocations in turn pose problems of major proportion for the nation as a whole.

In essence then, it is suggested that government at the local level consists of a number of organized procedures and roles designed to solve problems which stand in the way of achieving or maintaining locality order and integration. The way in which the local political system goes about its functions is conditioned in large part by the nature of the problems to which it must address itself, which in turn are largely a product of the locality's peculiar physical environment and social system, in conjunction with the demands of the external political system of which it is a constituent part.

The advent of independence and the conclusion of an era of colonial rule have radically altered and extended the society that Uganda's leaders would develop. The local governments not only are expected to direct their energies and resources to the solution of parochial threats to local order and integration, but more and more are required to contribute to national integration order and development. These new demands are severely challenging the local political systems that evolved predominantly in response to traditional and parochial needs.

In common with many former colonial territories, Uganda's major local government area—the district—also serves as the primary unit of central government administration. Uganda's fourteen districts can usefully be categorized into three general types:

1. Districts which coincide approximately with the former tribal kingdoms or amalgamations of former kingdoms.

2. Districts which coincide approximately with a recognized tribal unit which never possessed a centralized or highly specialized political system. In such districts the traditional political unit is of a small scale variety and rarely exercised authority over more than a lineage or localized clan.

3. Districts which are composed of two or more tribes whose traditional political systems in some instances approximate the first type and others the second. Districts of this nature are generally characterized by intra-tribal loyalty and inter-tribal conflict.

Before proceeding it is necessary to explain the basis on which the three areas chosen for intensive research were selected and the implications of the respective choices. In the case of type one, the study focuses on the problems of developing democratic local government and politics in a social system characterized by a tradition of autocratic centralization, and on the problems of integrating a former kingdom into a unified Uganda. The general problems faced in the second type are those inherent in institutionalizing a district-wide system of authority, by securing the consent and participation of a people possessed of a tradition of relative anarchy. The problems encountered in implementing a Western system of local government in a district composed of fundamentally differing tribes, each possessed of its unique social system and tradition, is encountered in the third type.

The traditional kingdom of Bunyoro-Kitara, now the administrative district of Bunyoro, was selected as representative of type one, Teso District coinciding generally with the region inhabited by the Iteso, Uganda's second largest tribe, is representative of type two, while Bukedi District in southeast Uganda, composed of a bewildering multitude of tribes and cultures, was chosen as characteristic of type three. (See Figure 1.)

Obviously one cannot generalize about all of Uganda on the basis of a study of only three districts. However, for the purposes of this study, the three districts selected are characteristic of the major types of local political systems in Uganda. Less intensive data and observations drawn from Uganda's other districts are employed wherever possible or desirable for purposes of contrast and illustration.

Uganda achieved its independence on October 9, 1962; in common with other African territories, this new nation is undergoing a period of rapid social, economic, and political change. The local government system currently being developed is designed to provide a means for

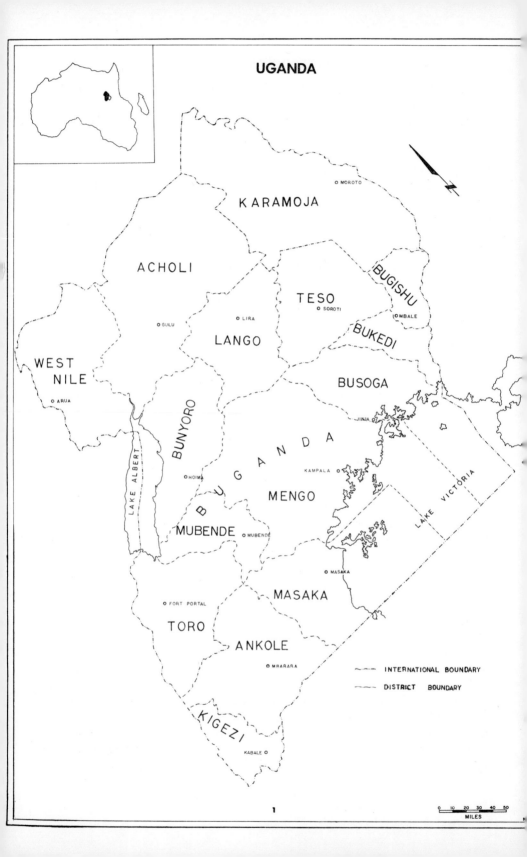

UGANDA

KARAMOJA

○ MOROTO

ACHOLI

BUGISHU

TESO

○ SOROTI

BUKEDI

○ MBALE

○ GULU

○ LIRA

LANGO

WEST
NILE

BUSOGA

○ ARUA

BUNYORO

JINJA

B U G A N D A

○ HOIMA

KAMPALA ○

MENGO

LAKE VICTORIA

LAKE ALBERT

MUBENDE

○ MUBENDE

○ MASAKA

MASAKA

○ FORT PORTAL

TORO

ANKOLE

○ MBARARA

INTERNATIONAL BOUNDARY

DISTRICT BOUNDARY

KIGEZI

KABALE ○

1

0 10 20 30 40 50
MILES

coping with new problems arising as a consequence of change. However, many traditional problems persist for which new political forms are frequently inappropriate. Under certain conditions, and in certain areas, the indigenous political systems continue to cope with traditional problems. However, in some regions, the traditional political systems have largely disappeared, and in still other areas, elements of the traditional system have been adapted to cope with new problems.

The rapidity and scope of change have been accompanied by the imposition of political structures with respect to problems which yet are unrecognized by the local inhabitants, by instances of disintegration and disorder, and by the informal evolution of political structures based upon both traditional and Western systems.

Uganda is a fairy tale. You climb up a railway instead of a bean-stalk, and at the end there is a wonderful new world. The scenery is different, the vegetation is different, the climate is different, and, most of all, the people are different from anything elsewhere to be seen in the whole range of Africa.

WINSTON CHURCHILL

CHAPTER TWO

Background to Uganda

In 1956 when the author made his initial visit, it appeared as if Uganda would be the first territory in British East Africa to be granted its independence. And the European population in the white highlands of neighboring Kenya and Tanganyika regarded Uganda's deliberate and rapid steps toward self-government with considerable anxiety, fearing the effect that an adjoining independent African country would have on their own political futures. However, to the surprise of many, Tanganyika won its freedom nearly a year before Uganda was granted independence, on December 9, 1961. The difficulty of integrating a complex of differing societies, traditions, and political systems into a unified independent state is primarily responsible for the delay; as there will be numerous occasions to note, this difficulty persists and poses a major obstacle to nation-building in Uganda.

An attempt has been made to present as balanced a background picture as possible, but the general description of Uganda and its people which follows is in no way meant to be complete. The purpose of this chapter is to draw particular attention to those facets of the physical and social environment which are particularly relevant to the evolution and functioning of government and politics at the local level.

GEOGRAPHY AND CLIMATE

Uganda is a land of lakes and marshes occupying nearly 100,000 square miles of the east central African plateau. Of this total area, however, approximately 14,000 square miles (14 per cent) consist of marshes and lakes. The River Nile, which has for centuries intrigued mankind, gathers its waters in Uganda—a part of the world about which relatively little was known until this century. Topographically, Uganda is fragmented by a maze of swamps and marshes flowing imperceptibly into small meandering streams which turn much of the country, for several months of the year, into semi-islands. This complex of streams and marshes in turn flows into larger streams and lakes, and eventually into the Nile.

6

George Homans once wrote that "landscape is the engraving of societies older than history."[1] Where it is thought relevant, variations in the landscape, and in the uses to which men have put the land which have affected the style and function of political organization, will be described and analyzed.

Considering its complex drainage system and great variations in altitude, it is not surprising that Uganda possesses a most varied climate. For example, the altitude averages about 4,000 feet but rises to nearly 17,000 feet in the Ruwenzori Mountains and falls to less than 2,000 feet in the Valley of the Albert Nile. The traditional social system is organized largely in terms of the primary problem of wresting from the earth the requisites of physical existence, while variations in climatic conditions significantly condition the types of problems the people must cope with in order to secure their livelihood.

There are three broad natural regions in Uganda. The northeast is the least fertile and most poorly watered part of the country. The seasons in this region are pronounced and though the countryside appears green and lush during the rains, it resembles the sand and scrub areas of Nevada and Arizona during the dry period.

Slightly more than half of Uganda's terrain is of the short grass savanna type and is characteristic of the northern part of the country with the exception of the desert scrub regions of the extreme northeast. It also dominates the landscape in the central part of the country as far south as the Kafu-Kyoga River system. People living in the savanna area practice a mixed agricultural and cattle herding economy.

The remainder of Uganda, which faces on Lake Victoria and extends south and west to the Congo border, is the most fertile and densely populated portion of the country. The dominant vegetation in this region is elephant grass and tree savanna with a rainfall ranging from forty-five to sixty inches. This area possesses some of the richest soil in East Africa which in conjunction with an even and adequate rainfall permits year-round cultivation. Uganda's ancient kingdom-states are located in this region.[2]

THE PEOPLE OF UGANDA

Uganda's population is slightly in excess of six and one-half million, but unlike the neighboring territories of Kenya and Tanganyika, does not possess a large European settler population. As will be noted, the absence of a permanent and sizable European minority has significantly affected Uganda's development and politics. The non-African population contributes less than 1.5 per cent of the total. The greater part of the 87,000 non-Africans consists of persons of Indo-Pakistani extraction. The European population is less than .2 per cent of the total.

TABLE 1

UGANDA POLITICAL DIVISIONS AND POPULATION (THOUSANDS)*

Province and District	Total Population	African Population	Land Area in Square Miles	Population Density Per Square Mile
Buganda Province	1,881	1,834	16,138	117
Mengo East	613	607	5,101	120
Mengo West	725	688	4,588	158
Masaka	444	440	3,781	117
Mubende	99	99	2,668	37
Eastern Province	1,903	1,873	10,971	173
Busoga	677	661	3,443	197
Mbale Township	14	8	9	937
Bukedi	400	398	1,575	253
Bugishu	353	353	1,638	215
Teso	458	453	4,306	106
Western Province	1,503	1,498	17,098	87
Bunyoro	129	128	4,723	27
Toro	349	347	4,745	74
Ankole	531	530	5,728	90
Kigezi	494	493	1,902	260
Northern Province	1,249	1,245	33,327	37
Acholi	287	286	10,783	27
Lango	354	353	4,464	79
Karamoja	172	171	12,216	14
West Nile, Madi	436	435	5,864	74
Total	6,536	6,450	77,534	

* In 1963 the provinces ceased to be official administrative units, but are still employed in the administration of services.

SOURCE: Uganda Protectorate, 1961 Statistical Abstract, East African Statistical Department.

The population averages 84 per square mile, but there are extraordinary variations in population density and distribution as can be seen in Table 1. Density running from a low of fourteen per square mile in Karamoja to a high of 260 in Kigezi (exclusive of Mbale Township) in conjunction with variable soil fertility and rainfall is a significant factor conditioning the constituent local political systems. For example, pressure on available land in some areas is so intense that political activity and organization tend to revolve about land tenure to the relative exclusion of other issues.

Settlement and migration patterns, as they affect the local political systems, are discussed in detail in Chapter Three. Here it will suffice to note that with few exceptions, the people of Uganda reside in scattered homesteads. The term "village" appears a number of times in this study; but it is important not to confuse the Uganda village with the compact concentration of homes which the term implies in the West. The village in Uganda is most often an area of scattered homesteads set off from similar concentrations by swamps, streams, forests, or uninhabited and fallow land. The major exceptions to this pattern are the relatively dense settlements which characterize the major towns and townships, a few fishing villages on Lakes Edward and George and, within the past decade, a number of African trading centers. Unlike parts of West Africa, there are no traditional cities in Uganda. Uganda's urban population (3.2 per cent) is among the lowest in Africa, and only 209,000 persons of all races live in the ninety-five gazetted towns; and of this total over one-third live in Kampala and Jinja, the two largest towns. The urban centers that do exist (five main towns with 10,000 or more population) tend either to be administrative or commercial centers, where the great bulk of the mercantile enterprise is in the hands of Asian merchants.

Although the density of Teso District, for example, is greater than one hundred people per square mile, it is possible to drive for miles through the countryside and, with the exception of local government public buildings, see few signs of domesticity. However, if one looks carefully along the side of the road, he will see frequent foot and bicycle paths leading into the bush. A five-minute walk along such a path usually leads to an enclosure where one might see four large and a number of smaller wattle huts, chickens, crying children and bleating goats. At the rear of the enclosure the path commences anew winding through fields of cassava and cotton until it reaches the next homestead. Where the terrain is level, as it is in much of Teso, the individual homesteads are rarely in view of one another. In Kigezi, however, where the density of population is more than double that of Teso and where the terrain consists of steep cultivated hillsides with homesteads clinging precariously to the slopes, a neighbor's house is generally visible and within shouting distance as well.

A scattered settlement pattern is not unique to Africa. The following description of the "tref" in thirteenth-century England could as well apply to present-day Teso or Bukedi. And there can be but little doubt that similar settlement patterns reflect comparable conditions.

Tref is not an isolated farm, neither is it a village, but something in between and consisted of about nine houses and could be said to be a hamlet and usually was a settlement which contained one plough and owned cattle in common (for Teso substitute "and herded cattle in common") . . . Such a unit was held together by economic bonds and kinship bonds . . . also descendents of a near and common ancestor . . . the tref settlement was the general rule in Brittany, Ireland, Scotland, Wales, and Cornwall.[3]

The towns of East Africa are essentially non-African institutions. In recent years, however, an increasing number of Africans are coming to regard the town as their home. This is particularly true in Kampala, Uganda's principal city and even more so in its extensive urban fringe. Two other towns, Mbale and Jinja, both in the Eastern Province, have also recently experienced rapid increases in their African populations. Kampala proper, in 1959, had a population of about 48,000, of which approximately one-half were Africans, 19,000 Indians, Pakistanis, and Goans, and 3,000 Europeans. Nearly surrounding Kampala, but lying outside the legal municipality, is Kibuga, a largely African urban area with a population in excess of 35,000. A study completed in 1955 by staff members of the East African Institute of Social Research estimated that the population of the "urban area as defined by ecological criteria, to be over 100,000."[4]

More important than the dispersal and density pattern of Uganda's population is its ethnic, tribal, and linguistic composition. On one occasion the author asked a young and educated member of a tribe in northern Uganda why the people in his small sub-district did not support amalgamation with the larger and adjoining West Nile District.[5] His reply is significant for it dramatizes the failure of the non-African to perceive and comprehend the significance of ethnological variation. To this query the Madi respondent replied, "We have nothing in common with the other tribes of West Nile than the color of our skin." That Uganda lies at one of the major crossroads of African migration is partially responsible for its unusual ethnological and linguistic diversity. The East African population census (1959) lists twenty-one main tribes with a population of sixty thousand or more while other sources claim as many as thirty-five.

Most anthropologists have classified the native population of Africa into Bantu, Nilotes, Half-Hamites, Hamites, and Negritos, though there is little agreement as to the criteria that should determine the category within which a given tribe should fall. More recently, a few scholars have sought to distinguish major tribal groupings on the basis of type of traditional political system.[6] Lloyd A. Fallers, who has explored this approach in considerable depth, concludes that, "The core feature of the complex is the institution of rulership."[7] The Bantu peoples of Uganda, in contrast to the Nilotes and Nilo-Hamites, traditionally tended to rule themselves through the institution of a centralized tribal-state. In such traditional kingdom-states as Buganda and Bunyoro, authority was exercised over the inhabitants of a circumscribed territory with relatively little reference to kinship. Although the ruling dynasty was ordinarily recruited on a kinship basis, e.g., a royal patrilineal descent group, there existed a relatively sharp distinction between political and non-political roles and functions.

The Nilotic and Nilo-Hamitic (half-Hamites) peoples on the other hand, tended more toward political organization on a much smaller, more diffuse and egalitarian scale. The unit of authority was generally an integral part of the kinship, or other segmentary system, and authority over people was determined not only according to shared territory, but on kinship and other non-spatial lines as well.

The peoples of Uganda are composed of numerous interspersed Bantu, Nilotic, and half-Hamitic peoples. The differences in culture and political organization of two neighboring tribes included within the same administrative district and local government area may be as pronounced as in societies separated by thousands of miles.

The Bantu tribes, which include the inhabitants of the four Uganda kingdoms (Buganda, Bunyoro, Toro, and Ankole) reside generally in the south and west of Uganda, whereas the Nilotic tribes make their home primarily in the north, and the Nilo-Hamitic tribes in the northeast. This generalization should be treated with caution because, as shall be seen, one of the major problems facing the development of local government and national integration in Uganda is the multi-tribal and multi-ethnic composition of some Uganda districts. Tribalism, along with the presence of the alien English rulers, has long posed a major obstacle to effective self-government.

Uganda: Its History

A written language was not indigenous to East Africa. For a history of the peoples now occupying Uganda it is necessary to rely largely upon verbal recollections, myth, and conjecture. It is known that Uganda was subject to periodic waves of invasion by nomadic tribes from the north and northeast. It is thought that these invaders found scattered groups of indigenous agriculturists already occupying the land in what is now southern and western Uganda. For reasons which are not clear, the invading pastoralists dominated the inhabitants of much of Uganda and, in the process of establishing their hegemony, relegated the indigenous residents to a status of near serfdom. Warfare was endemic among these interlacustrine kingdoms, and it is probable that if a written history covering the past six centuries did exist, it would tell a tale of the variable fortunes of expanding and contracting kingdoms.

Eastern Uganda probably experienced a slightly different form of settlement characterized more by gradual migrations of small kinship or age-set groups than by massive invasions of an alien people. As a consequence of this variation there did not evolve in the eastern regions the semi-feudal and politically centralized kingdoms that characterized the west. Violence, though on a smaller scale, was just as endemic, with clan fighting clan and on occasion tribe battling tribe. Thus, prior to the arrival of the Europeans, the western kingdoms and the eastern clans and tribes were most likely in a process of ebb and flow, with the fortunes of first one group and then another momentarily on the ascendancy. An important impact of British hegemony was that this fluid picture of a people in motion was suddenly stopped and the existing distribution frozen. As a consequence, one finds here and there the vanguard of what was once a tribal migration now cut off from its main tribal body and surrounded by traditionally hostile neighbors.

The era of English expansion in Uganda is even more crucial to an understanding of present-day local and national problems. European influence first entered Uganda in 1877 in the guise of the Church Missionary Society. This religious penetration occurred in response to Stanley's now famous and dramatic appeal published in the *Daily Telegraph* of November 15, 1875, that civilization, peace, order, and Christianity be brought post haste to the people of Buganda. The message was received and acted upon in Rome as well as in London; the Church Missionary Society (CMS) and the Catholic White Fathers arrived in Uganda almost simultaneously. The ensuing competition for the African soul led to the foundation of two competing hostile religious groups which, within a few months of their arrival, were deeply immersed in local politics and intrigue. As we shall subsequently note, this volatile mixture of religion and politics continues unabated and is a dominant theme in local and national politics to this day. Because the European missionaries initially extended their influence only to the Kingdom of Buganda, the Baganda achieved a lead of nearly a decade on their neighbors in speaking the white man's language, reading his books, and worshipping his God—an advantage which also continues as a factor in local and national politics.

The Chartered East Africa Company was relieved of its responsibilities in Uganda in 1893 when a reluctant British government finally agreed to assume control from the nearly bankrupt company.

The British Protectorate over Uganda was formally pronounced in 1894 with the signing of a treaty by the acting British Commissioner and Kabaka (King) Mwanga. Within three years, however, Mwanga became party to a planned revolt against the British which eventually led to his fleeing the country and to the accession of the regency of his infant son, Daudi Chwa. In 1900 the Uganda Agreement was signed between Sir Harry Johnston for Her Majesty's Government and for Buganda by the Regents of the infant Kabaka. As a consequence of the Agreement of 1900, Great Britain was committed to a treaty relationship with the kingdom of Buganda which legitimized the latter's political institutions and practices. In the course of time, this served to place Buganda, vis-à-vis other regions, in a special and advantageous position. This special status has significantly affected the development of local government in other districts as well as complicating the integration of the constituent districts into a unified nation state. Paragraph five of the original 1900 Agreement points up this ambivalency.[8]

> The laws made for the general governance of the Uganda Protectorate by Her Majesty's Government will be equally applicable to the Kingdom of Uganda (Kingdom of Buganda) except insofar as they may in any particular conflict with the terms of this Agreement, in which case the terms of this agreement, will constitute a special exception in regard to the Kingdom of Uganda.[9]

Not only did Buganda serve as the springboard for the subsequent extension of British rule into the outlying areas of Uganda, but it also provided a considerable portion of the armed forces and materials required. Thus, the Baganda, who were first to adopt Christianity and to sign an agreement with the English, became, in effect, a favored tribe and a privileged junior partner of the British in the subjugation of the remaining portions of the country. The Baganda were well rewarded for their cooperation. In 1896 the independent Kingdom of Koki, to the southwest of Buganda, was dissolved and incorporated into Buganda, and in 1901 a large slice of the kingdom of Bunyoro-Kitara was awarded to Buganda.[10] Furthermore, wherever the British flag was raised in Uganda an administrative system patterned on that which the British had first observed and learned to admire in Buganda was super-imposed over the traditional polities. Chieftainship posts in these newly subjugated areas were often filled by Baganda and to them went the spoils of domination.

British occupation and extension of authority in the remaining northern and eastern portions of Uganda took place gradually. The techniques employed consisted of a combination of Baganda mercenaries and administrative agents, localized military forces, and agreements with petty chiefs and clan leaders. The criteria of effective occupation and rule was the successful levy and collection of a hut tax. This process was finally completed in 1918 when the truculent Langi were convinced of the necessity of paying a tax to the imported Baganda chiefs.

It is tempting to read current significance into the selected historical events. Though one must guard against this inclination, there do appear to be a number of current-day problems which, in part at least, are attributable to certain historical events that we have briefly described.

1. British influence and occupation initially took place in the kingdom of Buganda, and gave to Buganda a special status and an advantage over its neighbors that it still maintains. The declared policy of Great Britain to develop a unitary state in Uganda ran headlong into the Buganda Agreement and the values which it ensured. The special federal status granted Buganda in the 1962 Uganda Constitution is but the latest example. Not only did this special status delay independence for Uganda but it also dictated the necessity of a quasi-federal constitution providing federal status for Buganda and to a lesser extent to the other kingdoms as well, within an otherwise unitary state.

2. The "Agreements" with the kingdom-states granted to one province (Buganda) and four districts (Bunyoro, Toro, Ankole and Busoga) a special status denied to the remaining districts. This policy has perpetuated the nationalism and separatism of the kingdom-states and posed an ideal status to be attained for the remaining "non-Agreement" districts.

3. The role of the missions and the religious wars have left a legacy of "religion in politics" which powerfully influences the local political system in nearly every district.

4. The use of Baganda mercenaries and the export of the Buganda system of government throughout Uganda is in part responsible for the general suspicion and distrust with which the Baganda are more or less held by most of their neighbors. The implementation of the Baganda system of chieftainship led to the institutionalization of a universal system of administration which in northern and eastern Uganda was in sharp contrast to the traditional local political systems.

5. The establishments of districts based wherever possible on tribal residence has contributed to a sense of district nationalism and separatism that in many cases did not exist prior to the arrival of the British and subsequent amalgamation of the parochial segments into single districts.

PATTERNS OF MEMBERSHIP, ASSOCIATION AND SOLIDARITY

Kinship

Traditionally the most pervasive and significant solidarity unit affecting political behavior in East Africa has been that based upon kinship. Kinship patterns for our purposes can be viewed as those social norms and institutions that determine a person's behavior, associations, and loyalties on the basis of biological (real or fictitious) relatedness.

Anthropologists are not agreed as to the exact nature of the unit to which they attribute the term tribe. Most agree, however, that tribe refers to a cluster or a group of people possessed of a common language, culture, and territory. To qualify as a tribe other anthropologists require the group to possess an ideological unity or shared dogma explaining its tribal origins. The tribe traditionally has served as a meaningful unit of association in the kingdom-states; for there political authority was centralized and was exercised over an extensive territory coinciding generally with the area of tribal residence. However, in the northern and eastern parts of Uganda, the tribe traditionally did not provide the major focus of communal loyalty; nor did it provide a basis for the exercise of political authority. The major unit of kinship association in many of the non-Bantu areas in northern and eastern Uganda was the clan. Agreement on the distinction between tribe and clan is not universally shared among anthropologists but generally clan refers to those members of the social system which trace their origins to a single (real or mythical) common ancestor. The clan is also that kinship unit within which exogamy is institutionalized. In some parts of Uganda, which are examined in detail below, the clan is subdivided into "lineages." A lineage, for our purposes, is a kinship association within which the members claim a common and real ancestor who generally is no more than two generations removed from the living members.

There is reason to believe that before the arrival of the pastoral invaders from the north, the indigenous people of Uganda were organized primarily on a kinship basis and that it was the invaders who superimposed over the multitude of kinship societies more specialized and extensive political-territorial systems. In the eastern regions of the country, however, localized clan groups served as the basis of authority into the present century. Within these regions the individual, even today, is held accountable to his clan and lineage mates in a specific and known manner. Upon occasion kinship obligations conflict with the individual's duties to other associations of which he is a member. A chief, for example, may find himself in the position of failing in his administrative duties because he is required to fulfill contradictory obligations to his kin. This conflict of new and more universal responsibilities with traditional kinship obligations is a dominant theme in the evolution of local government.

Religion

Christianity and Islam, though not indigenous to East Africa, wield extraordinary influence today. Religion tends to dominate the local as well as the national political scene in Uganda to a greater degree than possibly anywhere else on the continent. Parochial clan organizations possess well developed institutions for solving inter-clan disputes. However, the current religious conflicts which characterize much of present-day Uganda, are exceedingly difficult to cope with, for there exists no accepted machinery for solving such disputes. A fundamental understanding of this problem would likely require intensive psychological study not only of the Africans but of the missionaries as well. Religious factionalism affects every district in Uganda, but is more pronounced in some than in others. In Kigezi District, for example, solidarity oriented about Protestant or Catholic affiliation is so binding that it even tends to cut across kinship lines. Thus, a citizen of Kigezi sometimes feels more compelled to fulfill his responsibilities to his fellow Catholics or Protestants than to his kinship associates.

Some historical antecedents to this problem were noted above. Another factor contributing to the powerful impact of rival religious denominations on Uganda politics, has been the extraordinary influence of the Christian missions in the field of education. The early missionaries, cognizant of the relative advantages to be gained from obtaining the support of powerful chiefs, schemed and competed to attract to their respective schools the sons of chiefs and other important local dignitaries. And anti-Catholic and anti-Protestant teaching loomed large in early theological training as the missions vied for the secular support necessary to ensure their domination. Conflict between the missions and the chief frequently broke out over the use of compulsory labor on the estates of a rival denomination, the grant of native lands to the mission, the traditional obligations to the chiefs of mission African employees, teachers, and religious instructors, and the liability of mission-based Africans to communal labor, taxation, and adjudication. A tendency on the part of the missionaries to relieve the boredom of an isolated and primitive existence by dabbling in the intrigues of local politics also served to interject an unusually strong element of religion into local politics.

Political Parties

Political parties were relatively slow to develop in Uganda and it was not until two to three years before independence that modern effective parties were established. Uganda's peculiar political composition and evolution is certainly partially responsible for this retarded political development. The special status granted Buganda, and to a lesser extent to Bunyoro, Toro, and Ankole in conjunction with a policy of concentrating upon the development of district-tribal representative local government, served to concentrate political activity within the constituent districts and kingdoms. Furthermore, independence was promised by Great Britain almost before it was demanded and there were no European settlers to contest African preeminence. An excellent climate, good soil and adequate rainfall eliminated hunger or economic deprivation as a nationwide issue. On the other hand, the persistence of court intrigues and politics within Buganda and the other kingdom-states provided ample opportunity for the exercise of parochial factions and politics. Uganda's classic style of religious strife permeating every district also provided a ready-made issue upon which district councils and tribal politicians could differ. Thus in contrast to the importance of local issues, nationalist agitation and interest were relatively insignificant. History, like nature, has been kind to Uganda. Freedom came without a struggle; and the independence ceremonies and celebrations, though technically admirable, were surprisingly unemotional.

The first direct elections to the Uganda Legislative Council were held in 1958. The Uganda National Congress (UNC), the country's oldest party and direct descendant of the Uganda Federation of African Farmers, won five of the ten directly elected seats. The Democratic Party (DP), founded in 1956, was by design and practice a Roman Catholic political action group, though it has subsequently sought with little success to attract non-Catholics to its ranks. It managed to win only one seat in the 1958 elections, while independent candidates captured the remaining four.

Shortly after the newly formed Legislative Assembly met, a group of representative African members established a new party which in effect was directed against Baganda influence and domination. The tendency of the Nilotic and Nilo-Hamitic people of the northern and eastern regions to combine in opposition to the long dominant influence of Buganda, has increased as the educational and economic gap separating the two factions has narrowed.

The new party—the Uganda People's Union (UPU)—drew its support from dissident UNC legislators and from those non-Baganda representatives associated neither with the UNC nor the DP. D. A. Low, in his excellent study of Uganda political parties, concludes that the UPU was "an attempt to organize along new-style lines the non-Baganda parts of the country; and its formation represented not just a new outlook in the less advanced parts of the country, but a direct reaction to the establishment in a strong position within Buganda of the Baganda neo-traditionalists."[11]

Thus while the non-kingdom regions of Uganda were striving to develop nationwide modern political parties, traditional interests in Buganda, and to a lesser extent in Bunyoro, Toro, and Ankole, were at work to discourage and frustrate the development of modern political party organizations. An independent unitary Uganda, as the Baganda were quick to appreciate, would bring an end to the long history of Baganda domination and would surely place the kingdom and its supporting traditional institutions and interests at the mercy of a nonsympathetic antimonarchical majority.

In 1959 the situation was further confused by a split within the Uganda National Congress between its older relatively radical leadership and a group of younger, more pragmatic political leaders. The new UNC elected as its president, Milton Obote, who in three years was to become the country's first Prime Minister. A year later, and again in response to anxiety over Buganda's influence, the UPU and the new UNC merged to form the Uganda People's Congress (UPC) which rapidly emerged as the largest and most powerful party in the country. Even at this late date, however, party organization in Uganda, in sharp contrast to the extensive grass roots organization characterizing political organization in Kenya and Tanganyika, was weak and limited almost solely to the politics of the Legislative Council and the District Councils. The great mass of people were either apolitical or still obsessed with the parochial issues of Catholic versus Protestant appointments or inter-tribal (district) hostility. Even in those District Council elections where party labels are of significance, the parties, as is shown in detail in subsequent chapters, frequently divide along existing religious or traditional lines.

Before a special committee commissioned in December, 1960, to study and make recommendations on the position of Buganda in an independent Uganda could complete its work, the 1961 elections to the Legislative Council were held. The Baganda traditionalists, fearful that popular election to the central legislature would threaten their position, successfully discouraged the Baganda from participating in the election. And as is frequently the case in Uganda, the parochial behavior of a simple people, had nationwide ramifications. For although the UPC polled a majority of the votes cast, it received fewer seats in the legislature than the opposition Democratic Party. The DP received a majority of the relatively few votes cast by the Baganda, most of whom had boycotted the election, thereby capturing nineteen of the twenty Buganda seats; added to the twenty-four seats won elsewhere in the country, this gave them eight more seats than the UPC's thirty-five.

A gradual recognition that Buganda somehow would have to make its way within a unified independent country, plus the growing influence of Uganda nationalists within Buganda in 1961 led to the formation of Kabaka Yekka—an all-Baganda political party dedicated to the preservation of traditional interests within the framework of an independent Uganda.

The advent of the first direct elections to the Buganda Legislature (Lukiko) was the occasion which motivated the formation of Kabaka Yekka; for traditional vested interests in the kingdom realized that their very future depended upon defeating the Democratic Party candidates—not only in order to retain control of the "local" government but also, as it was likely that Baganda representatives to the Central Legislature would be indirectly elected by the Lukiko, in order to protect the position of Buganda within an independent Uganda. Thus, on the eve of the crucial April, 1962, pre-independence elections, the political arena was dominated by three parties: the predominantly Catholic Democratic Party which sought to add a popular majority to its majority of seats in the Legislature; the predominantly Protestant non-Baganda UPC which sought to turn its popular majority into control of the government; and Kabaka Yekka which, above all else, was determined to protect and if possible enhance the position of Buganda generally and the interests of the monarchy in particular. Politics in Uganda as elsewhere, makes for strange bedfellows as the 1962 alliance between Kabaka Yekka and the UPC demonstrated. The alliance held firm long enough for the coalition to win the 1962 elections and form the country's first independent government. The UPC won thirty-seven seats, which together with Kabaka Yekka's twenty-one Buganda seats provided a majority over the Democratic Party's twenty-two seats. Milton Obote of Lango became Uganda's first Prime Minister and won the privilege of ordering the raising of Uganda's national emblem at midnight October 9, 1962. As many expected, however, this unnatural alliance between a party dedicated to the preservation of parochial, traditional privileges and the other determined to build a modern unified state, began to break down within a few months of independence.

The relationship of Kabaka Yekka to the UPC at this writing is in the process of being fundamentally altered and it is conceivable that Kabaka Yekka will voluntarily be dissolved and absorbed into the

UPC. This unlikely eventuality follows from the amendment of the Uganda Constitution in October, 1963—one year after independence. In common with the pattern established by other former British dependencies, Uganda, after one year of independence as a dominion, has chosen to forego this last link with the United Kingdom. But because the declaration of a "republic" is odious to the powerful monarchical institutions in the kingdom states, the relinquishing of dominion status was not followed by the proclamation of a republic.

After considerable negotiations, the Kabaka (king) of Buganda was selected as Uganda's first President. It is this sudden fusion of the traditional Buganda kingship with the constitution of the modern state of Uganda that has drastically altered the relationship between Kabaka Yekka and the UPC.

Because our analysis of local government generally excludes the tribulations and politics of the quasi-federal state of Buganda, little attention is given to Kabaka Yekka.[12] However, the influence of the Democratic Party and the Uganda People's Congress on local government, politics, and administration within the districts intensively studied is of major importance and is treated in considerable detail below. It should be evident that the evolution of local government and its relationship to nation-building in Uganda today cannot be considered without reference to the important and growing role of this most modern form of solidarity and association.

Cooperatives

Today the people of Uganda are required to consider and sort out their relationships with their neighbors not only on the single criteria of kinship but on the basis of tribal, religious, occupational, and political party obligations as well. A number of other modern associations have also emerged to claim a portion of the individual's loyalty and obligation. The modern farmer, for example, in addition to the traditional and modern associations already noted, is probably a member of one of Uganda's seventeen hundred registered cooperative societies. In some districts as many as 20 per cent of the adult males belong to cooperative societies and although the cooperatives are primarily specialized producer and marketing associations, they have been closely related to the political life of the country from the very moment of their establishment.

The Uganda cooperative movement can be dated to 1933 and the formation of the Baganda Growers Association. In 1962 the Cooperative Movement could boast a quarter-million members participating in nearly seventeen hundred primary societies, most of which are affiliated with one of fifteen marketing cooperative unions. The economic significance of the cooperative is indicated by the fact that in 1962 approximately one-third of the total cotton crop was handled by the cooperative societies. In common with the evolution of other modern associations, the cooperative movement has been bedeviled by traditional interests and institutions which its growth seemed to threaten, and at certain stages in its development by the Colonial government.

After World War II an attempt was made to incorporate the multitude of private growers associations into a cooperative movement. Many resisted this attempt to circumscribe their activities under a Cooperative Society Ordinance and the movement in Uganda has long been characterized by conflict between the independent associations and the central government.

The significance of modern in contrast to traditional economic associations is the hierarchical manner in which they relate the formerly parochially oriented peasant to the nation-state and to a world market. A critical element in the nation-building process is the emergence of constituent plural institutions in place of parochial associations. In 1962 the Uganda-wide Cooperative Alliance Ltd. was established to unite all registered societies into a single nationwide organization. A Uganda Central Cooperative Union was also established in 1962 to coordinate and economize on the purchase and distribution of agricultural implements, fuel and related materials.

In Uganda as in Tanganyika and Kenya, the Cooperative Movement is employed as an instrument to limit and even to reduce the participation of the Asian minority in the commercial life of the country. The Indian community in Uganda has long controlled the lucrative business of processing primary agricultural produce. But beginning in 1952 the Uganda government began to encourage and assist African cooperative societies to purchase cotton ginneries. And by 1962 the cooperatives, with government assistance, owned and controlled about sixteen ginneries. An independent Uganda government in 1963 decided to move more rapidly toward a grower's monopoly of produce processing. In April of that year the Minister of Agriculture and Cooperatives in Parliament warned Asian ginnery owners to sell out to cooperative unions, for the government was about to loan cooperatives 90 per cent of the resources necessary to build their own ginneries.

Uganda's Cooperative Movement, successful as it has been, has been significantly retarded by tribal and administrative parochialism. With a shorter history and a less luxurious economic base, the Cooperative Movement in Tanganyika has rapidly assumed a major role in national development concerning itself not only with marketing of primary agricultural produce, but with retail and wholesale trade, banking, and education as well. The relative rigidity of kingdom and district boundaries in Uganda has acted to concentrate cooperative organization and activity within inflexible political compartments and generally delayed a trend toward a national cooperative union.

Traditional membership units, if they are to survive in face of modern problems and demands, are required to alter their organization. Traditionally, the leadership of the predominantly kinship type associations, for example, was of a hereditary nature. Today one can discern a change in the organization of these traditional associations as they respond to new problems in the face of a changing environment and social order. As people begin to move about to seek employment, they establish branches of their tribal associations throughout the country. We have observed the evolution of clan organizations along modern bureaucratic lines including the election of leaders on the basis of education and other cosmopolitan criteria. These new type clans hold regular meetings, lend money, form committees, collect dues, and issue printed receipts.[13]

Nation

Superimposing these emerging patterns of overlapping loyalties and associations is an embryonic sense of Uganda nationalism which is slowly but perceptibly gathering momentum. The concept of "nation" is probably the farthest removed from the cognitive range of the average peasant. He belongs first and foremost to his tribe, clan, and lineage. He most likely is a member of one of the Christian denominations as well as of one of the three major parties, but associates his membership with a local church or mission and with district or kingdom politics. Membership in a cooperative, though relating the individual to the national economy, is nonetheless oriented about a local branch or cotton ginnery. District, kingdom, or tribal nationalism, though on the wane in some areas, still overshadows a sense of Uganda nationalism.

Unlike Kenya, where powerful tribal factionalism has evolved in response to the conflicting interests of political parties and politicians, Uganda's constituent kingdoms and districts, from the very outset, were divided on a tribal basis. Thus, while tribalism in Kenya, in one important sense, is an expression of modern politics, tribalism in Uganda is a long standing problem. The most powerful forces seeking to maintain a high level of tribal-territorial autonomy and in the process to retard the evolution of a unitary centralized state are, of course, the traditional interests of Buganda. The traditional rulers, chiefs, and dignitaries of the other smaller kingdoms are relatively content with, or if not content powerless to oppose, political modernization and central government control. Preservation of the ceremonial customs and symbolic titles is about the extent to which autonomy has been granted to the smaller kingdoms. But Buganda has long enjoyed separate status and near exclusive control over a considerable portion of its domestic government. Thus, in Buganda it is not only a royal family and a group of elderly ceremonial office holders who have a vested interest in the perpetuation of the relatively autonomous kingdom, but a host of chiefs, sub-chiefs, ministers, and bureaucrats as well.

Traditionalism in modern Africa is regarded by liberal spokesmen as an embarrassing anachronism—and a remnant of a colonial policy of divide and rule. Many young and educated Baganda are uneasy about the perpetuation of their autocratic traditional institutions and deplore the fact that their government stands in the way of Uganda following the path of rapid mobilization and nationalism, as taken by Ghana, Guinea, or Tanganyika. Furthermore, spokesmen for the non-kingdom districts, even though jealous of the prerogatives of their own constituencies, are more inclined to support a unitary centralized state —no doubt in part because a unitary government would cut back the special powers and status of the kingdoms and thereby relatively enhance the influence of the nonmonarchical districts.

It is possible to detect in Uganda an emerging struggle for power on the part of the modernists in Buganda who seek to circumscribe the role of the monarchy and its supporting institutions and to further democratize the Buganda government. These young men, some of whom have broken off from Kabaka Yekka and established their own party in opposition to the influence and privileges of the chiefs and officials, are supported by leaders of the UPC, whose ultimate vision is of a modern, unified, and progressive Uganda nation.

A number of additional forces are at work in Uganda seeking to extend the citizen's cognitive range and thus to gradually incorporate him into ever larger and more inclusive associations. One such force is the rapidly changing economic system.

Uganda: Its Economy

> The development of the money economy, insofar as a pecuniary compensation of the officials is concerned is a presupposition of bureaucracy.[14]

In traditional Uganda the production and consumption of food, clothing, shelter, and tools were intricately meshed into the over-all social system. The thousands of parochial communities were nearly economically self-sufficient and there was little need for association with neighboring peoples on predominantly economic grounds. As one would expect, the centralized kingdom-states possessed comparatively larger and more specified economies. This was required if for no other reason than to collect from subject peoples a level of tribute necessary to support a hierarchy of specialist rulers. In the small-scale segmented systems of eastern Uganda it is likely that each kinship or other social segment grew its own food, organized its own hunts, and manufactured most of its own utensils. Little trade, with the possible exception of hoes, spears, and salt, took place outside of the locality. A legacy of small-scale economic self-sufficiency accounts, in part, for the relative capacity of some peoples in eastern Uganda to resist centralized administration.

The absence of hoardable wealth (except, of course, for cattle), meant that ruler and ruled alike generally wore comparable clothing and ate the same food, with the ruler differing only in a relatively greater consumption. The absence of a money economy also rendered chiefs, clan heads, and other traditional leaders particularly dependent on their subjects, for they looked to them for regular tribute of the perishable necessities of life. Today a chief receives a monthly pay envelope and is concerned with fulfilling his obligations to the bureaucracy more than to his subjects. The traditional tie of ruled to ruler was further reinforced by the authority of the ruler over the allocation of land. The introduction of cash crops and a money economy, which followed the establishment of British hegemony, significantly affected the traditional socio-political system. Today wealth can be accumulated and hoarded, and consequently has become a source of considerable power and influence. Cash crops and a money exchange have built roads and dispensaries, bought bicycles, radios, cloth, galvanized iron roofs, and education. All this is tending to render obsolete the hundreds of peculiarly local customs that sharply distinguished and isolated clusters of people.

The modern Uganda farmer earns a money income primarily from a return on the sale of cash crops (coffee, cotton, tobacco, and groundnuts) and cattle, or in the form of wages. With the exception of a few tea and sugar estates, nearly all commercial agriculture in Uganda is in peasant hands and small-scale commercial agriculture is now an integral part of the economic life of nearly all Africans in Uganda.

Two-thirds of the country's gross domestic product is derived from agriculture, and its foreign exchange is dependent almost solely on this source. The relative significance of commercial agriculture in contrast to subsistence farming is revealed by the fact that in 1961 the sale of agricultural products reached fifty million pounds and exceeded the estimated value of subsistence output by about ten million pounds.

It can hardly be said, however, that Uganda has experienced an agricultural revolution, for change has been remarkably slow. The World Bank study of the country's economy and development concluded that "Uganda's economic growth has been unspectacular but steady."[15] Despite nearly a half-century of attempts to improve agricultural practices and technology, there is little evidence that subsistence yield per acre has improved noticeably, nor for that matter has there been substantial improvement in the total production of coffee and cotton, the two major cash crops.[16] In contrast to neighboring Kenya and Tanganyika, Uganda possesses a relatively favorable climate and soil. This, in conjunction with the early encouragement and development of a peasant cash crop agriculture, has provided the Uganda African farmer with a comparatively high and steady income.[17]

Uganda's per capita cash income is approximately £23 per annum and although the over-all volume of agricultural production has increased steadily, the decline, from the mid-fifties onward, in world market prices for Uganda's major primary products has not only precluded a corresponding increase in export value and income to the grower, but in fact has reduced cash income. The value of Uganda's exports in 1960 (41.5 million pounds), for example, was less than in 1951. This decline in export earnings has been cushioned by large reserves accumulated by government controlled marketing boards during the years when the price of coffee and cotton on the world market was relatively high.

TABLE 2

PER CAPITA VALUE OF MAIN CASH CROPS TO AFRICAN GROWERS 1946-1959

(thousands of pounds)

Year	Coffee	Per Capita	Cotton	Per Capita
		Pounds		Pounds
1946	1,109	.2	4,002	.817
1952	4,331	.8	11,929	2.2
1954	8,290	.6	12,926	2.3
1955	16,070	2.8	11,584	2.0
1956	9,342	1.6	12,576	2.1
1957	10,574	1.7	13,081	2.1
1958	11,814	1.9	12,792	2.0
1959	13,725	2.1	11,720	1.8
1960	13,495	2.1	10,517	1.6

SOURCE: Uganda Protectorate Statistical Abstract, 1960

Acreage planted to coffee, cotton, and tobacco, the major cash crops, has doubled over the past two decades and today totals nearly two and one-half million acres.[18] There is, however, considerable potential for increased production, for in addition to the six and one-half million acres (approximately one acre per capita) planted in subsistence crops, there are nearly forty million uncultivated acres that could conceivably be put to commercial use. Despite a gradual increase in cotton planting up to nearly two million acres, there has not been a corresponding increase in production. In 1937/38 Uganda produced more than 400,000 bales of cotton, a quarter of a century later (1960/61) the cotton crop amounted to but 177,000 bales.[19]

Coffee production has increased more rapidly and by 1958 surpassed cotton as the most valuable crop grown. However, limitations imposed by international marketing agreements severely restrict the possibilities for future increase. A livestock census in 1960 showed that there were more than three and one-half million cattle and a like number of sheep and goats in Uganda. In 1960 nearly 100,000 cattle were shipped from the cattle producing districts. The livestock industry, it is thought, is capable of considerable development and large-scale ranching schemes have been launched, some in cooperation with local governments.

Cotton is grown in every district in Uganda except Karamoja and Kigezi, but major production is centered in Buganda, Bukedi, Teso, Lango, and Acholi. Nearly all the coffee is grown in Buganda, on the slopes of Mt. Elgon in Bugishu, the slopes of the Ruwenzoris in Toro and in the highlands of Ankole. Livestock production is centered in Karamoja, Teso, and Ankole. Wide variations in cash income are largely determined by this pattern of commercial agriculture. Per capita cash income ranges from about £3 per annum in Kigezi to nearly £20 in Buganda. In the northern districts of West Nile, Madi, Acholi, and Karamoja and in the southwest districts of Ankole and Kigezi per capita income is nowhere greater than £5 per annum.[20]

The development of Uganda depends primarily on a substantial increase in the production of primary products and particularly cotton. However, as a former Minister of Natural Resources noted, "There has not yet been an agricultural revolution. What has been achieved has evolved out of the traditional pattern of agriculture and radical changes are not yet apparent."[21] Less than a quarter-million Ugandans in 1960 were employed in other than peasant agriculture or domestic services.[22] Nearly all Asians and Europeans are included in this category and tend to monopolize the skilled and managerial positions in the nonagricultural sector of the economy.

More than half of all the employed Africans not occupied in peasant agriculture are with the public service (126,000) while slightly less than half (102,000) are employed by the private sector. The political and economic significance of local government is suggested by the fact that nearly two in every five public servants is an employee of a local government.

To date, industry has played a minor part in Uganda's economy. There do exist light agricultural processing installations such as cotton ginneries, coffee hulleries, and cottonseed oil mills. In addition, Uganda can claim two large sugar processing works, two tobacco factories, two breweries, a cement factory, two textile mills, and a smelter to handle the ore from the newly opened copper mine in the Ruwenzoris. More important than the physical plant is the impact of industrial wage earning on the social system. Working for a stranger-employer for an hourly wage is a new experience for most Africans. Walter Elkan notes that two centuries of industrial economy have developed certain attitudes in Western society. The Uganda native traditionally is used to working, resting, and eating when the spirit moves him. Walter Elkan adds:

> Qualities which single men out for praise or respect at home are not necessarily relevant in the factory and may be ignored there. The customary rhythm of work is the subject of derision on the employer's part, and is something for which he regards himself entitled to seek retribution. In these conditions the necessary meaning of labor efficiency often must be the extent to which men have acquired the attitudes which make them effective industrial workers.[23]

In many districts the government is the largest single employer and in a district such as Bunyoro it hires more persons than all other employers combined.

As early as 1928 the government, with the intention of aiding the growth of African trade, began to curtail the business enterprise of non-Africans. The development of an African commercial and business class of substantial proportions was long a major aim of the Protectorate government and though the success of earlier programs has been spotty, commercial enterprise on the part of Africans in Uganda is relatively more highly developed than elsewhere in East Africa. In 1961 the United States International Cooperation Administration (ICA), granted nearly $150,000 to Uganda for loans to be made to African businessmen and farmers, and since 1954 has granted more than $600,000 to Uganda to further African agricultural and commercial enterprise.[24]

The monopoly of the commercial life of the country by Indian merchants provided a basis for racial hostility and political agitation even before World War II. The British Colonial government, as early as 1925, began to curtail the commercial expansion of non-African entrepreneurs. The Protectorate government's policy, particularly after 1949, was one of developing an African commercial and business class of substantial proportions. Programs designed to encourage and facilitate the participation of Africans in commerce were accelerated as independence approached—in part in an effort to preclude a repetition of the anti-Asian boycott and riots of 1959. A variety of business loan and development funds have been established and designed to encourage and facilitate the entry of more Africans into the commercial life of the country. Programs of this sort plus a strong desire on the part of the African to participate in businesses have contributed to a rapid increase in the number of African shopkeepers to more than 15,000 by 1962. Nearly 4,000 loans totaling more than half a million pounds have been made up to 1962/63.

It is within this economic context that local government must obtain the human and physical resources necessary to cope with its portion of developmental problems and challenges.

UGANDA: ITS GOVERNMENT

The exercise of political authority was long understood by the peoples and rulers of the four kingdom-states as a specialized activity to be entrusted to specified role carriers. However, even in the relatively highly developed kingdoms, government was associated with religious and social institutions. In the non-kingdom areas the exercise of traditional authority over the locality was only analytically distinguishable from other aspects of social organization and activity. This important distinction between the relatively centralized and the diffuse segmentary types of political systems is analyzed in greater detail in the following chapters.

The ultimate locus of political authority in Uganda before October, 1962, and the acquisition of independence was Her Majesty's Government in the United Kingdom. In practice, of course, the Colonial Governor possessed considerable autonomy. From 1894 and the proclamation of the Protectorate to 1905, Uganda was governed by commissioners under the authority of the Foreign Office. In 1905 this responsibility was transferred to the Colonial Office and the first Governor was appointed. In 1920, a legislative and executive council was introduced. The Executive Council initially was composed of departmental (ex-officio) heads. The law required that certain matters be referred to the Executive Council but its decisions were not binding upon the Governor. The first Legislative Council consisted of the members of the executive council with the addition of the Provincial Commissioner of Buganda, and a number of unofficial members—usually two Asians and two Europeans, nominated by the Governor. The constitution gradually changed over the years with the first African being appointed in 1945. By 1950 the Legislative Council was composed of sixteen government and sixteen representative members of which eight were

African, four European, and four Asian. In 1954 the council was reconstituted and the novel institution of a "cross bench" introduced. The cross bench was drawn from the leading members of the public who could speak and vote as they wished except on matters of confidence, in which case they were required to support the government. A ministerial form of government was introduced in July, 1955, increasing the African representation in the Legislative Council from twenty, of a total membership of fifty-six, to thirty in a membership of sixty.

The composition of the Legislative Council (LEGCO) was altered in 1958 and again after the 1961 elections. The last government before independence consisted of a one-hundred-member Legislative Council of which eighty-one were elected from single member constituencies, nine specially elected by the elected members, three ex-officio members and seven nominees of the Governor. The leader of the Democratic Party, Benedicto Kiwanuka, was asked by the Governor to form a government.

The preparation of a constitution for an independent Uganda was preceded by a 1959 report of a specially appointed constitution committee which made recommendations on the composition of the future government; the report of the Uganda Relationship Commission which recommended that Buganda's relationship to Uganda be of a federal nature and which outlined a proposed governmental system; and finally by constitutional and independence conferences held in London in 1961 and 1962 respectively.[25]

The resulting 150-page constitution reflects the series of earlier debates and compromises, and sets out in considerable detail, first, the federal rights and privileges of Buganda, then the lesser prerogatives of the other three kingdoms and Busoga, and finally the position of the remaining non-monarchical administrative districts. The constitution defines Uganda as consisting of Federal States, Districts and the territory of Mbale. The Federal States are the Kingdom of Buganda, the Kingdom of Ankole, the Kingdom of Bunyoro, the Kingdom of Toro and the territory of Busoga. The districts are the Districts of Acholi, Bugishu, Bukedi, Karamoja, Kigezi, Lango, Madi, Sebei, Teso and West Nile.[26] The respective kingdom constitutions are included as schedules to the Uganda constitution. Whereas Buganda's legislature is free to alter its own constitution without recourse to the central government, constitutional alterations in the other kingdoms require central government approval. Uganda's National Assembly consists of 82 elected members from single member constituencies, and up to nine specially elected seats. The constitution gives special consideration to the number (21) and the manner of recruiting representatives from Buganda.

The most fundamental change in Uganda's constitution occurred on October 9, 1963—the first anniversary of her independence. On that date Uganda relinquished its dominion status and proclaimed itself "an independent sovereign state." The Governor General, as representative of the Queen, was replaced with a Ugandan President whose titular powers correspond approximately to those of his predecessor.

It was considerably more difficult for Uganda, given its quasi-federal constitution, to substitute an indigenous for a British head of state. For it immediately raised the issue of the balance of power between Buganda and the other kingdoms, between the kingdoms and the districts, and between the respective parties and factions.

Prime Minister Obote's announcement in September, 1963, that the Queen would be replaced as head of state by a Ugandan, at first elicited a negative reaction from Buganda—which feared that such a constitutional change would mean the establishment of a republic which in turn would threaten her monarchical institutions. The solution was to preclude the proclamation of a republic and to obtain the position of head of state for the Kabaka. On September 16, the Buganda Lukiko (legislature) unanimously approved the proposition that the Kabaka become Uganda's head of state.

After considerable debate it was decided that the President should be elected by the National Assembly. Prime Minister Obote proposed that the candidates be drawn from the hereditary rulers and the constitutional heads of the districts.

The issue was a crucial one for the political fortunes of Buganda. If the Kabaka were chosen, the kingdom's relative influence would increase. But if he were not, the monarchy itself might be in jeopardy. The latter alternative was unacceptable and to have forced it on the Baganda, the Prime Minister realized, probably would have subjected the new nation to greater strain than it was capable of withstanding. Nonetheless, the forces opposed to the Kabaka as head of state were substantial. Not only were many northern and eastern province leaders against designating a Bantu king as President, but the rulers of the smaller kingdoms were not pleased with the likelihood of the already more powerful Baganda achieving still greater influence.

The forces opposing the Kabaka as President, including the hereditary rulers of the three smaller kingdoms, settled upon Sir Wilberforce Nadiope, the Kyabazinga of Busoga, as their candidate.

The future of the new nation depended upon the reconciliation of this constitutional issue which threatened the vital interests of traditional and modern institutions alike. The Prime Minister's political skill and his awareness of the cruciality of the situation, in conjunction with an extraordinary cabinet meeting, brought a last-minute agreement that the UPC would support the Kabaka's candidacy. The confrontation was averted and the Kabaka became Uganda's first president.

Executive authority now resides in the President who in parliamentary fashion appoints the Prime Minister. The Cabinet, consisting of the Prime Minister and other ministers, is responsible to the National Assembly. Each of the federal states has its own Council of Ministers and an Assembly with powers confined to its own citizens and area of jurisdiction.

An expanded civil service has adequately kept pace with advances in the economic and political life of the country. In 1934 there were but 530 European officials, about 300 Asian clerks, and 130 Africans in pensionable positions.[27] In 1962 budgetary provisions were made for more than 25,000 positions. The central government in 1962 had on its payroll approximately one employee per 240 inhabitants in Uganda. In Bunyoro District the local government alone pays salary or compensation to nearly 700 persons or to one in every 180 Banyoro.[28]

Uganda's basic administrative units have been retained largely as they were before independence. The only major changes made in recent years include the creation of two new districts—Sebei (from a part of Bugishu) and Madi (from a part of West Nile), the elimination of the four provinces as administrative units, the establishment of Mbale Township as a separate territory and the additional constitutional distinctions between the four Kingdoms and Busoga, and the remaining districts. The District Headquarters (boma) since the first days of British rule has been the seat of authority in the respective districts. Sizable towns or townships have grown up around these administrative headquarters while the development of local government and tribal nationalism has given them the air of a regional capital. The boma dominates most administrative towns and its architectural style of adding an addition here and a new building there, is a visual record of the evolution and extension of government services. The history of the boma—in fact of British administration—is the story of the District Commissioner and his subordinate District Officers.[29]

As the most visible symbol of British rule, the office of District Commissioner in recent years has undergone considerable change. Unlike Tanganyika, which has eliminated the office and replaced it with a politically appointed official, Uganda has elected to maintain the position. However, a District Commissioner serving as late as 1954 would hardly recognize the position today, for the post-independence powers of the District Commissioner have been severely circumscribed. He no longer is the major authority figure in the District responsible for supervising a staff of five or six assistant district officers.

The separation of judicial and administrative functions and roles also deprived the District Commissioner of his important role as Chief Magistrate; and he no longer is responsible for supervision of the district and lower courts. Often located near the boma are the offices and Assembly Hall of the District Councils which have grown in size and significance with the decline in the importance of the District Commissioner and the boma.

The role of the expatriate British District Officer has not been an easy one; he has had the unpleasant assignment of working himself out of a job. The changing duties and powers of the District Commissioner relative to the local government system are examined in more detail in the succeeding chapters.

Having briefly sketched the pertinent aspects of the physical, social and political environment, it is now possible to proceed to an examination of the development and current status of local government in Uganda.

Imagine for the sake of argument that before the white man got to Africa we Africans were playing around in shallow muddy pools and dirty puddles in an effort to swim. Then the white men appeared on the scene and were shocked by the general state of the sport of swimming. "Look here you fellows," they said to the Africans, "What are you doing? That is not swimming and you have not even a swimming pool to speak of. We will build you a swimming pool if you will cooperate and we will teach you how to swim." So the white men set to work, leveled all the small pools and puddles, constructed one big one and soon started swimming. Now when we Africans come up to fall in, we find a notice: "No one must go into the swimming pool unless he can swim."

S. JOSHUA L. ZAKE, *Reform in Uganda*

CHAPTER THREE

Evolution of Local Government and Politics

CONSTITUTIONAL TRANSITION

British influence and administration in Uganda were first established in the Kingdom of Buganda. There the early English explorers, administrators and missionaries found a sophisticated political system replete with king, court and hierarchy of chiefs which resembled that with which they were already familiar. Surely then it was here in Buganda and in the other kingdom states that Lugard's principle of indirect rule was meant to apply.

Captain Lugard, who played an important part in establishing British rule in Uganda, was appointed High Commissioner of Nigeria in 1900 and it was there that he first explicitly developed the principle of indirect rule which has since come to be associated with his name.[1] Briefly stated, indirect rule consists of employing an existing indigenous political machinery to every extent possible in the administration of a colonial territory. The principle of indirect rule in a local government context was well stated by Donald Cameron.

[Indirect rule] is designed to adopt for the purposes of local government the tribal institutions which the native people have evolved for themselves, so that the latter may develop in a constitutional manner from their own past, guided and restrained by the traditions and sanctions which they have inherited, moulded or modified as they may be on the advice of British officers, and by the general control of those officers.[2]

But when colonial administration was extended into areas where an indigenous political system capable of providing a basis for indirect

33

rule did not exist or could not be determined, the principle ran into considerable difficulty. For example, early administrators in the Nilotic areas of the north, the Nilo-Hamitic areas of the northeast, and the noncentralized bantu areas of the southeast looked in vain for a Buganda-like hierarchy of chiefs. What they found was either a confusing array of clan leaders, some of whom appeared to hold sway over considerable areas and lesser clan leaders, or a system of political authority built about institutionalized age-grades. Who were they to recognize as the indigenous authority and subsequently to hold responsible for law and order and for the collection of taxes?

The Baganda willingly lent their assistance to the extension of British hegemony over these outlying areas. And many early administrators reasoned that, if not already existent, the Buganda system of a hierarchy of chiefs ought to be developed. For regardless of the peculiar nature of the indigenous system, it was necessary that officers be posted and responsibility assigned. The accepted basis for administering a colonial area depended upon the functioning of an all-purpose authority over a known and definable territory. As the Baganda already had an admirable system in operation, it followed that the solution to the impasse of ruling territories characterized by political anarchy was to superimpose a similar chiefly hierarchy over Buganda's "unorganized" neighbors. Thus, "indirect rule" in its original sense was replaced by an indirect style of indirect rule. Conveniently located or relatively powerful clan leaders were selected and charged with responsibility over specified areas. Over most local chief-designates was placed a Muganda agent; for who better, the British reasoned, than the Baganda to teach the intricacies of the Buganda system?

This pattern was formalized in 1919 in "An Ordinance to Make Provision for the Powers and Duties of African Chiefs and for the Enforcement of African Authority."[3] The duty of the chief was defined as that of maintaining "order in the areas within which he has jurisdiction."[4] This ordinance gave the chiefs of Uganda—both those possessed of traditional authority and those superimposed over clan or age-group societies—a degree of authority which greatly exceeded anything they held traditionally. Backed by the power of the Colonial government in the guise of the District Commissioner, the chiefs' powers of arrest and seizure, and control over the allocation and use of property were nearly unlimited. Paragraph seven of the ordinance made the chief, subject only to British administration, the sole source of legitimate authority. "Any chief may from time to time issue orders to be obeyed by the Africans residing within the local limits of (his) jurisdiction. . . ."[5] Although the general subjects over which a chief could issue such orders were specified, he also was authorized to issue binding orders on "any native law or custom in force for the time being in his area." As his decision as to the substance of native law or custom was final, his powers in fact were limited only by his accountability to the District Commissioner.[6]

In the kingdoms (Buganda, Toro, Bunyoro and Ankole) early constitutional arrangements were negotiated and formulated in the form of treaties or agreements. The Native Authority Ordinance applied to the kingdom-states as well as to the districts. In Buganda, however, a conflict between Protectorate government legislation and the Buganda Agreement was to be decided in favor of the Agreement. The principle of indirect rule, in its ideal sense, is concisely stated in this Agreement.

> So long as the Kabaka, chiefs and people of Uganda shall conform to the laws and regulations instituted for their governance by Her Majesty's Government, and shall cooperate loyally with Her Majesty's Government in the organization and administration of the said Kingdom of Uganda, Her Majesty's Government agrees to recognize the Kabaka of Uganda as the native ruler of the Province of Uganda under Her Majesty's protection and over-rule.[7]

Chiefs throughout Uganda, under the Native Authority Ordinance, were granted almost unlimited powers. But chiefs in the Agreement kingdoms continued to be responsible, at least in part, to the traditional political system as well as to their British indirect rulers. But this was not the case in the non-Agreement districts where the traditional systems did not provide for a hierarchy of customary chiefs. This important difference in the constitution of Uganda's many traditional political systems has given rise, over the years, to a number of interesting developments.

In eastern and northern Uganda the British administrators, or their Baganda agents, demarcated provinces, districts, sazas (counties), gombololas (sub-counties), mirukas (parishes) and batongoles (villages). A provincial commissioner was appointed and held responsible for the administration of the province to the Governor. District commissioners responsible to the provincial commissioner were also appointed. With few exceptions the saza chieftainships, in practice, were held by Baganda agents.

Although some of the expatriate Baganda agents were honorable, others regarded themselves as conquerors and superior to their backward subjects. They arrogantly confiscated for themselves choice lands, women, and food; needless to say Baganda chiefs were not overly popular. Nevertheless, effective administration over large areas was established, roads were built, and taxes collected. If the foreign chiefs were not traditionally responsible to their subjects, they were at least free from the likelihood of such obligation conflicting with their responsibilities to the district commissioner. It was not until the late 1920's and early 1930's, that the gradual process of replacing these agents with local understudies began. Most indigenous chiefs, selected to replace the Baganda, were clan or lineage heads who were nominated by the British and Baganda because they seemed to possess some local authority in the immediate area of the administrative headquarters; or in a few cases because they traditionally exercised a hazy sort of authority over a relatively extensive area. While serving under Baganda agents, the local chiefs possessed little real responsibility other than to traditional kinship or related segmentary groups. Once they replaced the Baganda agents, however, they frequently found their roles as government chief and clan leader incompatible. As primary loyalty was owed to their kin, they were inclined to avoid their obligations to the official administrative hierarchy. It is not surprising that the removal of Baganda agents was often followed by administrative chaos. As far as the people were concerned it was one thing to put up with the authority of a non-partisan—even though cruel and greedy—foreigner, but quite another willingly to subject oneself to the arbitrary rule of the leader of a rival clan. Faced with this conflict, the early chiefs often violated bureaucratic norms and many were removed from office after serving but a short period free of Buganda supervision.

Replacements for the discharged chiefs-cum-clan leaders were younger men who had relatively less obligation to the clan organization. Their authority was derived, like that of the Baganda agents, almost solely from the official authority hierarchy culminating in the person of the district commissioner. But unlike the Baganda agents, these local chiefs possessed neither a sophisticated knowledge of the traditional system nor of the relatively impartial bureaucracy. Many were opportunists who milked the job for what they could. Accountable only to a distant colonial official the new locally recruited chiefs were relatively free to exploit their subjects. The chief could, for example, arrest one of his subjects for failing to obey "the lawful order of a chief" which he had arbitrarily issued by virtue of the "native law and custom" clause of the Native Authority Ordinance; he could try the prisoner in his own court, pass judgment and levy a sizable fine or imprisonment.[8] It is ironic that this system should have evolved in areas where there never had existed tribe-wide native customs or a tradition of obedience to chiefs.

In this fashion, by the mid-1930's there arose in the non-kingdom districts a system of effective but completely autocratic chieftainship. This contrasted with the situation in the kingdoms where the chiefs were restrained by the accountability of traditional authority. In the early 1930's some British administrative officers were concerned about the autocratic nature and excesses of the Buganda system as it had evolved in the Eastern Province. Consistent with the English tradition, the institution called on to remedy this situation was the local council. It was thought that a large council might render the autonomous chiefs accountable, in some degree, to their subjects.

A precedent existed in the form of the regular meeting (lukiko) of chiefs which had been inherited as a part of the imported Buganda system.[9] It was common for the lowest level (miruka) chief, in a fashion reminiscent of the administration of sixteenth-century England, to hold daily public meetings which were open to all peasants. In a similar fashion the gombolola and saza chiefs held periodic meetings attended by the lower division chiefs falling under their respective authority. This system of councils provided a chain of communication from the king and the Great Lukiko through the hierarchy to the individual peasant.

And along with the hierarchy of chiefs and administrative areas, the Buganda Lukiko was also exported to the Eastern Province. However, it never filled the same function there as it had in Buganda. The equalitarian social structure of the Nilotic and Nilo-Hamitic peoples clashed with a rigid system of superordination whereby everyone's hierarchical status vis-à-vis his neighbors was firmly established. The Lukiko, in the non-kingdom areas, evolved into a meeting of government appointed chiefs. Thus, a Miruka Lukiko was composed of the miruka chief and all batongole chiefs; the Gombolola Lukiko of all miruka chiefs, etc.[10] Meetings of chiefs to which the term Lukiko applied, very much like a sixteenth-century Quarter Session, were held largely to try judicial cases and to pass information and orders from higher to lower levels.

Once a year it was customary for a central meeting of the higher echelon chiefs to meet at the district headquarters under the chairmanship of the District Commissioner to discuss problems of administration, chiefs' salaries, and to recommend modifications in customary law. Under the provisions of the Native Law Ordinance of 1919, those councils recognized or constituted by the government "have the power by resolution, to alter native law and to fix penalties for the breaches of the native law."[11]

It is not difficult to see how this system contributed to the evolution of a hierarchy of chiefs carrying out orders passed to them from above, making and executing others in their own right, sitting as judges in the local courts, and meeting periodically to change the native law which they subsequently administered and adjudicated. It is hardly surprising that the system tended to become autocratic.

War's end brought to the Colonial Office a realization that there no longer existed unlimited time to develop the colonial territories. A post-war sense of urgency over political development was reflected in a spate of constitutional reforms. The reform movement began with the now famous dispatch from the Secretary of State for the Colonies to the Governors of the African Territories of 25 February, 1947. In this confidential dispatch, Mr. Creech-Jones concluded that the "development of an efficient and democratic [later significantly changed to representative] system of local government" was the "key to the success" of the post-war period of political, social, and economic development.[12] Creech-Jones' definition of what he meant by "local," "efficient," and "democratic" spelled the doom of indirect rule and consequently of the autocratic chief as well.

> Local because the system of government must be close to the common people and their problems," "efficient because it must be capable of managing the local services in a way which will help to raise the standard of living," "democratic because it must not only find a place for the growing class of educated men, but at the same time command the respect and support of the mass of the people.[13]

In common with most large bureaucracies the Colonial governments were slow to respond to radical alterations in policy. And needless to say, the Secretary's dispatch did not immediately effect a political revolution. Local, democratic, and efficient local governments still do not exist in Uganda, although the trend is clearly in that direction. The years immediately following this dispatch witnessed a flurry of conferences and draft ordinances throughout the Empire. In Uganda, reform efforts led to the Local Government Ordinance of 1949.[14] Prior to this ordinance, the kingdom councils and those which had gradually evolved elsewhere, were only advisory in nature. The kingdom lukikos were legally recognized in the respective agreements, while the 1949 Ordinance served to legalize and grant corporate powers and responsibilities to the remaining district councils. The ordinance did little, however, to meet the principles laid down in the Secretary's dispatch. Chiefs continued to be appointed by and responsible to the Governor, "or by such other persons as the Governor shall authorize or has already authorized."[15] The 1949 Ordinance did not repeal the Native Authority Ordinance of 1919 which rendered the chief responsible solely to the Central Government and which granted him merely unlimited judicial, executive, and legislative powers. The ordinance did, however, place him in a somewhat ambivalent position and heralded a day when he would be required to serve a multitude of masters.

> Every chief shall administer such Protectorate laws as he is legally competent to administer and in particular he shall administer the provisions of the African Authority Ordinance and any by-laws lawfully made by the District Council.[16]

Under the terms of this ordinance the Governor was empowered to establish a District Council as well as a tier of advisory lower councils in any area of the Protectorate. An important implication of this legislation was that it established the district as the local government area in Uganda. As the administrative districts (including the kingdoms) generally coincide with tribal residence, the 1949 Ordinance in effect provided a legal basis for the institutionalization of parochial tribally oriented local governments. This decision, as we shall have numerous occasions to note, had long-range implications for Uganda politics and government.

The District Administration Ordinance of 1955: The ineffectiveness of the 1949 Ordinance led to disillusionment on the part of the Africans as well as among the more progressively minded district officers. Through the initiative of a new Governor this dissatisfaction, in 1952, led to a Colonial Office Inquiry into African Local Government in the Protectorate of Uganda.[17] The Uganda government accepted most of the recommendations of the Wallis Report as the basis for future policy and circulated this Report to the standing committees of the existing district councils for their consideration and comment. On the basis of reports from the districts, the government drafted a new local government ordinance—the District Administration (District Councils) Ordinance of 1955.[18]

Under the provisions of the 1949 Ordinance, local government consisted "of chiefs, a district council and such other councils as may be established. . . ."[19] Under the 1955 Ordinance, "a council under the provisions of this ordinance . . . shall be the district administration."[20] The 1955 Ordinance was of the enabling type. It set out the law, general provisions and procedures for the proclamation of a district council. The over-all system was to be uniform while individual variations were provided for in the implementing document which officially established the council. This ordinance, like those it preceded, was applicable to all Uganda districts except Buganda.

The 1955 Ordinance technically would seem to have satisfied the goals laid down in 1947 by the Secretary of State for the Colonies. It provided for the possibility of a District Council being authorized to carry out as many as twenty substantial services and functions covering the primary fields of agriculture, veterinary, law and order, forestry, famine relief, medical, education, buildings, water supplies, and local industries. The councils, in theory, were also empowered, subject to government approval, to pass bylaws on thirty-eight additional topics. A careful study of the ordinance, which served as the basis of local government development until 1963, will show, however, that the Colonial government severely hedged its devolution of authority to the District Councils. For example, the councils were granted substantial financial powers, subject in minute detail to the approval of the central government.[21] The power to borrow money was granted— subject to government approval. It could invest its surplus funds subject to government approval. The council possessed the authority to levy a tax on all African males on or above the apparent age of eighteen years residing within its jurisdictional area; the rates necessitated the approval of government. Government could also exempt any class of persons from liability for local taxes.

In the important area of recruitment and regulation of chiefs and officials the 1955 Ordinance made a radical departure from the 1949 legislation. It provided for an Appointments Committee selected by and largely from the Council, with considerable autonomy to recruit, discipline, and dismiss chiefs and other officials. This committee could recruit chiefs and officials without prior approval, but required central government approval before higher chiefs and officials could be suspended or discharged. This surprising freedom to recruit the chiefs upon which the central government relied for grass roots law, order, and administration was a radical departure from earlier practices; and a number of District Commissioners, cognizant of the resulting ambivalent and potentially conflicting positions of the chiefs, looked to the future with considerable apprehension and anxiety. Subsequent events gave support to this apprehension. For example, the central government in December, 1957, was faced with a conflict over the appointment of chiefs and officials in the Teso District of such serious proportions as to receive central government intervention.

A commission was assigned the task of inquiring into the "management" of the Teso District Council. Included in its recommendations to the government was a proposal to amend the 1955 District Council Ordinance, so as to substitute an appointments board nominated by the Governor in place of the Appointments Committee elected by the District Council.

It was not only the breakdown of local government in Teso that led the central government to the retrograde step of depriving the local governments of authority to recruit local officials. Party politics, religious factionalism and tribal differences in a number of districts influenced the selection of members of the crucial Appointments Committee. Chiefs and other senior local government officials were often subjected to considerable pressure by political parties or factionally dominated councils. It was evident to the Governor and the Provincial Administration that so long as chiefs were held responsible to the central government for law and order it would be necessary to insulate them as far as possible from local factionalism and party politics. To achieve this end, it was necessary to deprive the local government of its authority over the recruitment and supervision of chiefs that had been granted in the 1955 Ordinance.

The ordinance and the constituent constitutional regulations were subsequently amended and in 1959 a nominated Appointments Board was substituted for the Council-elected Appointments Committee. The Appointments Board, removed, it was hoped, from the political fray, was designated as the agency to appoint, discipline and promote persons in the local Civil Service. In the "agreement" districts appointments, of course, were made in the name of the king. The proceedings of the Appointments Boards were completely separate from those of the District Councils; not even the minutes were open for councillor observation or review. The Board was granted considerable discretion with respect to lower chiefs and minor officials but "when a person is selected to appointment to or to act in a post the holder of which is recognized by the Governor as a chief of or above the rank of sub-county chief, the Board shall report the matter to the District Commissioner who shall be responsible for seeking the Governor's approval for the appointment of such person."[22] To further insure the non-partisan nature of local government administration, staff regulations prohibited local officers, chiefs and employees from "engagement in political activity" including party membership or support in any form. It was probably inevitable that the system of recruitment as provided for in the 1955 Local Government Ordinance, would place the chiefs and the Appointments Committee in an intolerable position. Under the provisions of the 1955 act the chief became an official of the local government with his salary, discipline, termination, transfer, and promotion dependent upon an Appointments Committee elected by the District Council. However, under the provisions of the Native Authority Ordinance of 1919, the chief was still a central government official responsible to the District Commissioner for the good administration of his area. Thus while his security in office was determined by the local authority, his major obligations were to the central government. This ambivalency has not been completely clarified by subsequent changes in the law and continues to bedevil political modernization in much of Uganda.

Implications of Independence

A series of commissions of inquiry and conferences preliminary to the granting of independence in October, 1962, laid the groundwork for a redefinition of the relationship of the constituent kingdoms and districts in Uganda to the central government.[23]

The inevitable necessity of granting special federal status to Buganda encouraged the smaller kingdoms and Busoga to demand comparable reserved powers for themselves as well. The non-kingdom districts, not to be overlooked in the provision of special prerogatives and privileges, were quick to demand a similar right to hereditary rulership—as a matter of equity, if not of indigenous tradition. This, in conjunction with a long history of emphasis on the development of local government in Uganda, posed a most difficult problem for the constitutional draftsman.

Government at the local level in Uganda, thanks to the precedent set by Buganda and to a lesser extent by the smaller kingdoms, from the very outset had possessed quasi-federal characteristics and sentiments. The traditional suspicion with which Buganda had long been held by the peoples in other parts of the country was such that it was not politically possible to provide status for the kingdom states completely distinct and separate from the nonmonarchical districts. On the other hand, the special legal and customary position of the kingdoms, and especially Buganda, required that these monarchies be given separate status. The compromise which emerged granted federal status to Buganda and in the process provided the Kabaka's government with exclusive powers not only over customary ceremonial and traditional matters but over a wide range of public services as well.

The kingdoms of Bunyoro, Toro, and Ankole and the territory of Busoga were granted quasi-federal status with exclusive power over their hereditary and ceremonial offices and over traditional and customary matters. The major distinction between the kingdom and Busoga governments and the district administrations is symbolic and procedural rather than substantive. In recognition of their traditional status the kingdoms and Busoga were given all the trappings of a parliamentary constitutional monarchy while the constitutional arrangements for the districts resemble more orthodox local government procedures and nomenclature. With respect to actual power, however, there is little difference. And even these differences are gradually being narrowed as the prerogatives of the smaller kingdoms are progressively narrowed and those of the districts extended.

The constitution of Uganda, including its many appended schedules, devotes considerably more space to describing the governing system of its constituent kingdoms and districts and their relationship to the central government than it does to the organization and powers of the central government. The constitution of Buganda, Ankole, Bunyoro, Toro, and Busoga, for example, are included in separate schedules to the Uganda constitution. The boundaries of the federal states and districts cannot be altered without prior approval of a two-thirds vote of the relevant local legislative assemblies. The legislatures of the federal states (kingdoms and Busoga), have exclusive powers to make laws with respect to the office of the ruler of state; the powers, obligations and titles of the rulers of states as such; public holidays and festivals of the state; traditional and customary matters relating to the state alone; such other matters as may be agreed between the government of Uganda and the government of state.[24]

Local services in the federal states are provided by agreement between the central government and the government of the federal state. Such agreements can be terminated with respect to any service by a decision of the central government acting alone, except in the case of Buganda which has exclusive authority over its public services.[25] Whereas the Uganda constitution stipulates that the federal states shall have their respective police forces, the districts may do so under the terms of the 1962 Local Administrations Ordinance about which there is more below.

Chapter 8 of the constitution outlines the administration of the districts and specifies that each district shall have a council with "such functions in relation to the administration of the district as may be conferred upon it by law."[26] Although the councils are permitted considerable autonomy with respect to their own composition it is nonetheless required that nine-tenths of the members be directly elected from single member constituencies. Permission is granted to the districts to establish the office of constitutional head provided that the motion to do so is supported by two-thirds of the council and approved by the Minister of Regional Administrations. The permissive functions of such a constitutional head resemble, and in fact are patterned upon, those of the hereditary rulers of the federal kingdoms and are limited almost solely to ceremonial and symbolic functions. The federal states (the kingdoms and Busoga) and the District Administrations are required to establish land boards which must include persons representing the "traditional interest in the territory for which the board is established."[27] The land boards are custodians of all land vested in them by law and have assumed the general authority over land formerly invested in the Crown.

The functions of Uganda's district administrations and federal states (excluding Buganda) are set out in the Local Administrations Ordinance of 1962 and the Administrations (Western Kingdoms and Busoga) Act of 1963 respectively. The differences between the two systems are largely procedural and semantic. For example, the Kingdoms Act provides that the activities of the local government are to be carried out in the name of the hereditary rulers. The kingdoms, as minor federal states, have their respective "governments" while the districts must be content with "administrations." Whereas the legislatures of the district administrations are termed councils, those of the kingdoms enjoy the privilege of being referred to as assemblies; the Speaker of the Assembly in the kingdom is equivalent to the Chairman of the Council. The system of local government provided for in the 1962 Local Government Ordinance is generally similar to that set forth in the 1955 District Council Ordinance. The more recent legislation enables the local government to acquire many of the titular, ceremonial and prestigeful offices and functions previously prohibited; on the other hand, it also provides for more centralized control over local government than did the earlier 1955 Ordinance. As with the previous ordinance the 1962 system requires that the standing orders of the councils and staff regulations of the district councils be approved by the Minister of Regional Administration. In this respect there exists an important difference between the 1962 Local Government Ordinance and the 1963 Kingdoms Act which defines the local government systems for Busoga and the three smaller kingdoms. Government's proposals set out in the Western Kingdoms and Busoga Bill generated considerable opposition on the part of the spokesmen of the traditional kingdoms. They rightfully saw the proposal as an attempt to circumscribe the federal status they thought had been won at independence. However, the UPC government generally has been determined to limit the prerogatives of the kingdoms to minor ceremonial affairs. A series of conferences was held between spokesmen and officials of the kingdoms and those of the Uganda government. More than a hundred amendments, all designed to permit greater autonomy, were submitted with little effect by the representatives of the kingdoms. The Ministry of Regional Administrations ideally would have preferred to possess the power to appoint the members of the kingdom governments' Public Service Commissions as it did with respect to the District Administration Appointments Boards. However, as the kingdoms traditionally had greater autonomy over the recruitment and management of their chiefs and officials, it was not politically feasible to transfer this power, in one stroke, to a central government ministry. Thus, the Kingdoms Act authorizes the Kingdom Assemblies to submit a panel of names from which the Council of Ministers chooses the local Public Service Commission. This is in contrast to the District Administrations Ordinance which gives the central government Ministry of Regional Administrations through the Regions Service Commission appointed by the minister, complete power over the composition of the District Appointment Boards. However, the Ministry of Local Government, in large part, has seriously qualified the autonomy of the kingdom governments over staff recruitment and discipline by successfully including in the Kingdoms Act a provision authorizing the central government ministry, and not the local government, to make staff regulations "for all or any of the . . . purposes relating to the discharge by Government Public Service Commissions (local government) of their functions in relation to persons in or desiring to become officers in government."[28] This provision gives to the Region Service Commission of the central government effective control over the regulation of appointments and methods for applying for promotion as well as termination of appointments and dismissals.[29] It also provides for appeal from the decisions of the Local Public Service Commissions. The local autonomy of the federated kingdom states and Busoga over their staff is further circumscribed by a provision in the Kingdoms Act to the effect that any conflict between the standing orders made by the Kingdom Assemblies and staff regulations made by the ministry shall be decided in favor of the latter.[30] There is also a slight difference in the manner in which the life of the respective assemblies is determined. Both types of legislatures are to be dissolved on a two-thirds vote of no confidence of the members. But as the kingdoms possess a rudimentary ministerial system of government, the rulers may dissolve the assembly if the Council of Ministers tenders its resignation and the titular ruler finds that it is not possible to appoint a chief minister who is able to command the support of a majority of the assembly.[31]

The federal assemblies as well as the district councils elect, respectively, speakers and chairmen who can be turned out of office by a two-thirds vote of the legislature. Both types of local government are required to elect education committees composed of no more than nine members, two of whom are appointed by each school owner in the local government area educating 1,000 or more children; and two persons appointed by the Minister of Education to represent other schools and teachers. Decisions of the Education Committee are made available to the local governments for information only and in effect the Education Committee is a separate authority, albeit with more representation from local government than was the case under the pre-independence 1955 Local Government Ordinance. All local governments are required to appoint finance committees. The committee structure of the federal states is stipulated in the respective constitutions while the district administrations committee system is set out in the Local Government Ordinance and in subsequent arrangements with the central government. The constitutions of the four smaller kingdoms and Busoga authorize the establishment of a Council of Ministers composed of the chief minister normally called Katikiro and such other ministers as are included in the constitution or are later agreed upon by the federal and central government. The usual ministries provided for in this fashion are finance, works, education, social services, and health. The Local Administrations Ordinance, on the other hand, permits the Councils of Districts by resolution to decide, with the prior approval of the central government, to term any four of their committee chairmen "minister." In no case, however, can the Minister of Finance of either kingdom or district be in charge of the treasury, which must remain under the responsibility of an official designated by the Appointments Board or the Public Service Commission as the case may be. Most districts have sought to avail themselves of this opportunity and it is likely that the Minister of Regional Administrations will eventually be required to permit all districts to establish ministries with the result that the present officials will in effect become permanent secretaries. A proposal under consideration in 1963 will allow the districts to select not only ceremonial heads comparable to the hereditary rulers in the kingdoms but a politically recruited chief minister (Katikiro) and other lesser ministers as well. If this does in fact transpire, the official now termed the Secretary-General will become a secretary to the politically appointed Katikiro (chief minister), and the treasurer will become secretary to the Minister of Finance, though retaining control over the treasury. Although this would necessitate considerable additional expenditure, it is defended on the basis that it would serve to standardize local government and in the process narrow the distinction between the federal governments and the district administrations. It is also believed that it might remove political pressure from the officials now in charge of the respective functions. More important, however, is the likelihood that it will further politicize local government; and as the legislatures of all but one of the federal states (excluding Buganda) and the district administrations are controlled by the majority UPC, it would in effect extend central party control from the ministry throughout the local government system and thereby contribute to the fortunes of the party in power.

While the detailed functions of the Busoga and the kingdom governments is left to negotiation with the central government, the district administrations have been assigned a number of services which they are required to provide. Generally, however, the required functions of both styles of local government are similar, though somewhat greater than those that were devolved on local governments under the terms of the 1955 Ordinance. Major additions to local government responsibilities include the provision of primary, junior secondary, and technical education, as well as enhanced authority in the general area of medical and health services.[32] The powers of the Minister of Regional Administrations are such, however, that he can effectively redefine the list of mandatory services to meet the requirements and capacity of individual districts; and if he deems it necessary he can instruct a central government agency to take over all functions from the local government. The district administrations are further authorized to perform as many as thirty-five additional functions or services, most of which were permitted under the 1955 Ordinance as well. Unlike pre-independence legislation, the laws made by the district administrations are binding on all persons of Uganda regardless of race.

Central government control over the recruitment and regulation of local government staff, including the major officials, was firmly set out in the post-independence 1962 Local Administrations Ordinance. The membership, constitution, and regulations of the local appointments boards are determined by the minister. The powers of the central government over local staff appointment, tenure, and functions is greater than at any time since the introduction of modern local government. Even the chiefs, under the Native Authority Ordinance, retained relatively greater local initiative. The withdrawal from the council of control over the recruitment of chiefs and officials has not gone uncontested and resolutions deploring this decision and requesting that local prerogatives be returned are frequent in every district. As in other recently independent and developing states, local government in Uganda is regarded by the national bureaucracy as an agency of the central government to be employed, according to central direction, in the all-important task of nation-building.

Excluding Buganda there are more than 5,000 administrative areas in Uganda, including five federal states, ten districts, some eighty-five counties, nearly five hundred sub-counties, slightly less than two thousand parishes, and approximately 3,700 villages. Councils exist at the district, county, sub-county, and parish levels with a total membership well in excess of 50,000 or about one councillor for every thirty-six adult male Ugandans.[33] Only the district councils and governments of the federal states are corporate bodies possessed of taxing and bylaw powers; the county, sub-county, and parish councils, referred to as "lower councils," are largely advisory. Their significance varies from district to district depending on local conditions. In 1963 proposals were advanced to eliminate one of the two intermediate councils and chief-taincies.

Over the years minor financial responsibilities have been delegated to some county councils. But with few exceptions, the lower councils long have been the tools of their respective chiefs who, until 1963, were the de facto council chairmen. As the chiefs have gradually become responsible to the district local government, and as direct elections to the district councils have replaced indirect recruitment through a tier of local councils, two of the major justifications for the maintenance of lower councils have ceased to exist. In theory, the lower councils pass advisory resolutions on local matters to succeedingly higher councils for consideration and ultimate inclusion in the agenda of the district council. As a later examination of a lower council in operation shows, however, there is a considerable discrepancy between theory and practice.

THE LOCAL POLITICAL SYSTEM TODAY

The Men and the Jobs

A detailed analysis of various local authority roles is presented in the chapters treating with the three illustrative districts. At this stage it is important to describe briefly the more significant political and administrative roles and describe the manner in which these positions are filled and structured.

Literature, cartoons, and jokes have all helped to equate "chief" with tropical Africa. A hierarchy of chiefs did characterize the kingdom states of Uganda, but in the non-Bantu areas traditional chieftainship was as foreign to the people as it would have been to the inhabitants of Saratoga County, New York.

The present-day political system of a selected kingdom state is examined in Chapter Four. There traditional authority was exercised through a hierarchy of chiefs culminating in a divine right king. The kings, though wielding extraordinary powers, were surrounded by a court of officials and advisors, some of whom were selected on merit and others on the basis of hereditary right. The kingdom was divided into administrative areas ruled by a chief appointed by and responsible to the king. They, in turn, appointed (in some cases with the approval of the king) sub-chiefs to administer portions of their territory. The duties of these early chiefs resemble the obligations of bureaucratic chieftainship in modern Uganda. They collected taxes and maintained law and order, tried civil and criminal cases, and promulgated rules and regulations binding on the inhabitants of their respective territories.

Authority within the kingdom states was never completely monopolized by the king and his chiefs. The indigenous clan systems, which predated the kingdom, persisted and continued to adjudicate intraclan disputes, marriage dowries, inheritance and land rights.

In the non-kingdom areas of east and northern Uganda where kinship or age-grade organization prevailed, it was difficult to isolate specific political roles or define purely political functions. With few exceptions, there were no territorial chiefs in these areas before the British arrived. The basis of authority was oriented about kinship rather than personality or territory, and the leaders of the kinship segments exercised political authority as one aspect of their general powers. As is noted in detail in the following chapter, the supernatural played an important role in ensuring locality order and integration within the kinship group.

The changes that have occurred in the kingdom states are largely a matter of degree, for the general pattern has remained constant. The "councils" have grown progressively more democratic and influential while the ruler and chiefs were made responsible first to the government and more recently to the public through the agency of representative local councils. In the non-kingdom areas the amphorous authority of kinship leaders, ancestors, witch doctors, and rain makers has gradually given way to the all-purpose system of territorial and bureaucratic chieftainship. However, traditional roles and values have not completely disappeared, though in many instances the manner of recruiting people to fill these traditional roles has changed to meet new conditions.

It is possible to perceive considerable ambiguity in the present local government system attributable to a persistence of traditional practices. For example, the distinctions made in English local government between councillors and officials, or in the United States between executive, legislative, and judicial, are not so clearly perceived in Uganda. The policy of indirect rule, to the extent to which it preserved the kingdom states and transferred the same pattern to other parts of the Protectorate, has served to perpetuate much of the traditional system. The early district commissioners, like the traditional chiefs, were legislators, executives, and judges. The domination of local councils by chiefs has gradually been reduced and in most areas eliminated completely. However, during the post-war pre-independence era it was common for the chiefs to dominate the councils—particularly at the county, sub-county, and parish levels. It took a brave peasant indeed to rise to his feet in such a council meeting and disagree with or complain about the actions of a chief. For the remaining 364 days of the year he had to live in a community wherein this same chief possessed discretionary powers of arrest, judgment, and punishment. The penalties for violation of local legislation is the same in the federal states as the district administrations. Neither local court system can levy a fine in excess of fifty shillings or imprison for more than six months.

Surprisingly enough, the central government has greater control over the legislative process in the federal states than in the district administrations. The Kingdoms and Busoga Act requires that before a bill is introduced into the Assembly it must first be forwarded to and approved by the Minister of Regional Administrations.[34] The legislative process in the district administrations does not require prior approval of draft bills by the minister although his approval is required before local legislation becomes law.

Both varieties of local government are authorized in their respective ordinances to establish and proscribe the functions of local government councils in their constituent administrative counties, sub-counties, and parishes. Such local councils may be authorized by law, penalty powers up to 100 shillings.

Chiefs and Officials

It was noted above that the executive positions in the two forms of local government vary somewhat with the federal states generally possessing a ministerial structure while the district administrations, though tending in this direction, are more likely to be headed by a Secretary-General with powers and prestige slightly greater than those of the Treasurer and Chief Judge. In both systems however the authority, recruitment, and accountability of the chiefs have undergone significant change. The problems that have evolved as a consequence of fundamental alteration in the basic institution of chieftainship are a major factor in current politics and administration. This phenomenon is analyzed in some detail in subsequent chapters. Here it is only necessary to note that generally the authority of the chief has progressively declined while his accountability has shifted away from the central government's provincial administration toward the local governments. However, the chief's dual accountability to central and local government has persisted. For example, the most recent legislation holds the chief responsible to the directives of the District Commissioner in the performance of his responsibilities with respect to law and order.[35]

However, the way has been cleared for the first time to end the accountability of chiefs to the central government and thus terminate the ambivalency of serving two potentially contradictory masters. The Kingdoms Act as well as the 1962 Local Government Ordinance empower the Minister to transfer the law and order function of the chief to the police. Furthermore the chiefs' judicial powers have been gradually reduced to the point that in most areas the separation of the judiciary from the administration has been completed.

A chief's security in office long depended upon his superior's evaluation of how well he administered his area, which in turn was largely determined by the performance and cooperation of the chiefs who served under him. It was imperative, if administration was to be considered good, that the chief be in a position to influence who should, or at least who should not, serve as one of his sub-chiefs. For example, in a county torn by religious conflict, a Protestant county chief could hardly be expected to stand idly by and permit a local government appointments board to present him with a rabidly Catholic sub-county chief. Nor could he permit an avowed enemy sworn to supplant him as county chief, to become one of his sub-chiefs. As their authority and prestige have diminished and as they have come more and more under the control of a politically organized local government, the capacity of the chiefs to influence recruitment and place of assignment has declined to the point that today their position in many areas is nearly intolerable.

In one respect, however, the withdrawal in 1959 of the District Council's authority through its elected appointment committee and lower council advisory committee to recruit and promote chiefs served to improve the chief's position, for he was no longer required to take an active part in manipulating the composition of the councils which could determine his tenure and effectiveness. This earlier situation was further complicated by a tendency of deposed chiefs to seek retribution through council membership.

Although his capacity to manipulate the composition of lower councils has drastically declined, while the necessity of manipulating the councils is less critical, the chief none-the-less is still inclined to seek to control this expression of popular sovereignty and in the process makes use of political techniques common to democratic parties everywhere. For example, the virtues of his candidates are propagandized, as are the limitations (frequently fabricated for the occasion) of his more powerful opponents.

These illustrations are not designed as an exposé of chiefs, for what is described is probably inherent in the system. A chief, if he is to be successful, is placed in a position wherein he frequently has no choice but to deviate.

Before independence the District Commissioner maintained considerable control over local government as well as over the chiefs, and it was common for councillors to bring their complaints to him. But if this was done properly, that is through the chiefly hierarchy, the complaints frequently were lost, slightly altered or even dismissed. Frequently complaints against chiefs were sent to the District Commissioner directly or presented personally when he was on safari. However, such complaints were rarely successful for it must be recalled that the District Commissioner relied on these very chiefs for information. More important, he himself was caught up in the same ambivalent situation. He may well have known, for example, that the reputed results of a given election did not accurately reflect the wishes of the people. And he probably knew, as did the chief, that if the wishes of the people were respected the result would be more conflict and tension than already existed. So long as the chief and District Commissioner agreed that good government was preferable to self-government, local democracy was largely a fiction.

The game is a complicated and personal one. Certainly a District Commissioner could not tolerate blatant and extreme divergence from the ideal pattern. However, the county chief knew the limitation of the District Commissioner's tolerance and this became a part of his frame of reference. The successful chief was one who correctly assessed the extent of deviation permissible. The unsuccessful chief was one who either miscalculated the degree of deviation allowed and was reprimanded for interfering with the democratic process, or one who failed to deviate at all. The tactics a chief employed to manipulate and control the hierarchical chiefly organization to suit his administrative needs was not limited to playing a blind hand in local elections or in frustrating lower council resolutions, for he also could discredit a lower chief who, despite an earlier attempt to preclude his appointment, managed to secure a position within the hierarchy.[36]

Chiefly Hierarchy

It is important to distinguish between what are termed higher and lower chiefs. In recent years there is a tendency to recruit county and sub-county chiefs from outside the chiefly hierarchy and vacancies are increasingly filled by local government headquarters clerks, teachers, and central government officials. On the other hand, village and parish chiefs continue to be recruited and to serve locally.

The Secretary-General in the district administrations and the Chief Minister in the federal states are the major local government officials. In practice, however, their position varies significantly from their counterpart in the British system upon which Uganda local government is largely modeled. To the British, a local government official is a permanent career employee hired by the council and devoid of general executive powers.[37] The English system is built about the principle of the council as both a legislative and an executive institution. The distinction is a subtle one, as even Professor MacKenzie has had occasion to note:

> We all know the structure of the committee and the power and duties of officials; what we do not know is the answer to the question which any simple-minded foreigner would ask: "who runs this place?"
>
> To the outsider the oldest thing about an English local authority is that it seems to have no focal point of decision . . . this is on the whole the general weakness in English local government.[38]

The institutional absence of a distinct head or executive in the British model has caused considerable difficulty and some confusion in implementing this system of local government in Uganda; and as one might expect, it also has led to a number of deviations. For example, the Secretary-General in Uganda's district administration is quite dissimilar to the English town or county clerk. Unlike the English county clerk he does not act on the advice of committees or the council but rather advises them. Before 1962 the Secretary-General in most districts was chairman of the General Purposes Committee and was situated at the pinnacle of the hierarchy of chiefs. In the non-kingdom states he was the most powerful and influential individual in the local government.

Uganda's first crop of secretary-generals were recruited largely from the ranks of the county chiefs as many still are. However, in recent years it is more common for the successful candidates for these positions to be drawn from central government departments.

The Chief Judge and the Treasurer, along with the Secretary-General, are colloquially referred to as the "big three." And it is they, along with the chairman of the council (speaker in the federal states) who are perceived as the ones "who run things around here."

The importance of local government in the daily lives of the people can hardly be overemphasized. In taxes it absorbs a considerable part of the farmer's limited cash income. And unlike central government revenue, which is largely indirectly procured, local taxation is visible. In many districts and states it is the largest single employer. Through its regulatory activities, undertaken both in its own right and as the agent of the central government, it affects nearly every hour of the peasant's life.

A major problem facing every local government is that of securing capable junior staff. The country's secondary schools are only commencing to graduate sufficient numbers of students with minimum qualifications for positions with the local governments. The great majority of local government clerks and junior executives are rarely in possession of more than six years formal education. The proliferation of administrative staff, which has accompanied the growth of both central and local government, has created an exclusive economic and social class in many parts of Uganda. This growing cadre of functionaries is highly respected, if not feared, by the public and regarded as the agency for obtaining the amenities and services of government. To the average peasant, government is a complex and confusing phenomenon and he depends on a host of officials and clerks to work this complex machine. Involvement with either the central or local government nearly always involves papers and signatures. Only the functionary knows which paper or form to use and has the requisite skill to manipulate this intricate instrument. The county chief's clerk is the man who wields the all-powerful rubber stamp, and the "stamp" and stamp pad are everywhere symbols of modern authority replacing the spear and the shield.

The former local government hierarchy of officials and chiefs and the informal kinship authority system tend to blend into one at the lower levels of administration. The village chief, for example, is frequently a clan leader; he normally divides his village into hamlets over which he appoints, with the consent of the inhabitants, an unofficial sub-village headman who in turn is often a clan or lineage leader.

Changes that have taken place within the social system as to who wields influence in the locality has had an impact upon the recruitment of local government chiefs and officials. The 1955 Ordinance and attendant constitutional regulations, for example, stipulated that the Secretary-General was to be chosen by the council from among its ex-officio members (officials and chiefs).[39] In all but three of the districts operating under the terms of the 1955 Ordinance, the first chairman of the district council was also the Secretary-General. However, beginning in about 1959 with the abandonment of portions of the 1955 Ordinance, the trend has been to remove the Secretary-General, along with the chiefs, from the political arena and as far as possible treat them as non-partisan civil servants. Even though the post-independence Local Administrations Ordinance provided for the recruitment of the Secretary-General and other major officials by an ideally nonpartisan board, agitation for a broadening of the base for selection for the higher posts persists.

The high premium placed on education throughout Africa is well known and an educated person's status often approximates that of a chief—a situation, however, which often leads to local conflict. The bright young school master, for example, feels it is beneath his dignity to obey the "lawful orders" of what he conceives to be a backward and ignorant chief. The newly wealthy coffee or cotton farmer also finds it embarrassing to pay deference to the barefooted and tattered village chief. It is not surprising that at times it is beyond the effective power of a village chief to obtain compliance from his constituent wealthy planters or cattle owners for agricultural and veterinary bylaws which he is charged to enforce.

The lower chiefs in particular are finding it increasingly difficult to accommodate themselves to the complexity of the modern bureaucracy. To enforce the bylaws that accumulate at a bewildering pace, in the absence often of even minimum literacy, is extremely difficult; and to apply universal regulations without favoritism, as demanded by bureaucratic norms, often results in unpleasant conflicts with kinfolk and neighbors.

Even the informal kinship aspects of the local political systems are in a state of transition. In many parts of the Eastern Province in particular, numerous clans have altered their constitution and basis of leadership recruitment. Clan leaders no longer automatically succeed their fathers—nor are they necessarily elders as was required in an earlier day. A number of clans have extended their area of association and now elect their leaders from among the educated or wealthy, keep clan books and accounts, charge annual dues, and grant printed receipts.

Although the titles of chiefs and officials in the kingdoms (federal states) are traditional and have remained unaltered, their functions and obligations have changed considerably. The Secretary-General, Treasurer and Chief Judge in Bunyoro are entitled respectively Katikiro, Omuketo, and Omuramuzi. But to many peasants these titles infer certain powers and duties which no longer exist.

The kinship associations in those districts where kinship traditionally provided instrumental political authority continue significantly to affect the selection of local government officials, chiefs, and councillors. For example, in districts where the lower chief, until 1962, was selected by the people and where the area was dominated by a single localized lineage, election was often preceded by what corresponded to a clan or lineage caucus.

Allocation of chieftainship and other official positions within the local government hierarchy in the multitribal districts is most complicated. Ideally, chiefs should be selected and transferred within a district solely on the basis of merit. However, to transfer a chief who is a member of tribe A to a county where the predominant tribe is B, may actually pose a threat to the chief's life. Bukedi District's many tribes have a well-cherished history of intertribal warfare and transfer of local staff in Bukedi cannot be undertaken without regard to tribal frictions and solidarity. A would-be politician may possess all the superficial attributes for success, but if his clan or one of his near ancestors was known to have migrated from an alien tribe, his chances of success are slight. The security of tenure of a former Secretary-General of Teso District, for example, was constantly threatened by the rumor that his mother was not an Itesot.

Political authority and religon in most of traditional Uganda were diffusely interrelated and an inclination to mix politics and religion persists into the present. Religious association and conflict today probably have a greater over-all impact on the selection of local officials and councillors than does even kinship. Until the government restricted the recruitment powers of the local councils in 1959 by revoking the authority of the appointments committee, a Catholic majority on a council nearly always resulted in Catholic officials and a Catholic majority on all the important committees. In those areas caught up in religious factionalism the chief cannot separate his religious from his political role. A Protestant chief in those areas where religious conflict is pronounced is expected to favor his fellow Protestants and to make life difficult for his Catholic subjects.

The duties of the chief, even at the lowest local level, are daily becoming more complex and necessitate an increasing degree of specialist training and knowledge. The village chief, for example, must make crop, livestock, and census returns. He must enforce agricultural methods, ensure that latrines are of proper construction and size, and attend to other such matters.

The wide gap between the literate and knowledgeable official and the average peasant, combined with the growing complexity of government, has served to place in the hands of chiefs, clerks, and officials a powerful weapon. The trend toward increased corruption grows in proportion to the opportunities that are available and with the relative decline in the capacity of the electorate to hold their local officials responsible. On the other hand, the spread of knowledge and Western ideas of public service have served to liberate and activate those elements in local society that were previously subordinated and silent. Women, for example, are assuming political roles that were denied them in the past. However, the trend toward direct election of most councillors, which culminated in the requirement set forth in the 1962 constitution that nine-tenths of the membership of local legislature must be directly elected, has effectively decreased the number of women sitting on local councils. As educational opportunities and levels rise, the role of young men also increases in importance. Whereas the traditional criteria of political leadership put a premium on advanced age, modern leadership requires, above all, a relatively high level of education, and by and large it is the young who possess this valuable asset. Other traditional status distinctions which once determined the recruitment of chiefs have also given way to the demands of modernity. In the former kingdoms, for example, authority traditionally rested with the bahima—descendants of the original Hamitic invaders. Today, however, chiefs and councillors are recruited from the indigenous bairu (peasant) class as well.

Who Shall Guard the Guardians?

Consent of the ruled to being ruled is everywhere required to some degree, while authority based solely upon naked force exists nowhere. In Uganda's kingdoms the paramount chief traditionally ruled as the accepted hereditary claimant to divine authority. Even today he mystically symbolizes the embodiment of the collective values and unity of the tribe. Though his powers were enormous, the traditional ruler required a periodic expression of the consent of his subjects. If he failed to govern according to accepted norms, as occasionally happened, a revolution and the accession of a new ruler likely would occur. If a chief behaved autocratically and contrary to the interests of his followers he could anticipate that many of his subjects would pack up and move away to an area ruled by another and more sympathetic chief. As the number of subjects over which a chief exercised authority was a major factor determining his power and status, it behooved him to rule in their interests.

In the noncentralized kinship-oriented local political systems, organization was much more diffuse and democratic. The son of a clan leader did not always automatically succeed to his deceased father's position, for generally the entire kinship group met and democratically acted upon the accession. The constant possibility of clan fragmentation was also employed as a means of rendering the leader accountable to his clan mates. However, the introduction of British rule, and the superimposition of a hierarchy of chiefs, led to a breakdown in the traditional accountability structure. As noted earlier, neither the imported nor the locally recruited chiefs were responsible to their subjects and except for the limits set by their obligation to the central government, they ruled arbitrarily. Changes in the diffuse social systems also led to a breakdown of old patterns of accountability. The introduction of education and Western culture, for example, tended to lessen the obligations of the young and the educated to kinship authority with a resultant rise in normlessness. It has also required that local governments be concerned with regulating behavior that previously was the responsibility of traditional institutions. It was customary for deference and obedience to be awarded the elders, the wise, and those possessed of an extraordinary association with the supernatural. Education, a cash crop economy, and the new religions have altered this, and most traditional figures have lost their grip over their clan and lineage mates.

In bygone days the village was largely self-sufficient and only slightly susceptible to the centralizing pressures of external large-scale organization. Furthermore, a relative absence of economic dependency on the outside world served to reinforce the solidarity of the multitude of tiny parochial isolated units, while consent for centralized rule was retarded.

The introduction of cash crops has deprived the peasant of the freedom of mobility he once had and as a consequence he is no longer able to hold his leaders accountable by threatening to withdraw consent by moving to another area. At the same time the impact of a money economy has further diminished the necessity of the chief's obtaining the consent of those over whom he rules. In former days a chief or a clan leader received his compensation in the form of produce, the quality and quantity of which would in part depend on the subject's state of contentment with the ruler's behavior. Today's chiefs receive a monthly salary which is a part of the local government budget. The chiefs in the former kingdoms, as well as in the non-kingdom areas, are finding it increasingly difficult to gain acceptance for their authority. In the federal states most of the newly appointed chiefs are recruited on the basis of education and experience whereas traditionally a chief had to possess a number of hereditary qualifications as well. In the nonmonarchical districts chiefs were inclined to emphasize their obligations to their kin over those due the more modern bureaucracy. However, the extent to which this conflict exists today is often exaggerated for in those areas where a traditionally fragmented people were brought together within a single district administration, a new districtwide solidarity has evolved. In fact, district nationalism in these former segmented social systems is today little less than it is in the traditional kingdoms. New authority figures, such as the county chiefs and the local government officials, have come to be accepted as legitimate rulers. As an expression of this new-found unity, there is a universal demand in the non-kingdom districts today for a "paramount chief" similar to the traditional rulers of the kingdom states. The newly discovered unity has become so attractive that the people have willingly consented to a degree of centralization which would have led to bloodshed less than a half century ago. But, as will be seen later, it would be misleading to conclude that parochial loyalties which once characterized diffuse societies have completely disappeared.

The expanded areal scope of authority which characterizes political transition in Uganda is the product of a number of factors, some of which we have already noted. Diligent propaganda by the Colonial administration has played an important part, for effective administration required the acceptance of units of manageable size. Tribal identity and exclusiveness, until quite recently, were emphasized in government propaganda in order to build a sense of enlarged collective identification where previously only segmented sovereignty existed. For example, the Iteso were urged to grow more cotton, collect more taxes, and educate more children, so that they would not fall behind the Langi. It was through administrative devices of this nature that the Iteso came to perceive of themselves as a tribal entity and thus to consent to a degree of Teso-wide allegiance and authority. However, though it solved a thorny administrative problem, district chauvinism gave rise to a difficult political situation. The new unity was so attractive and evoked such a high degree of loyalty that subsequent efforts to submerge it within a larger unitary Uganda met with considerable opposition.

Influence deriving from a number of modern sources affects the scope and the nature of the consent that Ugandans are prepared to grant to the exercise of political authority. For example, the educational impact of the political parties has drastically altered attitudes as to what is and what is not a legitimate exercise of power. Party agitation initially was directed primarily against the district officer as the most visible symbol of Colonial rule. To the extent to which the chiefs were linked with the District Commissioner they too were labeled as instruments of Colonial exploitation and foreign domination.

Real and Ideal

The philosophy underlying the 1955 and 1962 Local Government Ordinances is that the consent of a taxpaying male population, through a system of democratic elections, should legitimize the exercise of authority. Consistent with English theory the local government officials and chiefs are accountable to a large unsalaried representative council organized for purposes of administration into a number of committees responsible to the full council. The committee system lies at the heart of English local government and the likelihood of transplanting English local government principles and practices to Uganda will depend in great part upon the success of transferring the committee system.

A contrast of transportation facilities in Uganda and England is hardly necessary here. The difficulties encountered when one hundred or more councillors from say, Teso or Acholi, are required to travel to the African local government headquarters to attend the quarterly District Council meeting is obvious. It can be argued that attendance, despite these difficulties, is surprisingly good. However, attendance is achieved at the sacrifice of another basic principle of English local government—the unpaid, public-spirited councillor. Not only are transportation allowances required but it has also been necessary to pay substantial attendance allowance as well. In many districts in Uganda the cost of compensating councillors for attendance is more than an incidental expense and has led to an attitude that compensation is the right of if not the reason for service.

A large council meeting infrequently and for supposedly short periods, can in reality provide little more than a negative check on committee work. One hundred men and women in the short time available, cannot acquaint themselves with the multitude of complex decisions that are of necessity made in committee. Their major contribution is a superficial check upon prior decisions and administrative acts. Observations of English local government suggest that the system, on the whole, works very well. But what are the relative factors which allow for good government under these circumstances? First, one should note the high level of education and information which prevails in England, making it possible for the average council member to possess at least a rudimentary knowledge of the technical aspects of local government service as well as the techniques of administration.

Secondly, the English councillor is a member of at least two or three committees and it is likely that he has had experience on others as well. Thus, he tends to conceive of the committee as an integral part of the whole council. His own experience in committee renders him familiar with much of the detail of council agenda in advance of the full council meeting, and enables him to have confidence in the committee work of his colleagues with which he is not familiar. The success of the committee system in England is due in part, at least, to this overlapping committee membership and to an intuitive knowledge built up through long years of experience which defines the limits to which the consent of the full council can be tried.

Not only is a sense of mutual trust required between the committees and the full council, but there must exist within the committee itself a tacit understanding that the members will abide by committee decisions. A minority committee report is unheard of in English local government. Were it not so, the advantages to be gained from the system would be few.

Accountability and the Committee System

The average district councillor in Uganda is a member of only one committee and likely sees himself as a delegate of a county, tribe, or party. He is highly suspicious of the complex agenda containing committee minutes and recommendations to which he is requested to give his approval. The committee to him is an alien institution; until 1963 its influential members tended largely to be officials or appointed members. Cognizant of the unrepresentative composition of the committees, the councillor did not feel that "it is our committee" nor, on the other hand, did the committee possess that sense or "feel" for the temper of the council which is characteristic of the English system. As a consequence, committee reports were rarely received with an assumption of acceptability necessary to the successful operation of the system. And on the contrary, the full council treated committee recommendations as they might suggestions from a European District Commissioner. There is a predisposition to dissent, with the result that most matters are debated anew, confusion reigns and much time is wasted. Before a council member can come to accept the committee as an integral part of the council, it will be necessary that he first serve for some years on a number of committees. He will then hopefully be more likely to expect council approval of his own committee recommendations and in turn be more inclined to give his approval to the policy of other committees.

So long as a local government performs relatively few functions over a large area with limited communications and few capable and available men, there will exist a tendency toward the establishment of an executive or general purposes committee which will appropriate to itself the bulk of the government of the area. This tendency, which has long been apparent in Uganda, is aggravated when the chairman of the all-purpose or executive committee is a salaried official of the local government as he frequently was until 1963.

The extent to which the major local government committees were responsible to the citizenry was investigated in 1956. In none of the five districts shown in Table 3 was there a majority of elected members on the three major committees. In West Nile District not one elected non-chief member sat on any of the three major committees.

The local government reform inherent in the Constitution and the 1962 and 1963 legislation no doubt will increase the proportion of responsible elected members in the major committees, but as is shown in subsequent chapters there continues to exist a tendency for a few persons to monopolize the important committee posts.

The 1955 Local Government Ordinance provided for a substantial number of nominated councillors and many of these seats were filled by Protectorate government officials who then tended to find their way on to the crucial committees.[40]

The paucity in most districts of experienced and educated persons capable of a major contribution to council work is a major problem throughout Uganda; for a variety of reasons the best people frequently do not stand or fail to win election. Nomination by the District Commissioner before 1962 and by the elected council since that date pro-

TABLE 3
ANALYSIS OF MAJOR COMMITTEE MEMBERSHIP IN FIVE DISTRICTS, 1957

| | DISTRICT COUNCILS | | | | |
	Acholi	West Nile	Bunyoro	Kigezi	Teso
Total Council Membership	56	89	75	61	89
Total Committee Seats	70	47	35	37	39
Number of Members with Seats	31	33	27	23	25
Number of Seats Held					
Chiefs	30	13	13	13	5
Local Government Officers	11	11	16	7	6
Central Government Officers*	4	10	3	4	3
Other*	11	13	10	5	9
Non-Elected Members	56	47	42	29	23
Elected Members	11	0	10	8	16
Unknown	3				

* Nominated members.
SOURCE: District Files.

vides an opportunity of obtaining the services of such persons. The District Commissioner's nominees usually included a number of central government officers.

As such services as primary education, agriculture, and water supplies were transferred from the central to the local governments, the central government officer formerly in charge of the transferred service in that district was seconded to the local government. This sometimes led to a situation wherein a seconded local government officer found himself an appointed member of a council which was at the same time his employer.

According to the English model, local government officials are but employees while the committees serve as the executive agents of the council, and in this manner decisional accountability to the electorate is maintained. In Uganda, however, the officials are not only the chief executives but in practice are largely responsible for policy formulation as well. It is, of course, contrary to English local government principles that officials be elected either directly or by the council, for in theory they should have no political responsibilities. So long as a Colonial government determined the direction of local government development, the councils were discouraged from seeking to elect these major officials who were sought through recruitment by a non-partisan appointments committee or board. Since independence, however, the desire for politically elected officials has received an added impulse.

The Judge and the Judged

The current process of adjudicating disputes resembles traditional practices and procedural values more closely than any other aspect of the imported local government system. Before the policy of separating the local judiciary from administration which began in the late 1950's had significantly altered this aspect of indirect rule, Uganda's chiefs served as judges as well. The two functions were interrelated and court sessions were often employed to pass on orders and instructions to lower chiefs.

Sidney and Beatrice Webb, in their account of the judiciary in eighteenth-century England, could as well have been describing the situation which existed in Uganda up to about 1961.

Even down to the nineteenth century, the administrative and judicial function of the judges were so intermingled that most writers give up the attempt to distinguish between them. Neither the individual magistrates nor the divisional sessions made any distinction between (i) a judicial decision as to the criminality of the past conduct of particular individuals; (ii) an administrative order to be obeyed by officials; and (iii) a legislative resolution enunciating a new rule of conduct to be observed for the future by all concerned. "All alike were in theory judicial acts."[41]

The Uganda chief and the eighteenth-century English justice of the peace issued general orders, apprehended criminals, adjudicated disputes, and pronounced sentences; and both were effective largely because they knew their subjects and litigants intimately. However, modern justice requires the judge or juror to disqualify himself if he is personally acquainted with the litigants.

Rapid social and environmental changes have brought confusion and indecision to an area that was traditionally precise and predictable. For example, district councils were urged by the Colonial administration to pass bylaws requiring the peasantry to dig pit latrines of specified dimensions within their homesteads. However, in some areas to dig deep holes within the family compound was prohibited for supernatural reasons. It is in this fashion that conflict between newly sanctioned behavior and traditional norms frequently erupts.

Rivalry between competing clans often culminated in violence. Feuds of this nature persist into the modern era and a study of numerous court cases indicates that the local judiciary has evolved as a substitute arena for carrying traditional feuds to a decision.

The impact of new and alien roles and status has served to circumscribe the coercive power of traditional leaders. In the non-kingdom districts, issues concerning dowry, inheritance, land tenure, and divorce were traditionally solved within the small-scale kinship association. Adjudication on these perennial issues is still initiated within the clan or lineage but today such cases frequently find their way into the official local court system. Local bylaws treating with dowry and rights of juveniles and wives are common in most districts and have emerged in response to the inability of traditional authorities to apply customary sanctions, or in some instances as a consequence of the ineffectiveness of traditional sanctions effectively to deter deviant behavior.

Cash crops and a money economy have significantly affected behavior that was traditionally sanctioned. For example, the value of land put to cotton or coffee is such that principles of customary inheritance are no longer acceptable or just. The temptation to obtain another man's property is naturally greater as the acquisition of nonperishable wealth becomes both possible and profitable. Disputes over land rights have increased in proportion to the utilization of land for cash crops. The large number of cases of civil debt which make up the bulk of local court adjudication are largely a product of a money economy and the availability of desirable hardware luxuries.

In traditional Uganda the individual rarely left his kin or neighborhood group and the obligation owed to neighbors and relatives was precisely known and a part of one's education. Conformity to explicit norms was ensured by a system of institutionalized sanctions. It was extremely rare, however, for traditional societies to distinguish between crimes against the person and the community. The individual per se counted for little, deriving his importance primarily as a vital link in the kinship chain. Thus, justice was not secured by punishing the deviator so much as by compensating the person or group which had suffered loss because of the deviation. As a fine or a prison term compensates no one, and in fact may make it impossible for a guilty party to render compensation, it is not highly regarded as deterrent, as will be noted below. Customary law more closely approximates "natural law" than it does the modern idea of law as the command of the sovereign. Thus, traditional norms are not regarded as a set of rules to be made but rather as a fundamental truth to be known or found. Viewed in this context, deviation is an attack upon the natural order and therefore is a sin against the supernatural source of law. It follows then that supernatural devices are frequently employed as coercive instruments to ensure conformity in the modern as well as the traditional sector. Compensation to a wounded party, like deviation from established norms, was rarely conceived as the duty of an individual but rather as the responsibility of the individual's kin or other constituent group. A kin group did not assume responsibility for the behavior of its constituent members out of a sense of social obligation, but because they realized that the empirical and supernatural forces of restitution alike would fall upon all clan members and not solely upon the deviant individual.

The successful blending of a modern judicial system with unofficial and traditional practices is partially explained by the relatively close resemblance of the new and the old. Even today most cases which reach the sub-county court (lowest official court) are first adjudicated by at least one nonofficial traditional institution. As a general rule a local magistrate will not hear a case unless it first has been tried and decided unofficially. Parish and village chiefs have no legal judicial warrants but they spend much time informally trying cases under a large tree or within their own homestead. The leaders of kinship associations also continue to play a major role in the process of adjudication. The individual who bypasses the kinship level of adjudication and proceeds directly to the sub-county court in most circumstances is harshly dealt with not only by his kin but by the sub-county magistrate as well.

The District Native Court was initially presided over by the District Commissioner, later by either a county judge on rotation or a panel of county judges, and now by a chief judge. Recently a nonofficial element has been introduced into the court system and one of the few functions of the sub-county and county councils is that of periodically electing a panel of court members, who along with the judge, constitute the constituent court.

The jurisdiction of native courts does not apply to proceedings concerning a charge of death or divorce in the cases of Christian marriage.[42] The native court's range of jurisdiction generally extends over "native law and custom . . . as far as it is applicable and is not repugnant to natural justice or morality . . ." or ". . . does not conflict with Protectorate law;" or with "all rules and orders made by the Provincial Commissioner, District Commissioner, or African authority under the African Authority Ordinance."[43]

The native court system increasingly has been granted jurisdiction over specified Protectorate government ordinances and particularly over those of a regulatory nature dealing with agriculture, trade, poll taxes and witchcraft.

The Modern Court System and Law Enforcement

Each court has its own warrant which can usually be found hanging alongside a picture of the Prime Minister in the local council hall; the warrant sets out in detail the court's jurisdiction with respect to criminal and civil cases. Social and environmental changes have taken place at such a rapid and differential rate that customary law has been unable to make the necessary adjustments. The trend toward professional judges and increasing human mobility means that litigation nowadays is often between individuals of different tribes, and to further complicate matters cases are frequenty tried by a judge from still a third tribe. The fluidity of the content of "customary law" has encouraged selective decisions, varying interpretations and nepotism. Customary law with reference to nontraditional problems is no longer natural law but has become what the judge or council states it to be with the result that the peasant is frequently confused as to what is and what is not sanctified behavior. Traditionally the flexibility of court procedures where the litigants, assessors, and judge were all personally acquainted acted to further substantive justice. Today, however, ad hoc procedures frequently lead to a miscarriage of justice. The open competition and rivalry for chieftainship has rendered the courts, in a number of instances, political bodies used to chastise rivals and to reward friends. Furthermore, the maintenance of two distinct court systems on the basis of racial difference is perceived by some as unduly expensive and discriminatory.[44]

Uganda's judicial system has undergone a series of fundamental changes over the past twenty years. In conformity with the tenets of indirect rule, indigenous systems purged of procedures which seriously violated a sense of English justice or propriety, were recognized and given legal sanction. A concomitant of indirect rule as it affected justice was the evolution of a dual system of courts—one by the central government for non-African, and one by local administration and restricted to the African population. The post-war rejection of indirect rule necessitated fundamental revision in the nation's judicial system requiring an integration of local and central courts and procedures, the separation of the judiciary from the administration, and liability of all citizens regardless of race or tribe. Considerable progress in this direction occurred in 1957 with the passage of the African Court Ordinance, which provided for the separation of judiciary from the administration. The African Courts (Amendment) Ordinance of 1962 completed the task. The amended ordinance provides for a District Court (including the kingdoms except Buganda) with jurisdiction over all races and a lower court at the sub-county level. Local judicial officers from the Chief Judge through the sub-county judges are appointed by the central government's Judicial Services Commission.[45] The judicial hierarchy has been considerably simplified by abolishing the county and parish courts. Supervision over local courts has been transferred from the central government administration (the District and Provincial Commissioners) to court advisors responsible to the Ministry of Justice. In criminal cases the reconstituted District Court can imprison up to four years and levy fines not exceeding 4,000 shillings; and may hear civil cases not including property or compensation exceeding 15,000 shillings. The sub-county courts are limited to twelve months imprisonment, fines of 1,000 shillings and civil cases up to 12,000 shillings. Appeals for decision of the sub-county court is to the District Court and from there to the Uganda High Court.

The 1957 African Courts Ordinance was the first step in integrating the multitude of local courts currently litigating a variety of customary and Protectorate government laws.[46] This ordinance throws more responsibility on the local courts by limiting the number of appeal stages and by increasing the local court's powers of jurisdiction in both criminal and civil cases. More important, however, the local courts "shall in regard to their practice and procedure be guided by the provisions of the criminal procedure code."[47] Whenever an offense is covered both by customary law and by the Penal Code or any other Protectorate ordinance, it is required that the local courts adjudicate on the basis of the latter criteria. In the past there was no limitation on the nature of evidence that was advisable. But since 1957 the local courts are supposed to take cognizance of the Protectorate government Evidence Code. The local courts have long been authorized to try cases involving violations of a number of Protectorate ordinances. However, few sub-county chiefs (judges) were aware of the existence of these ordinances and few local court cases in Uganda involved central government ordinances.

Disobedience to local laws accounts for the bulk of the criminal proceedings in most districts and the propensity for cases of this nature is indicative of the extent to which the formal court system has come to act as the chief's coercive agent. In Lango in 1961 there was a total of 18,000 official cases reported, with the court fees and fines alone exceeding one million shillings. The adult male population in that district in the same year was about 89,000. If one assumes a minimum of two litigants per case it is evident that on the average nearly every other adult male was involved in formal litigation in 1961.

Appropriation and Expenditure

In Acholi District, prior to the arrival of the Europeans, it was obligatory that the successful hunter give the hind leg of an animal, if speared, to the Rwot (chief). But if the animal was trapped the Rwot received a front leg. In the kingdom of Bunyoro the ruler, whenever the need arose, appropriated from his subjects sufficient cattle to assist those subjects whose herds had been depleted through misfortune.

Government, both in its positive aspects of cushioning the impact of a fickle fate, and in its negative role of enforcing conformity to certain norms, has always been a costly affair. If some members of the society are to assume positions of authority over the rest they must receive compensation and deference commensurate with their positions. Political organization inevitably implies some redistribution of available resources. In the kingdoms this redistribution was bureaucratically organized with the peasants being obliged periodically to provide to a representative of the chief or ruler specified amounts of grain and other food stuffs. These perishable revenues were collected at the local level; a set amount was retained by the collector and the remainder passed on up the hierarchy until eventually a portion reached the king. In return, the political organization dispensed a certain degree of security from external attack and from internal disorder. Accumulated livestock and food stuffs were used to provide for various schemes of social welfare for deserving and needy subjects.

In a subsistence society the most valuable resources are land and water. The allocation of rights over land and water in both the kingdom and segmented societies was closely associated with the exercise of political authority. So long as individual title to land does not exist, the produce of the land but not the land itself may be appropriated by the political system. A controversial and at times a violent issue in Uganda even today revolves about the question of land tenure.

The primary test of the initial extension of British colonial administration was the successful collection of a hut or poll tax. The object of taxation was not only to secure revenue to cover the costs of administration, but also to serve as an effective means of introducing a money economy. The African was required to pay taxes but he was also provided with the means of raising money to pay the taxes. The subsequent export of cash crops contributed an additional source of public revenue in the form of export duties.

Until 1938 the native local political units did not levy formal taxes and the Protectorate government received the entire income from the locally collected poll tax. However, the county and district Lukikos —forerunners of the councils—did possess small funds which were held in trust by the District Commissioner. In 1919 in Teso District, for example, court fines and fees which had previously accrued to the chiefs were paid into a Lukiko fund.[48] The chiefs, in the early days of the British administration, received their income from a variety of sources and techniques. For example, the peasants, under the Native Authority Ordinance of 1919, were obliged to work a given number of days for their chiefs.

The year 1938 saw the proclamation of the Native Administration Tax Ordinance which, for the first time, authorized the levy and collection of a local government tax on all adult males.[49] A major object of this tax was to obtain revenue to compensate the chiefs for the income which they had formerly derived from compulsory labor. For those who were unable to obtain cash to pay the tax, provision was made to discharge the obligation by labor. Theoretically such labor was to be restricted to Native Authority undertakings or essential public works projects. The penalty for failure to pay the tax or to work it off was a fine of three times the tax or imprisonment for two months. Those who suffered from imprisonment were the peasants cultivating cash crops or the relatively few wage earners. And as these were the same people who were most able and willing to pay taxes, imprisonment was a relatively ineffective policy. The chiefs collected and returned the tax receipts to the District Commissioner who maintained the local native administration accounts. Local tax rates were initially low, ranging from five to seven shillings per annum, but numerous amending ordinances and legal notices effected a gradual increase. Until 1949 the Protectorate government rebated from 30 to 50 per cent of its poll tax collection to the Native Authorities. After 1949 the rebate was abolished, the Protectorate government rate lowered, and Native Administration taxes raised accordingly.

The expenditures of local governments since World War II have increased rapidly. In 1940 no local government unit spent more than £70,000. By 1955-1956 no local government unit was spending as little as £70,000.[50]

In one important respect the development of government in Uganda has been unlike that which has characterized most Western democracies. In England and the United States the cost and administration of most social services initially were assumed by volunteer agencies and local governments, while over a period of years a number of services gradually were taken over by the state and central governments. In Uganda, modern governmental services were initiated and financed by the central government. After 1955, a few services, notably primary education, water supplies, and agriculture, were devolved to some district councils. Thus the major occupation of government at the local level, until recently, has been largely the maintenance of order and the collection of central government revenue. This heritage is reflected today in the relatively high proportion of local government revenue devoted to the costs of administration.

A significant transfer of services from central to local governments began in 1956. Generally, responsibility for local water supplies was the first to be devolved. In some instances transfer of services, however, has amounted to little more than a bookkeeping transaction. The transfer of education to local government, for example, generally required the reassignment of the central government educational officer to the local government and a grant-in-aid equivalent to the costs of the additional service. Modern local government services require the employment of a large number of highly skilled technicians. Though local governments in Uganda may be overstaffed on the administrative side, the paucity of trained specialists capable of assuming responsibility for the technical services is a major problem. Thus, the transfer of services has often involved little more than a continuation of the same functions by the same men with money from the same source.

An elaborate system of local government has been developed in Uganda which, in many respects, is disproportionate to the services and functions for which it is responsible. Rapid social and political transition have generated numerous problems of local disintegration. However, the modern local government system is not well equipped to cope with the conditions underlying these transitional problems. For responsibility remains largely in the hands of the central government.

An informal division of labor between central and local governments in Uganda has gradually evolved with the central government assuming major responsibility for the positive or integrative functions and the local government concentrating on problems of order. Since independence more substantial responsibilities, in theory, have been devolved on to local governments. However, it is unlikely that an independent central government will in fact give up control over the development of services to relatively inefficient local authorities.

The greater part of local government funds and personnel are devoted to the nonservice and regulatory aspects of government. Local government chiefs, as agents of the central government, perform a number of administrative functions. For example, in addition to their other duties the chiefs enforce central government ordinances and regulations.

Uganda's local governments receive the greater part of their locally derived revenue from a personal tax assessed on a limited graduated basis.[51] As the district councils and committees until 1961 were disproportionately weighted with officials, chiefs, and nominated members, it was not surprising that graduated taxes were long opposed by the local governments.

The introduction of cash crops, private ownership, and wage earning have created a greater diversification of consumption and accumulation patterns. Government has now assumed responsibility for providing services that were either not required in the past or were formerly supplied through the obligations inherent in nonpolitical associations. The problem of assessing relative wealth with the object of differential taxation has now evolved. Despite the presence of differential levels of wealth there is little popular support for graduated taxation and tax collection has fallen off drastically since independence. Furthermore, the problem of measuring a citizen's capacity to support government is difficult indeed.

The source and means of procuring local revenue depends in large part on the operating philosophy of local government. Local governments in England are referred to as local authorities and are perceived as corporate groups composed of local representatives who have been delegated authority over the administration of specialized services. Most British colonial administrators feared that if local authorities in Africa were permitted a broad and varied tax base they would cease to be local authorities and become local governments. Faced with a perennial problem of tribal and district chauvinism, English Colonial administrators were little inclined to allow local authorities to possess anything resembling sovereign power.

This fear was well grounded for district councils, by and large, do conceive of themselves as governments and not local authorities. Nor for that matter are they inclined to limit their concern to local government. Some local councillors and officials were of the view that independence would lead to the withering away of the central (imperialist) government at Entebbe and the assumption of complete sovereignty at the district level.

The degree to which a local government should be self-supporting so as to preclude central domination or local irresponsibility is a question close to the hearts of politicians and scholars alike. However, this issue cannot be viewed outside of its cultural context. The duties one normally associates with local government in the West often were gradually assumed by local authorities from voluntary or neighborhood agencies. However, local resources in many areas were not sufficient to finance the services demanded by a rapidly increasing population which, when combined with corresponding changes in attitudes as to the proper role of government, led gradually to central government assumption of what were formerly local government services.

In Uganda, however, the developmental process has been quite different. The emergence of new social problems necessitating the development of corresponding institutions has taken place at such a rapid and disproportionate pace that voluntary agencies capable of initiating such services have not had an opportunity to evolve. Furthermore, the philosophy of government transferred from the United Kingdom to Uganda was hardly that of eighteenth- and nineteenth-century liberalism, but rather that of the twentieth-century social service state. The provision of education, medical, agricultural, and other welfare services by the central government is not regarded by Ugandans as the culmination of a gradual process, but is regarded as the why and the wherefore of government. The provision of social services was not forced on government by a dissident populace, but rather was brought to Uganda as a consequence of the social values and political philosophy of the English administrators and policy makers. Having had no other experience, the Uganda citizen equates government with welfare service and is apt to judge a political system primarily on how effectively it provides such services. The pattern in Uganda has not been one whereby a central government gradually assumed the functions of local governments, but rather one of devolving services already provided by the central government on to the local governments. If the population is already accustomed to the provision of certain services by the central government it becomes extremely difficult to devolve such functions on to local governments whose lack of experience and resources is such that it is highly unlikely that the existing standard of service will be maintained.

This chapter began with a quotation from Mr. Zake, currently Minister of Education in the Uganda government. His analogy of the white man's construction of a swimming pool for the African, which upon completion he reserved to himself on the pretext that the African could not swim, was not directed toward the local government system in particular. The frequently heard accusation that Africans in Uganda were slow to achieve self-rule because the central administration established for their governance was operated almost solely by Europeans, was firmly grounded. At the local level, however, Africans from the very inception of British rule were involved in the governmental system. Nevertheless, Zake's analogy is still appropriate. True, a modern and impressive system of local government has been constructed along British lines, but the system has not successfully taught Ugandans how to swim English style, even though the pool is built to English specifications.

The following three chapters examine in considerable detail the inner workings of the local political systems in three selected Uganda districts. It is hoped that this approach will demonstrate the variable manner in which different peoples and sets of conditions adapt British principles and practices as well as their traditional local institutions to cope with situations that are at one and the same time traditional and modern. Having set the stage for our inquiry by setting forth the major theme and the dimensions of the problem, it is now possible to proceed with the analysis of the three regions and peoples that make up the greater part of this study.

CHAPTER FOUR

Bunyoro-Kitara: From Empire to District

The visitor to Bunyoro-Kitara District—the shattered remnants of the once mighty African empire of Kitara—is struck by an atmosphere of nostalgia which seems to blanket the people and country alike. The fact that Bunyoro was once the most extensive and powerful kingdom in East Africa colors almost every aspect of its current political system. The manner in which problems of local integration and order are perceived and dealt with cannot be intelligently viewed aside from a knowledge of Bunyoro's historical evolution. For though they now inhabit one of Uganda's smallest and poorest districts, the Banyoro once received tribute from or directly ruled over nearly all of what is now modern Uganda.

Today, life in Bunyoro is generally poor, hard, and dull, while the past is romantic and exciting; it is little wonder what the people of Bunyoro tenaciously cling to the symbols and habits of another era and strive to recapture that which has long since vanished.

THE COUNTRY AND ITS PEOPLE

Tukerabasaga Agutamba, the Omukama of Bunyoro, Sir Tito Winyi IV, C.B.E.—the present ruler—occupies the throne that his father surrendered to the British after a lengthy and bitter war. The area over which the Omukama (king) reigns today coincides with Bunyoro District—an area of less than 5,000 square miles. For its entire length of approximately one hundred miles, Bunyoro's western frontier is separated from the Congo by the eastern shores of Lake Albert. To the south of Bunyoro lie the outer reaches of the Kingdom of Buganda and to the north and northeast the Nilotic districts of Uganda. (See Figure 2.) Bunyoro's history and current political system reflect its proximity to both the Bantu Kingdom of Buganda and the Nilotic cattle people of the north.

Bunyoro is almost completely surrounded by water. To the west lies Lake Albert, to the north the Nile, and on the south and east the Kafu and Nile. In the center of the district, running from southeast to northwest, a ridge of hills gives rise to innumerable streams which feed the frontier lakes and rivers. This drainage system played an important part in the settlement pattern of the Banyoro.[1] The countryside, with the exception of the flat northern grasslands and the narrow lake plain lying beneath the Lake Albert escarpment, is checkered by a multitude of raised uplands, each surrounded by a swamp or meander-

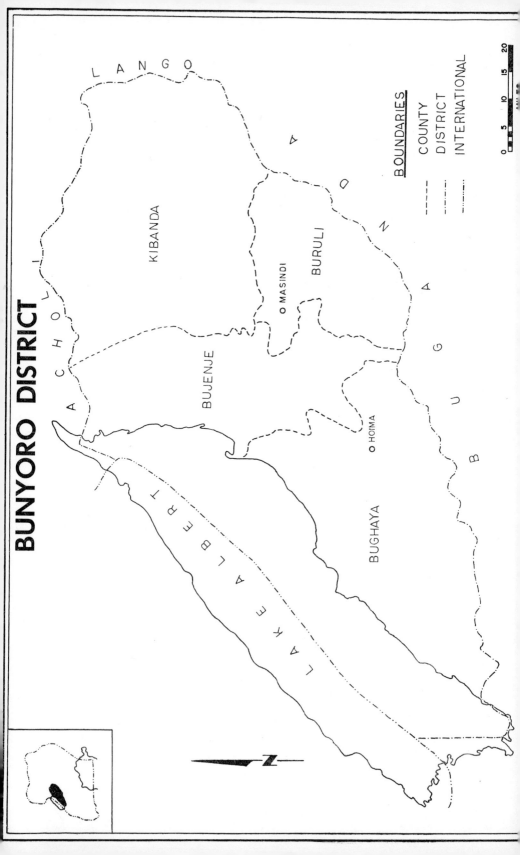

BUNYORO DISTRICT

LANGO

ACHOLI

KIBANDA

MASINDI

BURULI

BUJENJE

HOIMA

BUGHAYA

LAKE ALBERT

BUGANDA

BOUNDARIES

COUNTY
DISTRICT
INTERNATIONAL

0 5 10 15 20

N

ing stream. Homesteads, circled by mosaic patches of seemingly un-systematic cultivation, cluster at the center of these raised hillocks, which slope off into the swamps or papyrus-choked streams. John Beattie, who has intensively studied the culture of Bunyoro, attributes considerable significance to this topography.

> The topographical circumstance to a great extent determines the human settlement pattern in Bunyoro, for homesteads are found in the raised areas, and in the swampy boundaries tend to mark those areas off as separate units. This may be supposed to have enhanced in the past (it still does to some extent) the conscious-ness of land unity and mutual separativeness of the groups which live on them. Banyoro say that in former times each *mugongo* (raised area) was occupied by a separate *ruganda* (clan) and many stories are told of the mutual hostility of neighboring *ruganda*.[2]

Not only have the Banyoro suffered imperial shrinkage, but they possess the dubious distinction of being one of the few peoples in Uganda whose population is not rapidly increasing. This unusual state of affairs has been attributed to a variety of causes, ranging from poor nutrition to a heavy incidence of syphillis. Though inhabiting one of the more attractive parts of Uganda, supplied wth ample rain and fer-tile soil, the population is only twenty-seven to the square mile.

Bunyoro is divided, for administrative purposes, into four counties (saza): Bughaya in the south, Bujenje in the northeast, Buruli in the west, and Kibanda in the northwest. There are only two towns worthy of the name—Hoima, the district headquarters, and Masindi. The great majority of the Banyoro live within a radius of twenty miles of Hoima or within a swath extending northeast from Hoima to Masindi, while the sparsely populated counties of Kibanda and Buruli are heavily infested with game.

The Banyoro, along with the people of the other interlacustrine kingdoms, are classified as "Bantu." Their language, which many Banyoro claim is the mother tongue of the lake region, is a Bantu language and similar to that spoken in the Kingdom of Toro and in the surrounding portions of Buganda.

Though Bunyoro is a relatively homogeneous area, the Banyoro share the district with a number of other tribes. The most recent cen-sus credits the district with a population of 128,198 of which all but about 24,000 are Banyoro.[3]

The Banyoro share with the other lake kingdoms a history of Hamitic intrusion and conquest from the north. It is generally be-lieved that the land was once occupied by pastoral Hamitic people from north of the Nile. The bahima, as the descendants of the Hamitic invaders are termed, gradually mixed with the bairu (indigenous inhabitants) until today the distinction, though not unimportant, lingers on largely through clan names and generalizations as to social status.

The Hamitic invaders imposed on the indigenous clan settlements a more extensive and specialized system of centralized political authority. Beattie claims that the intrusion of the non-negroids from the north has fostered a dual social system which "expresses itself in political terms as the opposition . . . between the superimposed state, *obutemi*, and the underlying community of kin and neighbors."[4]

HISTORY

Bunyoro history fades gradually from that recorded since the arrival of the European, to a verbal history of recent dynasties and ultimately to a largely mythical antiquity. The lake kingdoms share the myth of a strange godlike people (Bachwezi) who, it is believed, mysteriously established kingdoms in the Lake Victoria region and then suddenly disappeared, never to be seen again. Roscoe claims to have found reference to nineteen of these mythical divine rulers.[5] They were believed to be quite unlike the people over which they ruled and are thought by some Banyoro to have been Caucasian. The Bachwezi dynasty was followed by another, linked to the first through the instrument of the supernatural. The Bachwezi priests are thought to have been the representatives or descendants of Bunyoro's supreme being, Rukanga, and it is these Bachwezi priests who link the mythical earth-walking deities to the human rulers which followed.[6] According to Roscoe, there have been twenty-three rulers of Kitara since the disappearance of the Bachwezi.[7]

The current dynasty (Babito) in common with earlier ruling families did not originate in Bunyoro but was summoned from across the Nile by some divine force to rule over the leaderless indigenous peoples of Bunyoro. Thus the present king, Tito Winyi IV, though neither a member of the peasant clans (bairu) nor of those clans claiming descent from the early Hamitic invaders (bahima), is recognized as the legitimate ruler of all Banyoro.

According to Banyoro myth, the first Babito were ignorant of the dominant cattle culture of the people over whom they were to rule and had to be taught the pertinent customs by an old woman, who had acquired her knowledge by secretly observing the practices of the previous dynasty. In reward for her instruction she was provided with a home and food and came to be called the Nyinamukama. It is customary to this day that an old woman from the same clan as the original Nyinamukama be designated as the official mother of the king. The woman receiving this honor must leave her home and village and live the remainder of her life in a distant sacred homestead.

The history of the kingdom from the time of the first Babito to the arrival of the European is one of warfare and territorial aggrandizement which reached its peak at about 1800 when Bunyoro-Kitara had extended its sway over most of present-day Uganda and parts of Kenya, the Congo, Tanganyika, and the Sudan. However, by the time the explorer Speke arrived at the court of the Omukama (king) the fortunes of Bunyoro-Kitara were already on the wane. During the rule of Nyamutuhura, the grandfather of Kamrasi, who was at the height of his power when the first Englishman entered the kingdom in 1861, a rebellious prince had successfully carved out an independent kingdom to the south. On the eastern frontier the younger and more vigorous Kingdom of Buganda was on the ascendancy and had gradually deprived Bunyoro-Kitara of its outlying southern provinces. However, there is little reason to believe that the fortunes of Bunyoro-Kitara were permanently doomed, for just prior to the conquest of Bunyoro by the British and their eager Baganda allies, Omukama Kabalega, successor to Kamrasi, was in the process of successfully reestablishing his suzerainty over a number of the disaffected outlying provinces.

The history of Bunyoro dating from the reign of Kabalega is particularly relevant to the present state of affairs in what remains of this once extensive kingdom. The story, of course, varies with the teller and the British acted largely on information supplied them by the Baganda, who were more than willing to join in a crusade against their traditional enemy. The interpretation of events that follows is largely based on Banyoro sources; in the opinion of the writer, this version more closely approximates the facts.[8]

Europeans Discover Bunyoro

Within a period of three years, East Africa's most famous explorers had called at the Omukama's court. First came Speke, in 1862, followed in the same year by Grant. In 1864, Samuel Baker and his wife passed through on their way to the discovery of Lake Albert. In 1870 Kamrasi died and after the traditional fight to the death among the princes of the realm, Kabalega was crowned. Surely no one who attended his accession to the throne could foresee that he would spend most of his life in exile on a lonely island in the Indian Ocean.[9]

In 1872 Samuel Baker, by then in the service of the Khedive of Egypt, returned to Bunyoro-Kitara as Governor-General of the Equatoria Province.[10] Baker was well received and the Omukama had a house built for him. But word soon reached Kabalega that Baker intended to annex Bunyoro-Kitara to Egypt's Equatoria Province. Baker revealed his true intentions when shortly after his arrival he asked Kabalega to call all his major chiefs together. At this meeting Baker announced the annexation of Bunyoro, ordered his troops to haul down the Omukama's standard, and then proceeded to raise the Egyptian flag. The Banyoro also maintain that the wily Baker tried to trick Kabalega into committing suicide; but the Omukama was too clever. Relations between the European intruder and Kabalega worsened rapidly and culminated in Baker's sacking Kabalega's palace and granaries and then fleeing the country. The Banyoro maintain that he planned to gather reinforcements and supplies and return to destroy Kabalega's army. Their subsequent reputation for being anti-British and warlike, the Banyoro firmly believe, was falsely attributed to them by Baker who sought to convince Captain Lugard that he should assist in their destruction.

These beliefs about the nature of the early contacts and relationships between a proud absolute monarch and a deceitful European explorer have left a powerful legacy. The words of the present Omukama, now an old man, who once lived with his father in exile, are illustrative:

> The first Europeans who came to this country of Bunyoro-Kitara, such as Samuel Baker, then Governor General of the Equatoria Province, Emin Pasha, Governor of the Sudan, General Gordon of Sudan, Major Casati and others lowered the prestige and name of the Europeans in the country from the beginning, and the distressing history that followed was because of this reason. They did not come here as guests or mere explorers, but they came mainly as spies and aggressors.[11]

Captain Lugard, by this time in the service of the Imperial East Africa Company and in the midst of efforts to pacify sectarian-torn Buganda, sought to enlist the remnants of the Sudanese troops which were camped south of Lake Albert within the territory of the kingdom of Bunyoro. In the course of his march westward to make contact with the Sudanese, Lugard reinstated the King of Toro who had been dethroned by Kabalega in his campaign to reconquer his insurgent principalities. Before returning to Buganda, Lugard established forts in Toro garrisoned with the newly recruited Sudanese troops. Lugard's Sudanese mercenaries continually harassed Bunyoro's southern flank, further inciting Kabalega's distrust of the Europeans.

During the religious battles in Buganda, the momentarily defeated religious factions often sought refuge in Bunyoro. Sanctuary was willingly granted, for the Banyoro were delighted to encourage rebellion in the ranks of their rival. The Baganda, however, were successful in convincing the British of Kabalega's warlike and conspiratorial intentions, and in November, 1893, during the interval between company rule and the formal pronouncement of the Protectorate in 1894, Lugard made preparations to destroy Kabalega's army.

On New Year's Eve, 1893, British and Baganda forces, led by Colonel Colville, crossed the Kafu River and marched on Kabalega's capital. They quickly overran the country and forced Kabalega to retreat northward into the nearly impenetrable forests and marshes along the Lango-Bunyoro frontier where for four years he continued to wage guerrilla warfare against his enemies. In 1898 Kabalega was joined by Mwanga, the deposed and exiled ruler of Buganda, but the following year both rulers were captured and imprisoned. In reward for their assistance in crushing the Banyoro, the British awarded the greater part of five and one-half Bunyoro counties to their Baganda allies. There is considerable confusion and disagreement surrounding these arrangements but it appears that Colonel Colville had promised his Baganda allies all of Bunyoro south of the Kafu River. The decision to honor this promise met with considerable opposition and two British officers serving in Bunyoro resigned their commission in protest. In 1900 the Uganda Agreement, including a provision giving legal sanction to the inclusion of all of the territory south of the Kafu to Buganda, was signed between the British government and the kingdom of Buganda.

A summary of the conflict over the lost counties is necessary at the very outset of this chapter because the issue dominates the political life of Bunyoro.

Lost Counties

The reason why I am constantly claiming these territories is because when I look at my Banyoro subjects' life under foreign rule, it appears to me as if a child was taken from its parents and given to another person. In a case like this the real parent cannot help weeping when he sees his child in bondage. . . .[12]

The question of the lost counties is truly a national obsession amongst the Banyoro. Old men can relate in infinite detail the series of events that led up to the loss of their beloved territory. School children can, and frequently do, sing mournful verses about the suffering of their fellow Banyoro in the lost counties. Important issues involving Uganda and Banyoro development are ignored while minutiae relevant to this burning issue claim hours of Rukurato (District Council) debate.

Contemporary Bunyoro history is dominated by events revolving around the lost counties issue. In 1901 Kabalega's successor resigned as Omukama in protest over the reputed persecution of his countrymen in the lost counties south of the Kafu. An attempt to introduce Baganda chiefs in Bunyoro at about the same time met with an armed uprising. In 1921 a group of Banyoro supported by their Omukama, formed the Mubende-Banyoro Committee dedicated to the task of restoring the Bunyoro counties now in Buganda.

The Banyoro claim all of Mubende—Buganda's westernmost district and portions of Singo, Bulemezi, and Bugerere counties. The areas in dispute and their population by tribe are shown in Table 4.[13]

TABLE 4
TRIBAL DISTRIBUTION IN THE LOST COUNTIES

	Baganda	Banyoro	Other Tribes	Total
Buyaga Saza	2,340	32,991	5,704	41,035
Bugangazzi Saza	4,230	16,675	1,165	22,070
Buwekula Saza	21,730	4,716	9,518	35,964
Singo Saza (Five gombololas)	29,812	2,522	16,896	49,230
Bulemezi Saza (One gombolola)	1,423	45	2,446	3,914
Bugerere Saza	30,433	407	56,805	87,645
Buruli Saza	13,972	531	8,737	23,240
Bunyoro	882	103,137	22,856	126,875
Buganda	1,006,101	71,306	756,721	1,834,128
Uganda	1,044,878	188,374	5,216,306	6,449,558

SOURCE: *Report of a Commission of Privy Councillors on a Dispute Between Buganda and Bunyoro.*

Bunyoro spokesmen, led by the Omukama, since the turn of the century have waged a ceaseless and to date a fruitless campaign to restore the lost counties to Bunyoro. No fewer than twenty formal appeals and petitions addressed to the British government have been made over the years.[14]

The burial places of the Omukamas are considered as national shrines and they play an important part in Bunyoro custom and pageantry. Except for the graves of the two rulers who have died since 1900 the tombs of all other Omukamas are located in territory that is now part of Buganda. No aspect of this emotional issue is

more humiliating and each day of veneration and each annual ceremony of the accession to the throne is a perpetual reminder of this
degradation. To make matters even worse, the most hallowed traditional Bunyoro shrine—the witch tree located on the sacred Mubende
hill—is deep in what is now Buganda. The witch tree and Mubende hill
are important in the lore and ritual not only of Bunyoro but of the
Baganda and Batoro as well.

As independence for Uganda approached, agitation for a solution
to this problem increased in intensity. There was considerable fear
with what would seem to be good reason—that if the issue was not
resolved before the British left, the preponderance of Buganda in an
independent Uganda would forever preclude a favorable solution. In
1958 the Omukama formally petitioned the Queen requesting that
Bunyoro's claims be judged by a judicial committee of the Privy
Council. However, this tactic fared no better than those of the past
for the Secretary of State for the Colonies informed the Omukama
that the question was not a legal issue. In January 1961 the Bunyoro
government voted to send a three-man delegation to London to discuss the lost counties issue with the Secretary of State for the Colonies.
However, the Secretary of State refused to meet the delegation and
advised them to present their case to the Relationships (Munster)
Commission. In March of that year the case of the lost counties was
duly lain before the Munster Commission which was the first official
body to indicate that the Banyoro's case deserved serious consideration, not because of a historical injustice but because "Bunyoro has
never accepted her dismemberment. While feelings remain as they
are at present the dispute is likely to make it impossible for Buganda
and Bunyoro to coexist amicably."[15] The Munster Commission Report further recommended that a referendum be held in Bugaya and
Bugangazzi Saza (county), where there was conclusive evidence of
a Banyoro majority and a strong irredentist movement.[16] The report
also suggested, though less strongly, that a referendum be held in
any one of the other three counties claimed by Bunyoro as well. The
arrest in July and subsequent violent death of Bunyoro's Prince John
Iukidi at the hands of the Kabaka of Buganda's police, brought tribal
tempers to a new high. The following month the Omukama flew to
London with his two advisers to see the Colonial Secretary. In September he went to London again to attend the Uganda Constitutional
Conference but refused to participate in the meetings unless the
agenda included the lost counties issue. The Secretary of State found
it impossible to include the item on the agenda but did agree to request the Prime Minister to appoint a committee of Privy Councillors
to inquire into the problem.

In desperation the Rukurato passed a motion in October declaring that the disturbed counties had reverted to Bunyoro. Rioting and violence broke out in Bugangazzi County. The central government rushed special police to the area and declared the greater part of the lost counties a disturbed area.

In December 1961—less than a year before independence—a Commission of Privy Councillors was appointed to investigate the lost counties issue and make recommendations for its specific solution. The situation by this time was critical, for petitions and delegations had given way to a violence born of desperation. From October, 1961, to January 24, 1962, more than two hundred offences had been committed against the Baganda and Banyoro believed to have been in sympathy with the Buganda case.[17] Nearly all of these incidents—consisting primarily of crop slashing, arson, and threats of violence, occurred in the predominantly Banyoro populated counties of Buyaga and Bugangazzi.

The Privy Councillors, after receiving voluminous testimony and holding hearings throughout the areas in dispute, recommended that Buyaga and Bugangazzi be transferred from Buganda to Bunyoro before independence day, for as the Commission perceptively noted, "If a Prime Minister of an independent Uganda were dependent upon the Baganda bloc for staying in office, he would find it difficult to support any concessions to the Banyoro."[18] The Commission sounded a grave warning that unless the issue was reconciled "civil strife would gradually develop into a civil war, which would not be confined to the disputants if the Banyoro succeeded in enlisting the support of neighboring tribes. Even if violence were localized, conditions in the disputed area would come to resemble those in . . . the Congo."[19] The Commission further recommended that the remainder of the area in dispute continue to be in Buganda but that Mubende town, including Mubende hill and the witch tree, be designated a municipality and thereby withdrawn from the jurisdiction of either Buganda or Bunyoro.

The June 1962 Uganda Independence Conference, held in London, nearly foundered over this still unresolved issue. Buganda spokesmen refused categorically to consider any transfer of their territory to Bunyoro and would not accept the idea of a referendum. However, before the conference ended, the Secretary of State for the Colonies reluctantly took matters into his own hands and decided that "there would be no immediate transfer of territory; the administration of the two counties of Buyaga and Bugangazzi would be transferred to the central government; after not less than two years from the time of transfer the National Assembly of Uganda would decide upon a date for a referendum in these two counties in which the electorate would be asked to express their preference between the following choices—to be a part of Buganda . . . to be a part of Bunyoro . . . to be a new district."[20]

Milton Obote, Uganda's new Prime Minister, "undertook on behalf of the Uganda Government to accept responsibility for the administration of the lost counties."[21] The Bunyoro delegation, dissatisfied with still another delay, walked out of the conference. The Buganda delegation, though remaining, stated that the decision was unacceptable to them as well.

The summer of 1962 saw continued sporadic rioting and disorder in the contested counties generally, but particularly in Buyaga. Crowds of five hundred or more were dispersed with tear gas and on occasion by rifle fire. Dr. Beattie knew from his long research that Bunyoro nationalism was intense and warranted more serious attention than it had received. Writing from Oxford he warned of the dangers to Uganda that the "almost total surrender to Buganda pressure" might entail. He added that the government was underestimating the strength of local patriotism and loyalties which "are still an essential condition of social and moral stability and cohesion."[22] Independence Day— October 9, 1962—found the new nation of Uganda torn by a number of unresolved fundamental conflicts, not the least of which was that of the lost counties. Within a month of independence the two Democratic Party National Assembly members from Bunyoro began to agitate for the Prime Minister to honor his obligation to assume administrative control from the Kabaka's government in the two contested counties. The Prime Minister did appoint an "administrator" for the two counties but the administrator's powers were only vaguely defined and his role has generally been ineffective.

At this point it is important to recall that Obote's UPC was able to form a government only through coalition with Kabaka Yekka— the Buganda Party. This expedient alliance has already given evidence of breaking apart and the Prime Minister was painfully aware that he could honor his obligations vis-à-vis the lost counties only at the cost of the fall of his government. The situation was all the more embarrassing because the 1962 London Conference agreement had been incorporated into the Uganda constitution.[23]

The issue of the lost counties—a substantial threat to the peace and tranquility of this new nation in its own right—rapidly became a ploy in a still more fundamental conflict—the struggle for power between Buganda and the central government. Although Kabaka Yekka could not hope to form a government by itself, its twenty-one seats did give it an effective veto and as a consequence the Kabaka held the sword of Damocles over the worried brow of Prime Minister

Obote. As the break between Kabaka Yekka and the UPC widened, a possible rapprochement between the DP and the KY became evident. Up to this point the Democratic Party had been a champion of Bunyoro's claims, while the UPC in alliance with the KY had attempted to straddle the issue but when required to take a stand was inclined to side with the Baganda. The flirtation of the Democratic Party leadership with the Kabaka Yekka and the widening split between the UPC and KY significantly affected Bunyoro politics as well. Covert discussions were held between UPC national and local leaders and the two nominally DP Banyoro members of the National Assembly. The stakes were as high as they were obvious. If Bunyoro's two representatives were to cross over and join the UPC, Prime Minister Obote's party would have a slim majority in its own right and would no longer be dependent upon the Kabaka Yekka support. And obviously if UPC was free of its Buganda alliance it would be able vigorously to implement Section 26 of the Uganda Order in Council. In May 1963, after many rumors to this effect, Mr. Kukihya, one of Bunyoro's two elected representatives, crossed the aisle and joined the UPC.

In the meantime the situation was rapidly becoming more critical. In February, 1963, following the arrest of the leader of the Mubende-Bunyoro movement, six hundred Banyoro nationalists went on the rampage in Buyaga County, burned the Baganda saza chief's home and destroyed the county headquarters. Weapons were stolen and a number of sub-county chiefs were attacked and their homes destroyed. Baganda chiefs were able to collect taxes and to administer the two most troubled counties only with the aid of large police contingents—many of whom were claimed by the Banyoro to be Kabaka Yekka thugs.

In April 1963 a new and dangerous episode in the lost counties drama began. Early in the month, the Kabaka, accompanied by three hundred Baganda ex-servicemen, decided to make an extended "hunting trip" to Buyaga County. The central government Minister of External Affairs, on the pretext of protecting the Kabaka's life, declared the county a disturbed area. The Buganda government was outraged that the central government should have the affront to take such a step particularly when their king was in the county. The Bunyoro Rukurato (legislature), meeting in emergency session, demanded a commission of inquiry to investigate the action of the Kabaka and his soldiers. Road blocks were set up along the frontier by spear wielding Banyoro accompanied by tribal war drums. The Kabaka, surrounded by two thousand followers, calmly established a semi-permanent residence in the sparsely settled reaches of Buyaga. Plans were drawn up to allocate plots of land in the outer reaches of the kingdom to former servicemen. An air strip was surveyed and a road to Lake Albert projected. Obviously looking ahead to the 1964 referendum, the Kabaka was no doubt confident that he could bring more than enough followers into Buyaga to ensure a majority vote in favor of Buganda. By May 1963 there were already more than two thousand ex-servicemen in the area and plans called for settling at least three thousand more. As there are probably no more than seven and one-half thousand adult Banyoro males in Buyaga, the implications of this politically motivated immigration are evident.

In response to this threat the Banyoro UPC held a mass rally; the Katikiro (Chief Minister) warned his countrymen to be ready for action. A call went out instructing all ex-servicemen and able bodied young men to report to their sub-county chiefs. Four days later more than two thousand Banyoro, armed with spears, shields and knives, gathered at the capital ready, if need be, to march across the Kafu as their forefathers had done in the past. Fortunately, however, a major conflict was averted.

Each incident adds another insult or injury contributing to the likelihood of large-scale violence and diminishing the possibility of a compromise solution. In May 1963 the head of the Buganda princes (Sabalangira) was arrested by Bunyoro police while he was passing through Hoima on his way to visit the Kabaka at his camp in Ndazi, Buyaga.[24]

By June the situation was so tense that rumors were circulating in Kampala that the central government was planning to arrest the Kabaka if he did not leave the disturbed lost counties. Violence and threats of violence, maneuver and counter maneuver of the Kabaka and government police characterized the summer of 1963. It was only the election of the Kabaka as Uganda's first President and his subsequent return, after six months in his "hunting camp" in Buyaga, that relieved the tension. Though the situation is yet to be resolved and the referendum has not yet been scheduled, the incorporation of the Kabaka as President of all Uganda has reduced considerably the likelihood of large-scale violence between Bunyoro and Buganda, or for that matter between the quasi-military and police forces of Buganda and the central government.

This then is the explosive setting within which local government in Bunyoro has evolved. The problems of local order and integration in Bunyoro are quite unlike those anywhere else in Uganda and certainly different from the kinds of problems and conditions characteristic of an English county council. Having reviewed the background and development of this conflict, it is now possible to proceed with an analysis of Bunyoro's local political system.

ECONOMY

Bunyoro society has been described as a cattle culture *sans* cattle. Early reports and present customs indicate that there were many cattle in Bunyoro during the nineteenth century and that the dominant activity of the bahima was the herding of their striking longhorned cattle. The ravages of war and disease wreaked havoc upon the cattle economy. During the six years of sporadic warfare the herds were neglected; many cattle died while others were driven north and eastward out of the district. A rinderpest epidemic, which destroyed a large part of the cattle population throughout Uganda at the turn of the century, killed off the few that the vicissitudes of war had spared. In 1955 the cattle population numbered only seven thousand, but by 1962 the herds had reached nearly 19,000.[25]

Beattie notes that the Banyoro, almost to a man, believe that the loss of their cattle "was not only due to rinderpest and trypanosomiasis, and to capture and confiscation during Kabalega's wars, but also to the deliberate policy of the Protectorate government. . . ."[26] Many Banyoro, ever suspicious of government, believe that the antibiotics of the veterinary department were secretly designed to kill their cattle. This followed from a conviction that British, and now independent Uganda, policy continues to be one of deprivation and chastisement for the people of Bunyoro.

In 1932 the total value received for agricultural produce in Bunyoro was approximately 402,000 shillings. In the same year total taxation amounted to 327,000 shillings. In 1935, crop returns rose to 831,000 shillings, while taxation only increased to 485,000 shillings. In 1938, total taxation was less than in 1935, whereas crop values continued to rise.[27]

Per capita income from sales of farm produce and fish is relatively high. Land is abundant and the rainfall generally adequate, permitting a shifting pattern of agriculture that is capable of a good return with relatively little physical investment. Wage labor has rapidly assumed importance as a means of securing money both to pay taxes and to procure an increasing range of new products. Of the 42,000 adult males in Bunyoro, about 8,000 are employed, and half receive their income from either the local or the central government.[28]

TRADITIONAL BUNYORO SOCIETY AND POLITICS

The bairu (indigenous bantu), the bahima (invading Hamites), and the Nilotic royal Babito clan—which together constitute Nyoro society—were traditionally organized on a totemic clan basis in addition to their common citizenship in the Bunyoro-Kitara state. Roscoe maintains that the Banyoro belong to more than one hundred clans which belong to one of three categories: (a) the pastoral clan, (b) a mixture of the pastoral and bahima and the agricultural bairu clan and (c) the agricultural bairu clans.[29]

In addition to these three categories it is important to add the special clan of the ruling dynasty, the Babito. Bunyoro clans are relatively unimportant today and play but a minor role in the political life of the people. But as we shall have occasion to note, leadership positions still tend to be filled from the royal Babito and the high status pastoral clans. Formerly the clan leader was instrumental in the allocation of land, but this important responsibility is now held by the lower official chiefs. Before the advent of colonial rule, the authority of the state resided in principle and in practice with the semi-divine Omukama. He granted land rights resembling fief-hold to subordinate chiefs who in turn reallocated their holdings and in turn received tribute from and ruled over the inhabitants.

In those societies characterized by potentially competing kinship and territorial authority it is common for still a third association to exist which, by cutting across other membership units, contributes to local cohesion and integration. In medieval England, for example, the frankpledge fulfilled this function, while at the same time acting as a primitive form of police.[30] The frankpledge was composed of groups of ten adult men, one of whom served as leader, who pledged themselves to accept responsibility for one another's behavior. In the chapter on Teso District we describe how the age-grade association served to maintain local order in a manner resembling the frankpledge. In Bunyoro the institution of "blood brotherhood," though less important now than in the past, continues to play a similar role. Like the medieval frankpledge and the Iteso age-grade association, blood brotherhood effectively integrated aspects of the community not bound by ties of kinship. The act of blood brotherhood is made between two close friends and is solemnized in an elaborate ceremony wherein the blood of one is mingled with that of the other. Traditionally blood brothers were obliged to come to one another's assistance whenever called upon; to fail to abide by this oath would bring the wrath of the Omukama down upon the pair.[31]

Traditionally, the Omukama held almost absolute power. He could, and often did, run roughshod over the demands of the kinship association. Upon occasion blood brotherhood even served to ally two men in opposition to capricious action on the part of the chiefs or the Omukama.

Political authority in the kingdoms, although deriving some legitimacy from the state religion, was relatively distinct from other aspects of the social order. The Omukama appointed a hierarchy of chiefs who were selected and discharged primarily on the basis of their ability to fulfill their obligations to the ruler. The political function of the various clans and clan leaders were of a minor nature and generally limited to ceremonial and symbolic functions. With the exception of Buganda, which underwent a series of religious wars at the turn of the century, the kingdom states appear to have successfully separated politics and religion—this in marked contrast to those districts where religion was an integral part of political and social life.

The relatively homogeneous Banyoro shared the same monotheistic god or creator, Rukanga. This religious tie along with centralized government and a common language, enabled the Banyoro to develop a large unified state, which in turn facilitated subsequent Colonial administration and organization. The semi-divine nature of the monarchy served to legitimize the role of the Omukama. The various Banyoro medicine men, rainmakers and diviners, all entrusted with specific functions, were organized within the state system and were accountable ecclesiastically and secularly to the Omukama.

The King and His Kingdom

As late as 1948 the Omukama felt justified in stating that "the Omukama was, and still is, the real ruler of the people of Bunyoro. He ruled over many clans and tribes. He had no other ruler above him."[32] Possessing supernatural legitimacy, the Omukama was a divine king who held the power of life and death over his subjects. The state was divided into administrative and military divisions, the number depending upon the size of the kingdom at the moment. Just prior to the war with the British and Buganda, Bunyoro-Kitara was composed of ten divisions.[33] Each division was ruled by a chief appointed by, and responsible to, the Omukama. Although the Omukama on occasion appointed chiefs from among the bairu clans they were nearly always chosen from among the pastoral bahima. The Omukama was able to ensure the accountability of these powerful chiefs through the customary requirement that they be in permanent attendance at the king's court. As a consequence of this practice the divisions were effectively ruled by deputies and assistants accountable to the major chiefs. The deputies, however, had no independent authority and acted only in the name of the absentee chiefs. The major chiefs as well as their sub-chiefs were charged with responsibility for maintaining the Omukama's peace; and for the security of his and their subject's cattle.

In addition to the hierarchy of administrative territorial chiefs, there were a few important special purpose authorities. The herders of the king's cattle, for example, all fell under the authority of a special chief who was responsible in most matters only to the Omukama. Authority was further diversified by the king's bestowment of what were in effect fief-hold grants on loyal and favored retainers, who in turn exercised authority over the peasants actually cultivating the land.

The early kings of Bunyoro-Kitara moved about extensively, but in the declining days of the kingdom the ruler lived more or less permanently at a fixed court. The Omukama's palace and court consist of a large enclosure, with a circumference of two miles or more, surrounded by an elephant grass fence. Inside are numerous huts of varying sizes and symbolic significance.

The largest of these buildings was the great court house (Kaluzika) where the Omukama dispensed justice and issued executive orders. Today the District Council meeting hall located within the palace gates is termed Kaluzika. The local government councillor must pass through the palace gates, guarded by the Omukama's personal police, to attend meetings. The Kaluzika is an open building enabling a councillor to gaze out upon such symbols of the Omukama's traditional authority as the five sacred huts, the regalia men, and the throne room. Not only is a councillor apt to be somewhat intimidated by what he sees, but the periodic thunder of the king's drums no doubt reinforces the omnipresence of the monarchy. The lowing of the sacred cows as they graze near the rear of the royal enclosure is a reminder of the days when the Omukama was considered to own all the cattle in Kitara. Under the terms of the Bunyoro Agreement, effective local authority in Bunyoro is vested in the council. But it takes a sophisticated councillor indeed to display his independence and equality while in this awesome shadow of the throne.

Traditionally the Omukama appointed whomever he pleased to fill the hundreds of official positions in the kingdom. However, the sons of chiefs, with the prior approval of the ruler, generally succeeded their fathers. It was customary for the Omukama to send a special and trusted messenger to the inheritance ceremonies of a deceased chief to mourn in the name of the king. However, his real task was to determine whether or not the deceased chief's son was fit to assume his father's position and prepared to serve the Omukama.

Special duties often associated with the Omukama's person or household were reserved to members of certain clans and, though the Omukama could veto a clan's nomination, he could only designate a person from the clan traditionally responsible for that function. Included in this category were men responsible for the accession ceremonies, the royal tombs, sacred buildings, and the regalia of the kingdom.

It is important at this point to recall that the Babito traces its origins to the lands north of the Nile, and its legitimacy is in large part a consequence of this exclusiveness.

Paramount chieftaincy was common among the Nilotic tribes of northern Uganda. But unlike the exclusive nature of the Bunyoro dynasty, a paramount chief amongst the Nilotic Acholi, for example, was recruited from a royal lineage of an indigenous Acholi clan. The relationship of kinship and ruling lineage were very close. In Bunyoro, however, the Babito are not regarded as an indigenous Nyoro lineage, but rather as a revered but alien element brought in from outside the country.

The throne of Bunyoro-Kitara was not reserved to the eldest son of a deceased king. The Omukama took as many wives as his fancy inclined and the number of children he sired was accordingly great. The sons of a deceased Omukama had to prove their worthiness to rule by exiling or killing rival claimants. The death of the Omukama often was followed by as many as three years of turmoil and chaos while rival brothers and their supporters fought one another for control of the kingdom. When Kamrasi, the first ruler to see a European, died, Kabalega and his brothers fought for a year before Kabalega was able to triumph over his rivals. The procedure of accession to the throne is a long and complex one, designed to reinforce the symbols of legitimacy and the supernatural ordainment of the dynasty.[34] The coronation ceremonies are particularly revealing as they indicate both the limits and the extent of the Omukama's power. He must rule his people peacefully; he must love his subjects equally, however poor they may be; he must look after the orphans, and he must justly "cut cases" (adjudicate). During the ceremony he is handed a ritual spear (kinegeno) and told, "you have been put in possession of your country; should any person despise you, kill him." In like fashion, but through the agency of a different clan, he is handed a shield symbolizing his obligation to protect the country from invasion; he is given a dagger indicating that he must adjudicate cases "justly and well."[35] The Omukama receives a stick symbolizing the necessity of controlling his wrath and indicating that he should beat rather than kill minor offenders; he is handed a hoe demonstrating that he "has become father of his people and that all persons must cultivate and he must see that food is grown in order to avoid famine."[36] Within the royal enclosure there grows a large garden of papyrus to remind the Banyoro that the ancestors of their Omukama came to rule over them from across the Nile.

These extensive ceremonies which are held every year provide a visual demonstration of the Omukama's power and accountability and serve periodically to reinforce the allegiance of chiefs, officials and subjects. The Omukama traditionally was not an absolute ruler. In addition to the obligation inherent in the contract of accession, he was constantly surrounded by a large body of advisors, including his powerful divisional chiefs. The chiefs, upon occasion, acted on their own initiative and if need be were frequently able to deceive their Omukama. The chiefs sometimes hid people fleeing the wrath of the ruler and on occasion connived with a Babito prince to overthrow the Omukama. The royal enclosure was surrounded by the smaller courts of the divisional chiefs. This arrangement protected the Omukama from attack, but it also served as a reminder of the military power of the chiefs and of his dependence upon them. The power of the divisional chief was a constant threat to the stability of the realm and a variety of devices were employed to ensure their loyalty. For example, during the initiation ceremony of a chief, the king would relate before the solemn gathering of chiefs and other important persons the retribution that would fall to the new chief if he was so foolish as to be unfaithful. The new chief in turn responded by giving gifts to the king and swearing his loyalty and fidelity.

Traditionally every moment of the Omukama's day, including even the hours of slumber, were ritualized; the organs of his body were termed differently from those of anyone else. His hair, toe, and finger nails, for example, were considered sacred and carefully preserved until the day of his burial. It is not without purpose that the present Omukama has revived many of the ceremonies associated with the legitimacy of his position, which had lapsed during Kabalega's war.

The contrast of the past and the present in Bunyoro is nowhere more striking than in the role of the Omukama. On one occasion the writer found the Omukama awaiting him on the porch of his palace (Karuzika) nattily attired in eggshell blue slacks, pink socks and wingtip shoes. He was stylishly groomed and wore an open necked sport shirt and a plaid sport jacket. The audience was held in his comfortable living room and tea was served. He chatted amiably and informally in excellent English. Visiting him on another occasion, however, we were met by the Omukama's uniformed personal secretary and ushered formally into an anteroom. The Omukama made his regal appearance, shook hands and sat down. All conversation had to pass through the secretary, for on this occasion the Omukama had reverted to his traditional prerogative wherein he spoke to no one directly and knew only his own language.

Adjoining the Western style salon is the throne room with the traditional elephant tusk still guarding the entrance. In days gone by to step over the elephant tusk unless properly authorized would bring instant death. Traditional spears, bows, drums and other regalia of the kingdom surround the throne which consists of a large stool covered with layers of cattle, lion, zebra, and leopard skins.[37]

Each morning the Omukama performs a series of ancient rituals. Dressed in bark cloth robes, he walks slowly through a series of five sacred huts located within the royal enclosure. However, having completed his vigil he might well change into a pinstripe business suit, summon his chauffeur and drive to Kampala in the large official Chrysler which flies the royal standard.

Royal Justice

The traditional judicial system in most respects was surprisingly similar in form to contemporary practice. The higher and lower chiefs, for example, were magistrates as well as administrators; litigants, including even the lowest peasant, could appeal through the chiefly hierarchy to the Omukama himself. While hearing cases, the Omukama was attended by a special orderly who held the sacred double-edged sword (busitamu).[38] If angered, or if an individual's behavior was found displeasing, the Omukama would reach out his hand for busitamu and put an end to the case and the litigant in one blow. A person found guilty was liable to a fine of cattle and to physical punishment. However, the dignity of authority roles was upheld; a chief, for example, could not be degraded by being put into the stocks and if he required punishment it was limited to loss of position. On certain occasions litigants were ordered to prove their innocence by ordeal, which usually took the form of poison or fire.

The land and the cattle of traditional Bunyoro-Kitara belonged to the Omukama. The individual possessed his cattle and land only through the grace of the king. At periodic intervals the Omukama's chief tax collector was sent throughout the realm to assess and levy the Omukama's tax. While collecting taxes the collectors were also on the lookout for young and comely girls for the Omukama. Like taxpayers the world over the Banyoro cattle owners were inclined to depreciate the size and condition of their herds and hid as many cattle as possible from the inquisitive eyes of the collector. It was common to offer the collector a gift in appreciation of his nearsighted assessment. Young and lovely girls were also hidden away for, though some prestige was won for the family having a daughter at court, her subsequent adultery or desertion would bring the terrible vengeance of the Omukama down upon the parents.

As the administrative chiefs moved from time to time in search of pasture and water it was necessary to construct new camps. The peasant clans were required to provide the labor for the chief's buildings and kraals. A divisional chief, however, could not levy a labor tax on the peasants directly, but had to go through the channels of the bureaucratic hierarchy. To have allowed indiscriminate labor recruitment would have destroyed the authority and responsibility of the lower chiefs. Thus, the lower chiefs, upon demand, would supply labor to the higher chiefs who, in turn, frequently provided labor for the maintenance or building of the Omukama's palaces.

The army, except for the Omukama's personal division, was under the command of the divisional chiefs, who frequently led raids into neighboring kingdoms to obtain cattle, slaves, and women. It was customary for the divisional chief to present such booty to the king who would take a portion for himself and distribute the remainder among the warriors and their leaders.

The critical relationship of political authority to the possession and allocation of land and cattle cannot be overemphasized. A chief was obeyed not because he was chief, but because he was recognized as the extended arm of the Omukama. His rule was regarded as legitimate because he had authority over the land. His sub-chiefs in turn ruled over these people who cultivated or grazed their cattle on the land falling within their respective jurisdictions. This traditional identity of land-holding and political authority poses a major problem in present-day Bunyoro. As a consequence of modern changes in land title and in the method of recruiting chiefs, the roles of landowner and chief no longer coincide. The authority of today's chiefs is legitimized through the modern local government system. However, a number of important but nonofficial persons exercise the authority of chiefs within their respective communities because of their title to large sections of land. Needless to say, the two forms of chieftaincy are often in conflict and the peasant is frequently placed in the ambivalent position of choosing between contradictory norms.

POLITICS AND GOVERNMENT IN CONTEMPORARY BUNYORO

The defeat and exile of Kabalega was followed by the enthronement of his son Karukara. Dissatisfied with their choice, the British subsequently replaced Karukara with his brother Andereya who reigned under the direct authority of the British conquerors until 1924. In that year Andereya died and was subsequently succeeded by Tito Winyi IV, the present Omukama. From the date of the extension of the Protectorate over Bunyoro (1896) until the Bunyoro Agreement of 1933, the Omukama ruled as the titular head of what was in effect a conquered and occupied state. Insult was added to injury by the appointment of a number of Baganda chiefs. From 1900 to 1933 the British administration, in common with practice elsewhere in

Uganda, gradually built up councils of chiefs. These councils were hardly a novelty in Bunyoro-Kitara for the Omukama traditionally had ruled with the advice of a council of chiefs. However, neither the Omukama nor the council of chiefs had any real power, for important decisions were made by the British administration and even minor acts had to be cleared with the District Commissioner.

In 1933, the British government decided to grant to the Omukama and people of Bunyoro-Kitara Agreement status as had been done thirty years earlier in the other kingdoms. However, Lord Hailey in commenting upon this Agreement remarked that "in the circumstances the Agreement must be considered as a declaration of Government's policy rather than having the character of a treaty."[39] Nonetheless the Omukama and his countrymen did not regard the Bunyoro Agreement of 1933 as a "statement of policy," but rather saw it as a treaty between the British government and the Omukama. Much to the distress of the Omukama, the 1933 Agreement was not between himself and His Majesty, the King of England. Negotiations which led to the 1955 Agreement provided the Omukama with an opportunity to rectify this earlier slight. The 1955 Agreement was made by the Governor of Uganda "on behalf of Her Majesty's Government in the United Kingdom and Sir Tito Winyi IV, Knight Commander of the Most Excellent Order of the British Empire, Rukerabasaya Agutamba, Omukama of the Kingdom of Bunyoro-Kitara."[40]

In some respects the 1933 Agreement gave the Omukama powers that the office had never held in the past. For example, none of the traditional advisory bodies were included within the scope of the Agreement while the Omukama was officially granted nearly all of the powers he held traditionally, except that he was required to obtain the approval of the central government before he could exercise his authority. The Omukama was recognized as the native government. If he so desired he could "establish and maintain posts of ministers, chiefs and other persons as may be approved by the Governor."[41] Although he required the permission of the Colonial administration before he could appoint or discharge major chiefs and officials, he had a completely free hand with respect to the hundreds of lesser chiefs. It, however, was obligatory that "in order . . . to assist the Omukama in the Native Government . . . he shall maintain a native council to be known as the Rukurato."[42] The duties of this forerunner of the District Council were to deliberate on matters referred to it by the Omukama and to advise him on matters of state. But the Omukama was in no way formally obliged to accept the advice of his council.

The Rukurato, as specified in the Agreement (paragraph 17), was composed almost entirely of chiefs and officials. Any change in its composition required the approval of the Omukama. Thus in 1948, when Lord Hailey viewed the council, it was composed of seventy-two members including sixty-eight chiefs and officials and four representatives of the people (bakopi).[43] When the 1949 Local Government Ordinance was applied to Bunyoro, the Omukama reluctantly agreed to permit the inclusion of ten indirectly elected bakopi which in 1952 he agreed to increase to twenty.[44]

Paragraph 1 of the 1933 Agreement stipulated that the Agreement would remain in force until annulled or amended by agreement between the Governor and the Omukama. This clause was a constant frustration to the efforts of the young educated Banyoro to liberalize the constitution. The Omukama tenaciously clung to his prerogatives and, while other districts moved rapidly toward a system of modern democratic local government, Bunyoro remained largely as it had been for the past half century.

The impact of the Wallis inquiry into local government, described in Chapter Three, plus the constitutional negotiations in Buganda gave impetus to an anti-Omukama faction. A committee of fourteen was formed and Sir Keith Hancock, the constitutional advisor who had come from England to assist in rewriting the Buganda Agreement was invited to Bunyoro as well.

The composition of this committee is revealing of the sources of the liberal anti-Omukama sentiment. In certain respects the movement for reform was a palace revolt, for the committee included the Katikiro (Prime Minister), the Omuramuzi (Chief Judge), the senior county chief, and the secretary of the Rukurato (District Council). In addition, it included a number of young, relatively well educated central government officers such as the senior assistant agricultural officer (later Katikiro), Bunyoro's representative to the central government Legislative Council and the Community Development Officer. Also in the group were two influential private medical practitioners, the manager of the local cooperative society, the ex-Omuramuzi and two school teachers.

Pressure against the autocratic rule of the Omukama was building up from yet another quarter, for the central government was seeking to bring Bunyoro into line with political developments in the other districts. Government officials, including the Governor, held a series of meetings with the Omukama to convince him of the wisdom of gracefully surrendering most of his authority. Having spent a number of years with his father in exile in the Seychelles, and ever-conscious of the fact that only a few years earlier the Kabaka of Buganda had been spirited away into exile in Great Britain, the Omukama was well aware that his position was in serious jeopardy. It is not surprising that the negotiations which led to the signing of the agreement on September 3, 1955 were characterized by intrigue and bitterness. The Omukama attempted in every way possible to equivocate and to stall the proceedings. He pleaded ignorance and misunderstanding of the terminology in his meetings with government officials while, with the aid of his legal advisors, he skillfully studied the draft proposals clause by clause and by altering a word here and there, sought to dull the edges of a document which was designed to shear him of his regal powers. He sought in vain to retain control over the appointment of chiefs and to relegate the Rukurato to deliberation on matters referred to by himself. He insisted that all committees be constituted only with his approval. In desperation he sought to have all Rukurato resolutions passed to him for study and comment (or delay) before going to the central government for approval.

The men who spearheaded the reforms had much at stake, for failure would—at the least—have led to their spending the rest of their days in the political wilderness. The Omukama sought to discredit them and actively pursued a policy of vengeance. The forces allied against him, however, were too strong. The educated elite of his kingdom, with a small but influential following of its own, was dedicated to the achievement of a political system that would grant them greater influence and provide them with security against the whims of an old and embittered Omukama.

It would be misleading to assume that the Omukama resisted the changes purely for personal reasons. He sincerely felt that a mistake was being made. During the deliberations he once stated that it was imperative that he be informed of the council's activities so he "could raise his voice against them if they did wrong."[45] Finally forced to accept the majority of the reforms, the Omukama was nearly given a new lease on life by the actions of the Colonial Office in London. This incident is worth noting because it provides an illustration of the problem of communication between the Colonial administration and the Colonial Office. The lengthy negotiations had required an extreme degree of patience and diplomacy on the part of the District Commissioner in Bunyoro. Having finally secured the Omukama's reluctant agreement to every word, the draft was sent to the Colonial Office for approval. But the bureaucrats in London found a number of minor phrases which, in their view, required alteration, and therefore submitted an amended version back to Bunyoro certain that such minor changes would be readily acceptable by everyone concerned. However, this situation provided the Omukama with another opportunity to delay his capitulation and, as the District Commissioner anticipated, he refused to sign the amended version. In the original draft the agreement was to be made between Her Majesty's Government and the Omukama. The Colonial Office amended this to read "Her Majesty." The Omukama refused to sign on the grounds that Queen Elizabeth, possessed of a mortal soul, would one day die and that the Colonial Office version was little more than a contract which would expire when death claimed either of the signatories. The Katikiro also refused to sign on behalf of the Rukurato for he felt that he could not take this responsibility and stated that it would be necessary to recall the Rukurato into special session. The Governor of Uganda, cognizant of the significance of the impasse, saved the day by somewhat arbitrarily ordering that the original version prevail and that the Colonial Office amendment be dropped.[46]

The Omukama has found it difficult to accept the spirit of reforms which in theory rendered him a powerless constitutional monarch. He regarded the incident as an inevitable capitulation, to the detriment of his people, forced upon him by the British government. The Omukama is so convinced of the impracticability of local democracy he is inclined to think that when the system breaks down, "as it inevitably will," the country will regain its senses and revert to the old system. And though this breakdown may be inevitable, the Omukama is not beyond giving fate a helping hand whenever the opportunity arises.

Constitution of Bunyoro-Kitara

The pre-independence constitution of the government of Bunyoro-Kitara was first outlined in the 1955 Bunyoro Agreement, the District Administration (District Councils) Ordinance of 1955, and the Bunyoro-Kitara Rukurato Constitutional Regulations of 1956. The post-independence constitution is based upon Schedule Three to the Uganda constitution which specifies the special provisions relating to the kingdom of Bunyoro, and the Administration (Western Kingdoms) Ordinance of 1963.

The 1955 Agreement theoretically removed the Omukama from the sphere of politics and transferred the local government of the kingdom to the Rukurato. However, the stipulation that the District of Bunyoro would henceforth be termed the Kingdom of Bunyoro-Kitara signaled the growing contradiction between the trend toward constituent federalism and a declared policy of developing English style local authorities within a unitary Uganda.

The changes that have occurred since 1955 have provided for a transfer of executive responsibility from the Omukama to the Rukurato acting through its officials and committees; the composition of the Rukurato has become progressively more representative and democratically recruited. Nevertheless, all acts of the Rukurato are still done in the name of the Omukama. The most significant alteration in the local power structure was the withdrawal of authority over chiefs' recruitment and accountability from the Omukama and its assumption first by an elected Rukurato Appointments Committee and subsequently by an independent Public Service Commission.

The fundamental difference between the government of Uganda's kingdoms and districts was outlined in the preceding chapter. Before examining the operation of Bunyoro's local political system it is necessary to summarize its formal government structure in somewhat more detail.

Although the Bunyoro government possesses no more real powers than Teso or Bukedi District, it has all the trappings of a sovereign constitutional monarchy. The Omukama is the legal head of the government but with the exception of matters and appointments relating directly to traditional and ceremonial functions and the succession, he acts only on the advice of his ministers.[47] The Chief Minister (Katikiro) is the leader of the majority party in the Rukurato and is officially appointed by the Omukama. The remaining ministers are chosen by the Katikiro from among the members of the Rukurato and serve at his pleasure. The Council of Ministers is required to tender its resignation if a motion of no confidence is carried by the Rukurato.

The current Rukurato was elected in November 1960 and therefore does not yet conform to the requirements laid down in the 1962 Uganda constitution. It is composed of fifty-two directly elected and eleven ex-officio members. The UPC with 32 seats has an over-all majority.

Elections for a new Rukurato to conform to post-independence legislation were held late in 1963. The Rukurato consists of the Speaker, the Ministers, from fifty to seventy elected members and up to seven specially elected members, the Okwiri (Head of the Babito clan) and two persons selected by and from the Babito.

The members of the next Rukurato will hold their seats for five years unless two-thirds of the voting members request its earlier dissolution, or unless the Council of Ministers resigns as a consequence of a no-confidence vote. The Rukurato elects its own speaker (Omutalindwa) who does not necessarily have to be a member of the legislature. The enactments of the Rukurato are regarded as laws and published in the official Uganda *Gazette*. In common with the other kingdoms (except Buganda) a copy of every bill must be approved by the Minister of Regional Administrations before it can be introduced into the Assembly.

The 1962 Constitution authorizes the Rukurato to establish standing and ad hoc committees but requires the establishment of an education committee. Provision is made for a standing committee chaired by the Katikiro; a finance committee chaired by the Omuketo, a social service committee chaired by the Minister of Social Services, and a works committee chaired by the Minister of Works. At least two-thirds of the members of a committee must be members of the Rukurato.

In common with neighboring kingdoms, provision has been made for a Public Service Commission composed of a chairman and five members. The members of the commission are chosen by the Council of Ministers from a list of twelve persons submitted by the Rukurato. The Public Service Commission, within the limitations of staff regulations which must be approved by the central government, is responsible, in the name of the Omukama for the appointment, dismissal and discipline of the public service.[48]

Unlike arrangements in the non-kingdom districts, the saza chiefs in Bunyoro are ranked according to customary seniority and importance. Thus the county chief of Bughaya is termed the Mukwenda, followed in importance by the Kaigo of Bujenje County, the Kimbugwe or saza chief of Buruli and the Sekibobo of Kibanda County. The sub-county chiefs also are graded in a similar manner and possess titles equivalent to their rank. Lower councils in Bunyoro have been relatively ineffective. A visit to the most populous and important sub-county council, for example, revealed that the sub-county chief was ignorant of the basis of council membership. Sessions were held whenever he felt inclined to call a meeting.[49]   *141585*

Before the lower council system was installed, the people of a village met whenever called together by a clan leader, chief or other important person. They informally discussed local problems and sought to agree on a means of solution. If they failed, they placed their problem in the hands of the official chief. Informal meetings of this nature are still held in most Bunyoro villages.

The tier system of local councils evolved in response to administrative necessity and to the existence of a comparable system in Buganda. It was a natural development to seek to turn the chiefly hierarchy into something corresponding to the English system of county, district, and parish councils. In the United Kingdom every level of local government, except the parish council, has significant financial and decisional powers. The English parish council is viewed primarily as an advisory body and soundingboard of public opinion. In Uganda, however, the county, sub-county and parish councils, when and where they exist, possess even fewer powers and resources than an English parish council. As there is considerable overlapping membership on the many councils, they have provided an important communication system which, in theory at least, effectively disseminated government policy and directives to the community level. An illustration of the use of the lower councils can be seen in the following incident. In a letter to the county chiefs the Katikiro noted that the Omukama is concerned that "girls are being pregnated before they complete their studies, and the country loses the benefit of their girls; therefore a way must be found to put a stop to it."[50] The county chiefs were then instructed to order their parish chiefs to call the parish councils to discuss this problem and to resolve their views as to:

(a) punishment for the seducer,
(b) how to keep the girls safe,
(c) the amount of compensation to be paid to the parents who have spent their money educating the girl,
(d) what to do with those already pregnant.

The parish councils were to meet on this issue in December, the sub-county councils in January, and the county councils in February. In March all resolutions, as they had filtered through the hierarchy, were to be sent to the Katikiro for consideration by the District Council Standing Committee. The distilled resolutions were then included as part of the agenda for a subsequent meeting of the Rukurato.

In practice, however, the lower councils do not always effectively inform the local and central government administration about local opinion. As we have had occasion to note, complaints are frequently short-circuited, particularly if they tend to affect a chief adversely.

Although its resources and powers may be comparable to those of an English county council, the Banyoro do not perceive of their kingdom or its government as a local authority. The emergence of Bunyoro as a quasi-federal state, replete with all of the trappings of a constitutional monarchy, has added to the image of a sovereign state. Neighboring kingdoms and districts are regarded as foreign countries and great store is set on the location of frontiers, national flags, and culture. As far as the Banyoro are concerned there is little *local* government in Bunyoro. The lower councils which might conceivably qualify are not corporate bodies, have no financial powers and cannot pass bylaws.[51]

Bunyoro, along with the other districts falling under the provision of the 1963 Western Kingdoms and Busoga Act, may establish "local government councils in counties and other administrative sub-divisions," and can set out the appropriate functions including the power to make bylaws. However, before local councils can be delegated any real authority, the permission of central government is required.[52]

The manner in which these lower councils are perceived is suggested by an item which appeared on a Rukurato agenda.

the people who are selected as representatives of the people in *Gombolola* (sub-county) and *Miruka* (parish) councils do not like to attend this council when they are told to do so. Their excuse is that they do not get pay for the council.[53]

In practice the councils at the parish level are attended by all who wish to be present and are regarded more as community gatherings (barazas) than as meetings of constituency representatives. The following excerpt from a letter reveals both the changing role of women in Nyoro society and the tendency to view council meetings as open to anyone:

> We would ask you to kindly to be informed us [*sic*] when Miruka Councils are to assemble so that we can prepare to attend. You know we the *Bakyada* [housewives] of Bunyoro are not considered much in councils of this district, men alone cannot save the country, we need to collaborate.[54]

Little knowledge of the purposes or composition of local councils exists in Bunyoro, and although this is generally true throughout Uganda, it will be noted that in those districts characterized by small-scale kinship-based societies, relatively more interest and emotion are invested in lower council membership. The permissive functions of the Bunyoro government are those set out in the first Schedule of the Western Kingdoms and Busoga Act and summarized in Chapter Three. With the exception of slightly increased responsibility in the field of education, the government of the 1963 federal state of Bunyoro, has no more significant authority than the 1956 Bunyoro District Council. Bunyoro possesses neither the technical personnel nor the revenue capacity to undertake a wide range of permissive public services and the transfer of some agricultural services, primary education, rural water supplies and forestry has been largely a transfer in name only, for much of the work and supervision continues to be handled by central government departments. Technical personnel seconded to the local government continue to be formally responsible for certain matters to a central government department. Funds for transferred services are provided by Protectorate government grants roughly equivalent to the entire cost of maintaining the "transferred" service.

Kings and Chiefs

When viewing the rule and significance of the present Omukama, it is important to recall that he dates his birth from the time of the British and Baganda invasion of his kingdom. He was with Kabalega during the lengthy period of guerilla warfare, and joined his father in exile from 1910-1920. Certainly the wounded and embittered Kabalega recounted to his young son in great detail the treachery of the Europeans and Baganda, and he must have reminisced about the grandeur that once was Bunyoro-Kitara's.

In his youth the present Omukama served as the personal servant to a missionary in Hoima. Later he worked as a clerk in the District Commissioner's office. In 1922 he was appointed a sub-county chief and upon the death of his half-brother in 1924, he succeeded to the throne. After concluding the 1933 Agreement he was awarded the C.B.E., and after affixing his signature to the 1955 Agreement he was granted a Knighthood. He is reputed to have nearly seventy children (thirty-two admitted) and complains that the education of his family absorbs the larger part of his official salary.

It was noted above that before the arrival of the Europeans, chieftainships were granted by the Omukama and conferred authority over people occupying a specific territory. Although the traditional and modern hierarchy of chiefs are generally similar, the authority of the former depended more on the manner in which the chieftainship was acquired, one's personal relationship to the Omukama, and the number of subjects ruled.

The Colonial administration, limited in field personnel, took only a slight interest in the recruitment of village and parish chiefs. Selection of village chiefs was left to the people themselves while parish chiefs were generally appointed by sub-county chiefs with the approval of their superiors. Central government control over the appointment and dismissal of county and sub-county chiefs, however, has always been intense.

A significant distinction is made between higher (county and sub-county) and lower (parish and village) in Bunyoro. There is some traditional basis for the important status distinction between higher and lower chiefs, for in the days when Bunyoro-Kitara was a force to be reckoned with in East Africa, the higher chiefs resembled feudal lords and commanded large armies, while the lower chiefs were minor functionaries dependent upon the favor of a gracious king or major chief. The higher chiefs, when not conducting military campaigns or paying short visits to their respective domains, were in attendance at the king's palace where they could guard and be guarded.

British rule tended to perpetuate this important distinction, for the higher chiefs were few and accessible while the lower chiefs were numerous and blended imprecisely into the ranks of landholders and peasants.

The important difference is readily perceived by the Banyoro and is not unlike the distinction the New England villager makes between a resident constable and the transient state police. The lower chiefs, and in particular the village chiefs, are not subject to administrative transfer as are the higher chiefs. They tend to serve their own neighbors and kin until they retire, die, or, as is more often the case, until they are discharged.

The recruitment and role of higher and lower chiefs in Bunyoro varies from that of the non-kingdom states, as the following chapter will show. The difference is in part a consequence of variations in the manner of landholding and tenure. The Banyoro chief had authority over the land and therefore over its inhabitants. He granted secondary rights over portions of his fief-hold to his chief who in this fashion assumed authority over the inhabitants as well. For the Banyoro, right to land implies a right to exercise authority over its occupants, and the early chiefs derived their income from their tenants. The introduction of a cash economy gradually led to the transmutation of tribute into a cash payment, and by 1933 the chiefs were receiving from five to seven shillings per annum from each adult male within their jurisdictional area.[55]

The cash economy, however, served to dry up the sources of tribute which had traditionally filtered up to the Omukama, with the result that it became increasingly difficult for him to support his relatives and retainers in their accustomed style. The Omukama reacted to this situation by granting fief-hold title over portions of the kingdom to old friends, relatives and to others to whom he was traditionally obligated. These estates differed from the holdings of the chiefs who were required to relinquish their lands and authority if transferred or dismissed. However, the personal estates granted by the Omukama were outright and permanent gifts to a specific individual. Nevertheless the tenacious customary association of landholding with the exercise of authority over its inhabitants was such as, in effect, to grant to the estate holders the powers of a chief over their tenants. Thus in the midst of the territorial responsibilities of the official chiefs there emerged islands of nonofficial authority with the result that conflict developed between bureaucratic chiefs and large landlords.

To cope with this situation the government implemented a new form of land ownership and issued certificates of occupancy to the actual cultivators of the land, thinking in this manner to uproot the rapidly developing feudal system. Coincident with this "reform" was the replacement of the official chief's tribute by a regular salary. The success of a system of this scope required that it receive the support of the Banyoro who, for obvious reasons, did not enter into the spirit of the reform. In effect, few changes were made and the large landholders continue to possess their rights and thus their unofficial authority over the tenants.

Frequently the official and the unofficial chieftaincy system tend to blend into one another, for the official chiefs, upon appointment or promotion, seek to obtain landholdings commensurate to their position. In addition, official chiefs are often recruited from landed families. Thus the association between landholdings and authority is maintained despite all the efforts that have been made to divorce the two.

An understanding of the recruitment and role of the lower chiefs is best provided by a hypothetical description of a chief (for our purposes named Joseph) based upon accumulated data.[56]

Soon after finishing his primary education in a mud and wattle mission school within walking distance of his father's home, Joseph found himself a member of The King's African Rifles. This experience took him to Kampala, Nairobi, Mombasa, and to India and Burma. He returned a hero of sorts, wise in the ways of the outside world. His father, as one of the larger local landholders, held beer parties and dances in his compound which provided an opportunity for Joseph to relate his fascinating experiences. While in the Army he had learned to read, write, and speak English. He put this knowledge to use by working, for a time, as a headman for an Indian rubber and tobacco merchant. Later he served for a few years as a local government policeman. Finally, at about the age of thirty-five, he returned to his village to cultivate his land. The village chief died soon after and the people meeting together and conscious of his worldly experience chose Joseph as their new chief. The parish chief, a long-time friend of Joseph's father, approved of Joseph, concurred in his election and reported his approval to the sub-county chief who in turn brought the new state of affairs to the attention of the county chief. Joseph was then confirmed in office. He held a big beer party and everyone got moderately drunk.

Joseph's new position would not allow a life of ease, for his income as a village chief was only £24 ($67) per year.[57] Outwardly, he resembled his subjects, but if one were to look closely, he would see that Joseph always had a pencil and some papers stuck into his shirt pocket. He continued to live in his own house, which if not already more impressive than those of his subjects, was soon enlarged accordingly. Joseph's work was complicated by the fact that he was not the sole authority figure in his domain, for the head of the largest of the twenty to thirty Kibanja (landholdings) in his village exercised considerable authority over his numerous tenants. At times, it was extremely difficult for Joseph to enforce planting and harvesting regulations which were passed on to him by the parish chief. Within his village lived two young school teachers. Being very wise and haughty, they delighted in making Joseph look stupid and in refusing to consent to his authority.

Two days a week Joseph called all the people to work for two hours on local bush paths which he sought to convert into a road. He hoped that the local government ambulance and the cooperative cotton lorry would then be able to drive to his village. If Joseph's subjects refused to do as he ordered, he reported the offenders to the parish chief and, if still disobedient, the deviators were charged at the sub-county court for refusing to obey the lawful orders of the chief. People with petty disputes were always coming to Joseph's house and he spent a great deal of time listening to and pronouncing judgment on a variety of cases. If the litigants refused to accept his decision they would usually take their case to the sub-county court. But as this involved them in formal litigation and required the payment of court fees, Joseph's informal judgments generally prevailed.

Joseph's village was not a homogeneous unit. True, its boundaries were well known and it was required that he walk the borders when he assumed office. But within the village were three clusters of homes. In each one Joseph informally appointed a leading individual as his assistant. The assistant was likely a parish councillor who joined Joseph at the infrequent meetings of the parish council. The assistant received no pay, but had added prestige and could justifiably invite himself to more beer parties than before. Joseph was a popular chief. He was welcome in everyone's home and no special arrangements were necessary when he made his informal visits. Upon leaving he was often given a couple of eggs, but not necessarily so. If, however, the sub-county chief happened to be touring Joseph's village, everything was put in order. Joseph's subjects helped him to tidy up his compound, to prepare food and to build a shelter for the sub-county chief to sleep. On such occasions Joseph led a procession, including the sub-county chief, his accompanying policemen, and the local councillors, on a tour of his village. They stopped their bicycles at various homes (Joseph had already warned the selected families), and Joseph pointed out the cleanliness of his village, the excellent state of the crops, and the progress he was making on the roads.

Joseph was frequently called upon by a villager accompanied by a friend. The villager would tell Joseph his friend's history, testify to his good character, and request that his friend be allocated some land in the village. Joseph considered this request and, if he approved, he walked the boundary of the plot allocated and sent a message to the parish chief that the new arrival was to be entered on the tax register at the sub-county headquarters.

If it was necessary that Joseph see all of his subjects at once, he would beat a large drum and everyone would gather and listen while Joseph informed them that the village was to be honored by a visit from the county chief, and warned everyone to prepare for the great event. As village chief, Joseph was always on call. He often had to rise from his bed to restore order at a village beer party or to lead his villagers in pursuit of a chief. On occasion he organized hunts to rid the area of crop destroying animals. Frequently a local government policeman from the sub-county headquarters appeared with a warrant to arrest one of Joseph's subjects. Usually he assisted the policeman; but at times, if he felt for personal reasons that the charges should not have been made, he frustrated the askari's efforts and warned the wanted man to flee.

At tax collection time Joseph was exceedingly busy. Pressure was exerted throughout the hierarchy and Joseph hurried to the cotton buying stations carrying the tax tickets given him by the parish chief. He demanded payment while his subjects had the money. His possibilities of promotion depended, in large part, on how effectively the tax was gathered in his village. His assistance was also sought during the period of tax assessment when the village was visited by a committee of the sub-county council. Joseph provided the committee with information as to the relative assets and liabilities of his people.

Although he inherited land from his father, Joseph felt that as a chief he should acquire more. He bent every effort to do so, particularly when he was informed that the county council had selected him to become the new parish chief. As a parish chief, Joseph's duties were only slightly different from before. His pay was increased to £38 per year and he was required to spend considerable time calling on the three village chiefs serving under him.[58] He added a new pair of shoes and a khaki jacket to his wardrobe and more papers and pencils protruded from his pocket. With the assistance of a government loan he bought a new bicycle and spent less time at home. The sub-county chief made frequent calls and related to Joseph what the important people in Hoima had decided and what he was expected to do. Furthermore, Joseph was now a sub-county councillor and met more important people. He saw the District Commissioner about twice a year when he inspected the sub-county records and met with the sub-county council. Joseph wished he could be promoted to sub-county chief one day, but he realized that this was hardly likely, for by that time only clerks, school teachers, and other educated people were likely to become higher chiefs.

After ten years he became disillusioned; his health failed and he sought more and more consolation in the beer pot. His more enlightened subjects and ambitious village chiefs began to grumble and Joseph soon found himself replaced. He retired, but as he had accumulated rather large holdings of land he continued to exercise considerable authority over his tenants. In his bitterness he sought at every turn to make life difficult for the new and younger chiefs.

The sub-county chief, unlike lower chief Joseph, is a bureaucrat. He has an official forty-nine acres and a house built for him by the local government. In close proximity to his house is a large open building which, until 1962 and the separation of the judiciary from the administration, served both as the chief's court and as the council meeting hall. The sub-county chief's office, replete with a clerk and well-thumbed files, is located at one end of this permanent concrete building. If the sub-county chief is fortunate he drives an automobile, but more likely he must make do with a motorcycle. He does not know his subjects intimately and cannot approach them unannounced as do the lower chiefs. Though the sub-county chief is granted the use of forty-nine acres of land (county chief—eighty to one hundred) he is technically prohibited from raising cash crops, for it is felt that this would detract from his official duties or lead him illegally to recruit local labor. The higher chiefs solve this problem by raising cash crops in the name of their relatives. In this fashion the sub-county chief's annual income of about £220 is significantly augmented by the sale of cash crops.

A significant number of the higher chiefs are from the royal Babito clan and are more likely than not to be the sons of chiefs or other notable persons. In part this accounted for the fact that the chiefs were among the few people with sufficient resources to purchase an education for their children. Of the twenty-five sub-county chiefs in Bunyoro in 1956, four were relatives of the Omukama and eight were either the sons of chiefs or of other Bunyoro officials. Twenty of these chiefs were either of the royal Babito clan or of the high status pastoral Hoima clans.

It is rare today for a sub-county chief to be recruited from the ranks of the parish chiefs, and the gap between the two offices is continually widening. The parish and village chiefs continue to be community leaders, whereas the higher chiefs are in effect bureaucratic and professional civil servants; and it is from the ranks of the local government clerks and teachers that today's recruits for the positions of the higher chiefs are chosen.

The county chiefs in Bunyoro command considerable respect and deference which, as subsequent chapters show, is in marked contrast to Teso and Bukedi Districts. They own motor cars purchased with the assistance of local government loans, wear business suits and ties, and live in large, comfortable homes provided by the local government.

Democracy in Bunyoro-Kitara

It was noted above that under the present constitution, the chief and local government officials are technically the salaried officers of the local government and responsible to the people through the agency of the Rukurato and the Public Service Commission. The modern system has largely inherited the legitimacy of the old, though many peasants, either through ignorance or preference, still regard the Omukama as an absolute ruler. The change in Bunyoro is not as sweeping as in Teso or Budeki, for in the former area the similarity between the traditional and the modern system acts as a conservative influence. Political transition in Bunyoro is of an evolutionary nature and is based solidly upon precedent. A sense of district nationalism is traditional and effectively legitimizes new districtwide political institutions. Furthermore, the obsession with the lost counties issue has siphoned off political energies and ambitions that might otherwise have been directed against the existing system. Institutional changes in neighboring districts, and particularly in Buganda, are carefully observed, not for fear of being left behind in the process of political modernization, but for fear that Bunyoro's relative status may be affected.

In the forefront of the struggle to regain the lost counties are the officials of the local government, the leaders of the UPC, the Mubende-Bunyoro Committee, and the Omukama. In the eyes of the public this activity, which frequently borders on violence, reaffirms a legitimacy to exercise authority. More prestige is associated with District Council (Rukurato) membership in Bunyoro than anywhere else in Uganda except Buganda. The Rukurato has existed since time immemorial—only its membership changes. The Great Rukurato is required to meet at least four times each year; but in practice it is convened four or five times. The convening of the Rukurato is an impressive event and is illustrative of the importance of tradition and on occasion of the conflict between the past and the present.

On the opening morning, Rukurato members begin to drift into the palace gardens, some on foot or on bicycles, others riding motorcycles, while the chiefs and officials arrive in their own automobiles.[59] All must pass through the palace gates guarded by the Omukama's soldiers. The Rukurato Hall is decorated with papyrus, symbolizing the Nilotic origin of the Omukama and a reminder that he was called by the forefathers of the present Rukurato to rule over them. At the front of the hall is a raised platform covered with bark cloth and leopard and lion skins. To the rear of the platform is one large ornate chair and two slightly less impressive chairs. On the wall hangs a picture of Her Majesty Queen Elizabeth, slightly beneath and to the right of a photo of Kabalega and Prime Minister Obote. Between the raised platform and the rows of councillors' chairs is a large table with two conventional chairs and one special ornate chair strategically located. Here sit the Minister of Finance, the Secretary to the Katikiro, and in his special chair the Katikiro, splendidly attired in a blue robe embroidered in gold.

Suddenly the Omukama's royal drums break the silence. A woven carpet is unrolled stretching from the Rukurato Hall, through a small gateway in the fence that partially separates the Hall from the sacred huts, then through the first sacred hut to the Omukama's palace—a distance of at least 350 yards. The gossiping and good-natured chatter abruptly cease and the Rukurato members rise to attention. Through the gateway stride the royal drummers, followed closely by the royal trumpeters. In the background, smartly at attention, stands a detachment of the uniformed local police, with rifles held stiffly at present arms. The Omukama appears dressed in a gold-trimmed gown, purchased, as tradition requires, in Egypt. The medallions of his knighthood and C.B.E. blend well with the gold thread and braid. Behind the Omukama walks the District Commissioner attired in full-dress uniform. The two men pause and salute the police contingent and then proceed together into the Rukurato Hall. The Omukama takes his seat upon the throne and the District Commissioner seats himself lower and to the left. Without fanfare the Queen shyly takes her position alongside the Omukama.[60]

After a short prayer the Katikiro rises and speaks. He can be counted on to give the Rukurato a pep talk and bring them up to date on the "lost counties" issue. The District Commissioner rises and, with the aid of his interpreter, speaks at length, urging moderation on the lost counties issue and emphasizing the relative importance of the preliminary estimates with which the Rukurato must now deal, and the requirements of Bunyoro development. The District Commissioner will almost surely remind the gathering of an impending deficit and, on the basis of his intelligence reports, seek to anticipate specific complaints that will be raised during the course of the session. He knows, for example, that the issue of elephants destroying crops will arise; to forestall or to mitigate this, it is likely that he will inform representatives of the work of the game department and the number of elephants that have been shot.[61]

The Omukama slowly rises; the councillors chant traditional phrases of fidelity. The Omukama speaks softly of the need for higher education and encourages the inclusion of women in the political life of the kingdom. The Omukama urges caution and patience; he reminds the

chiefs of their key role in the development of the kingdom and urges
that they carry out their duties honorably and honestly. The new
Rukurato members and newly appointed chiefs come forward one by
one and kneel before the Omukama;

> I swear by Almighty God that I will serve the R.A., the Omukama,
> and the people of Bunyoro-Kitara honestly and diligently to the
> best of my ability, and that my counsel shall be devoted to the
> program and welfare of the Kingdom.[62]

The meeting adjourns temporarily while the District Commissioner
and the Omukama take their leave accompanied by renewed drumming
and bugling. The throne and skins are removed, the Katikiro and
county chiefs shed their traditional but uncomfortable robes and return to their chairs in business suits. The meeting is called to order.
An impressionistic description of the 1956 Rukurato session will provide the tone and style of Nyoro politics:

The Katikiro addresses the Rukurato for the second time, but
now less formally than before. He takes advantage of the opportunity
to impress the members with his dedication by maligning the British
government in general and the District Commissioner in particular,
whom he accuses of prejudicing the views of the Ministry of Local
Government with whom he is negotiating approval of the £5,000 "lost
counties" expenditure. Members from the floor support him in this
view and accuse the government of "playing on time." "We should
send an ultimatum to the minister that unless action is taken we will
act," says one. Another member rises and reminds the Katikiro that
the power of the Rukurato is greater than that of the Standing Committee and that the Rukurato must be allowed to approve committee
resolutions as well as to amend them if so inclined.

The general conduct of the meeting is orderly and rational compared to those in Teso where the chairman is frequently unable or
disinclined to maintain order. After some debate, the Rukurato, by
show of hands, votes to send a telegram of congratulations to the
new Governor. A committee of six is selected to draft a telegram to
be sent to the Minister of Local Government with reference to the
£5,000. The six are selected from the educated elite and they immediately leave the hall and cluster under a tree while a scribe, bent over
the fender of a new German Mercedes, records their judiciously
worded plea. In the meantime, the meeting continues. The Katikiro
educates the councillors about the danger posed by the East African
High Commission, particularly as to its recent action which concerned
the organization of the East African military forces. The Katikiro
takes the line assumed by nearly all educated Africans and warns his

councillors that this is but another example of the underhanded way the British are attempting to force an East Africa Federation on Uganda.[63]

A committee is selected to draft a resolution to the Colonial Office in opposition to the High Commission.

The declared purpose of this Rukurato session is the consideration of the estimates, but finances must await more important, better understood and more exciting matters. The council fulfills the District Commissioner's premonition and concerns itself with the devastation of crops by what it refers to as "vermin" and by what the Game Department perceives as the noble "elephant." The government claims the elephants are a national asset and must be protected. The peasants deliberately plant their fields where the elephants are likely to graze in the hope that upon their complaint the game guards will shoot the elephants and a feast of fresh meat will ensue. The local council regards the elephants as pests worse than rats because they are more dangerous. The Game Department offers no protection and merely frightens the elephant away. "If the government wants to consider buffalo and elephants as sacred animals, will they pay compensation for our crops?" "If my neighbor's goat or cow strays into my garden and eats my crops, my neighbor is fined and pays me compensation," are typical comments.

In the discussion of the estimates, it is possible to detect the evolution of nontraditional special interest groups. The teachers are particularly concerned about the education grant, the farmers about the price of crops and cooperatives, while the chiefs and officials are concerned about taxation and administration—but all share an emotional preoccupation with the lost counties. The Omukama himself has two direct representatives in the Rukurato.[64] In addition a number of the representative members are obligated to him either on a clan or personal basis. Thus, the Omukama also has his pressure group which initiates motions to increase his income and defends his position in debate. For example, some of the anti-Omukama councillors once accused the ruler of padding his mileage allowance and recommended that he be told to maintain an itemized account. His friends defended him by drawing attention to the heavy petrol consumption of big American cars.

In 1960 the Omukama, supported by the ex-officio councillors, attempted to preclude direct elections to the Rukurato, and did manage to delay the crucial election for nearly two months. The Rukurato passed a motion in favor of direct election by only three votes. On November 8, 1960, Bunyoro held its first direct elections to the Rukurato. No longer could the chief-dominated county councils determine the composition and policy of the Rukurato and the preponderant influence of the alliance of Babito, higher chiefs, and officials was broken forever.

The UPC won twenty-nine of the fifty-two elected seats (subsequently increased to thirty-two when three independents declared their affiliation) as 72 per cent of Bunyoro's 33,567 eligible voters went to the polls. The DP candidates successfully contested eleven seats while the Bunyoro Public Party won five. A single seat went to the Uganda National Congress while the remaining six were captured by independents. The importance of this election is suggested by the fact that only thirteen of the new Rukurato had been members of its predecessor, while thirty-nine members had never before sat on the Rukurato. Even more revealing is the change in occupational representation. Teachers have always played a relatively large role in Nyoro politics and as early as 1955 nearly one-third of the Rukurato members were schoolmasters. However, direct election increased this number to more than half of the total membership—a proportion equaled nowhere else in Uganda.

Reference was made earlier to the four general clan categories: the Babito royal clan, the bahima pastoral clans thought to be of Hamitic origin, the mixed clans, and the bairu or indigenous agricultural clans. Little emphasis is placed today on the status distinctions that were traditionally associated with these clan groups. In the kingdom of Ankole, however, the royal dynasty was not imported from an alien people as were the Babito in Bunyoro. The Omugabe (king) of Ankole is a bahima, and in that country the distinction between the high status bahima clans and the low status bairu clans is maintained to this day—persisting as a major divisive factor in local politics. For historical reasons, the bahima were largely converted by the CMS and the bairu by the Catholic missionaries. Today most bahima are Protestant and most bairu Catholic. This, when added to the religious basis of the political parties, goes far to explain the extreme factionalism and latent conflict that characterizes much of Uganda. In Bunyoro, however, there has been considerable intermarriage among the various social classes. Even before the arrival of the Europeans the Omukama occasionally selected his chiefs from the agricultural class. Nevertheless some aspects of this status differential persist into the present.

The rapid democratization of political life throughout Uganda has severely shaken the position of the traditional dominant elite in all four kingdom states. The 1960 election in Bunyoro dealt a serious blow to the preponderant influence of the royal Babito and the high-status pastoral clans; the 1963 elections served to further this trend.

The pre-independence period, however, was dominated by an elite which, regardless of its modern ideas, drew its support from the pastoral and royal clans. A study made in 1956 of the last indirectly elected Rukurato is indicative of the transitional influence of traditional forces.

A survey of sixty-four Rukurato members revealed a disproportionate number of Babito and pastoral clans on the council. Of the sixty-four Rukurato members, ten were Babito, thirty-three were from the high status pastoral clans and twelve from non-pastoral.[65]

Probably more significant is the relationship of council membership to kinship association among the Bunyoro chiefs. In traditional Bunyoro the chiefs represented legitimate authority. It is quite likely that the villager who traces his ancestry through a long line of chiefs is today regarded as a more proper Rukurato member than his less illustrious neighbor. The sixty-four councillors questioned claimed a total of 111 chiefs or ex-chiefs as relatives.[66] Thirty-nine (or 61 per cent) reported that their father is or was a chief; twenty-one (33 per cent) claimed a brother; twenty-five (39 per cent) a grandfather; and twenty-six (41 per cent) either a father-in-law or brother-in-law as a chief or ex-chief. Only twelve of the sixty-four councillors sampled claimed no such ties with a chief or ex-chief and of the twelve, nine were of the former serf clans. It is not likely that the voters consciously ponder the clan category of Rukurato candidates, but it is probable that leadership characteristics are associated for traditional reasons with the descendants of the pastoral and royal clans.

It is important to note that the twelve Rukurato members who reported no relationship to chiefs or ex-chiefs have a significantly higher level of education. Only four of the sixty-four Rukurato members had attended the University College of East Africa (Makerere College); two of the four are among those who claimed no relationship to chiefs or ex-chiefs. Of the remaining ten, five have either attended secondary school or teacher training courses. It is apparent that Rukurato membership tends to correlate with chiefly background, which in turn is associated with the high-status clan categories.

Education is rapidly replacing traditional criteria as the basis of leadership. This has not, however, resulted in a drastic change in the sector of society from which Bunyoro's leaders are recruited, for with some notable exceptions the fathers and grandfathers of today's aspiring Bunyoro leaders were chiefs, large landholders, or officials. And though the criteria for leadership are changing, the traditionally based elite has been better able to equip its sons with modern credentials. This, in part, explains why the pressure to liberalize and modernize the political system was initiated by the elite and not by the peasants, who are inclined to support the status quo. The new leaders, though they inherit from their forefathers a certain amount of traditional legitimacy, prefer to base a right to rule on the acquisition of an education or on other forms of modern accountability. But ironically, education and modernity have set them against the traditional system.

Patterns of Obligation

The Rukurato, the chiefs, the officials, the Omukama, the political parties, and the District Commissioner all have their respective roles to play in the local political system. These multiple roles, however, are interdependent and frequently overlap while a transitional environment has contributed to numerous conflicting obligations. For example, the Omukama in recent years has toured his kingdom semi-annually. On such occasions he is presented with food and gifts as tradition requires. Since, however, the gifts and much of the food must be purchased, the burden this places upon his subjects is heavy. In 1954 the Rukurato resolved that these visits be limited to once every three years. Obviously incensed, the Omukama replied that, "It is not fit to set laws for your Omukama." Furthermore, the tours are absolutely necessary "to the people who are oppressed and unjustly treated by the unscrupulous chiefs. . . ."[67] In anticipation of these royal "safaris" the Katikiro warns the county chiefs that they must refrain from offering "gifts" to the Omukama with the intent of securing promotion. The Omukama's reaction is that it is customary and right that the chiefs give "gifts" to their king. This situation illustrates the conflict of chieftainship as a gift bestowed by the Omukama, which in turn entails gifts to him and the bureaucratic requirements of a modern-day local government civil service.

The appointment of the official mother (Nyinamukama) of the Omukama further illustrates the conflict of traditional patterns of responsibility with the present-day values of Western justice and the inviolability of the individual.

In 1953 the Nyinamukama died. The clan leaders met and selected a new Nyinamukama. Her husband was not pleased by this turn of events for the honor did little to compensate him for the loss of a wife. He took his complaint to the District Commissioner and related that: three men "called to my home and deceived me that they were collecting the relatives of the late Nyinamukama to take them to Hoima on the death ceremonies, and that they shall return them on 26-2-53. Through this deceitful information I was deprived of my wife, called X. Since then my wife never returned and I never saw those men who took her."[68] Asked about the propriety of this alleged abduction, the

Omukama informed the District Commissioner that, to the best of his knowledge, the woman was recruited without force and was selected by a meeting of her relatives. The ruler expressed deep sympathy with the complainant but said that the matter was not of his doing and must be so.[69] Some of the younger Banyoro expressed indignation over this event. They felt that nowadays the individual should be free from such outmoded demands. But in Bunyoro, where the past and the present often blend, custom exerts a powerful influence. The problem of reconciling the modern-day values of individual security with the demands of tradition still exists.

Despite the constitution and the provision of the Western Kingdom and Busoga Act, the Omukama continues to wield considerable influence through the realm. The chiefs are well aware of this and it places them in a difficult position, for they cannot afford to ignore the Omukama's wishes, but if they comply they may risk conflict with the District Commissioner, the local government officials, and political party leaders.

The chief's position in Bunyoro, in spite of the tradition of authority and consent which surrounds him, is not an easy one. The strong chief commands the respect of the conservative elements of the community but often elicits the emnity of the influential educated elite. If the chief is weak and rules solely according to modern-day standards, he has little control over his lower chiefs who show their lack of respect by acting in such a way as to discredit him in the eyes of the administration and Public Service Commission.

Having been largely but not completely freed from their obligations to the Omukama, the chiefs have not substituted an accountability to the local government officialdom or to the Rukurato. Traditionally, the higher chiefs were not accountable to their respective clans and in recent years the Omukama's and District Commissioner's authority over them has been largely removed. It is difficult to be accountable to an amorphous committee or council composed of one's subjects, thus Bunyoro county and sub-county chiefs find themselves in a relatively normless situation. The sub-county chiefs who, until 1962 were still serving as judges are tempted to act irresponsibly, and often decided cases arbitrarily with little concern for proper procedure or for the views of the official court members. The frequency of misappropriation of funds is also indicative of the breakdown of channels of accountability, as is the repeated failure to include certain people on the tax register. Even the chief judge has been accused of taking a personal interest in civil cases, of refusing to allow certain evidence, and of destroying important documents.[70] Because they can no longer hold a chief accountable by moving away from his particular area and because the lower councils, in particular, have proven ineffective, the peasants have come to look to the District Commissioner and more recently the party leaders as their only hope.

Accusations of bribery and misconduct against the chiefs are regularly made and, in many cases, are unwarranted and undertaken for personal reasons. Therefore, accusations of misconduct and irresponsibility are usually treated with suspicion and no action is taken until direct evidence makes the misbehavior clear beyond doubt. Charges against a chief are extremely difficult to prove. If a chief is accused of accepting a bribe he may force some and solicit others to testify that he is being spitefully and wrongly accused. The higher chief generally supports his subordinate.

The men in charge of the medical dispensaries have been known to demand as much as twenty to thirty shillings pocket money before they will treat the sick. If the chief is receiving his cut it is extremely difficult to render anyone accountable. Cases in which chiefly candidates buy their appointments from higher chiefs are not unknown. When the District Commissioner discovered such a case he ordered the Katikiro to take action. The action consisted of ordering the chief to return the bribe with the implication that he be more discreet in the future.[71]

If the chiefs are not accountable to the people through the agency of modern local government system, neither are the councillors upon all occasions concerned only with the welfare of Bunyoro. Hardly a Rukurato meeting goes by without an effort to vote increased attendance allowances. Were it not for central government control over the budget it is likely that the councillors would vote themselves a significant proportion of total revenues. The full council rarely discusses in any detail the mundane problems of government but, as already noted, tends to concentrate on resolutions and petitions to the central government and on increased salaries while important decisions are made by the committees and officials. The Finance Committee, for example, is extremely powerful. It decides on personal loans to local government officials and chiefs and frequently authorizes warrants for special expenditures without the approval or knowledge of the Rukurato. It also establishes salary scales and fringe benefits for all local government employees. As the local government is the largest employer in Bunyoro, the economic and political significance of expenditures on salaries is clear. It allocates housing to the officials, clerks and chiefs, establishes and votes pensions and gratuities, makes loans to nongovernment associations, establishes and allocates transportation and safari allowances and decides on most staff increases. This is, of course, in addition to its responsibility for revenue and estimates.

The General Purposes Committee decides on amalgamations of administrative units, acts on lower council resolutions, determines the composition and functions of lower councils, discusses and decides on constitutional organization, and defines the local government's attitude to the central government and other local governments. The central government administration and departments deal with the General Purposes Committee as if it was independent from the Rukurato—which in practice it often is. Finally, the General Purposes Committee is responsible for the consideration of all local government bylaws.

Local government by committee is not inconsistent with the English model so long as committee membership accurately reflects the composition of the democratically recruited council. But in Bunyoro, until 1961, the committees were dominated by the nonrepresentative members who would not be permitted to sit on the council in England. In 1957, for example, the six local government officials held all but one chairmanship and seventeen of the seventy-nine seats, while the four ex-officio county chiefs held ten committee positions. Ten of the fourteen Rukurato appointed members were in possession of twenty committee seats and of these appointed members it is worth noting that the three holding five seats were sub-county chiefs.

Under the Local Government Ordinance of 1949, the representative members of the Rukurato were indirectly elected through a hierarchy of lower councils as described above. Although the representative members selected in this manner tended to be the choice of the chiefs, the system did possess the advantage of ensuring a continuity and overlapping of membership throughout the council hierarchy. A representative Rukurato member, prior to the 1955 reforms, was therefore also a member of a county, sub-county and parish council. Under the present system this overlapping of membership, vital to communication in an underdeveloped area like Bunyoro, does not automatically follow. Thirty-seven of the sixty-four Rukurato members polled in 1957, for example, claimed membership in no lower council, two reported themselves as members of a county council only, four of the parish council only, and twenty stated that they served on both sub-county and parish councils. It is too soon to gauge the significance of this altered pattern, but it would appear that the gap between the Rukurato and the lower councils will widen.

Maintaining Law and Order

As a centralized kingdom with a paramount semi-divine ruler, Bunyoro has traditionally maintained a sophisticated system of justice based on a universal and accepted knowledge of a set of sanctioned norms and coercion required to ensure compliance. The king was the supreme judge as he was the supreme law-giver. The judicial system was hierarchically organized with a highly developed procedure of appeal in some cases to the Omukama himself.

The court system in modern-day Bunyoro is similar in outline to that described in Chapter Three. The court of first instance is at the sub-county level; appeals can be made within a period of thirty days to the county court. The courts not only try cases involving native law and custom, but those dealing with infractions of local government bylaws as well. Bunyoro courts did not fall under the terms of the African court's ordinance until late in 1961. From that date county chiefs have been disassociated with judicial work. County courts are now presided over by county judges and two assessors. The central government judiciary has long appreciated the value of the latitude permitted by customary procedure and on occasion cases have been transferred to the native courts so as to take advantage of this flexibility. This has been particularly evident in cases where sufficient evidence for conviction in a Protectorate court was not available.

The Native Courts Ordinance of 1940, as applied to Bunyoro, recognized the Rukurato as the highest native court.[72] At that time it more closely resembled the traditional organization than it does today. The Omukama was President and was joined by the Katikiro, three higher chiefs, one parish chief, one village chief, and one representative of the people. Today the Omukama no longer plays an official role in the judicial system.

The local government maintains a central prison at the district headquarters in Hoima, and county prisons in each of the four counties. The twenty-four sub-county headquarters maintain temporary lock-ups. During 1962, 630 Banyoro (or approximately one in every forty-five taxpayers) spent some time in custody.

No longer able to employ traditional coercion to ensure conformity, the chiefs more and more rely upon the courts to enforce their orders. The sub-county chief, who as late as 1962 continued to serve as justice of the sub-county court, is most inclined to employ judicial coercion. This dual role renders the sub-county chief extremely powerful and provides numerous opportunities for personal gain. For example, he can arrest a person on a fictitious charge and subsequently convict him of that charge in his own court. The chief, as judge, must listen to the opinion of his court advisors, but is not required to take their views into account.

The uncertainties of a transitional era have given rise to multiple and sometimes contradictory standards of behavior. In many situations customary law is unsuited to modern conditions and is rapidly developing into ad hoc judge-made rulings. The absence of codification frequently results in arbitrary decisions and the denial of substantive justice while the nonexistence of well-defined and accepted norms contributes to anomie and furthers disintegration of the political system.

Acquisition and Allocation of Local Resources

The allocation of rights to land in Bunyoro differs from that in the non-kingdom districts. Bunyoro's population density is relatively low with the result that it has been spared the social and political problems of land pressure common to Kigezi and portions of Bukedi. Furthermore, the allocation of land in Bunyoro traditionally is associated with the person of the Omukama.[73]

A history of centralized land control and the granting of fief-hold-like titles to the chiefs, plus the introduction of certified holdings in 1933, has resulted in a predisposition to accept the idea of private ownership in Bunyoro. Thus land tenure proposals did not meet with anywhere near the degree of resistance as they did in Teso and Bukedi, where traditional custom and transitional problems are completely different. The relatively stratified status system which characterizes Bunyoro contributed to the acquisition of large holdings by the few, and a subservient tenant status for the many. In Teso District, as is shown in the following chapter, every man is entitled to equal rights in the land, and any attempt to deprive him of this prerogative is regarded as a denial of his birthright.

Traditionally, the Nyoro peasant paid a tribute to the land authority (chiefs and ruler). Today, the income of the ruler and chiefs has been monetized and the peasant pays a local government tax. But the idea of deference due the chiefs and the ruler in the form of produce still persists and the chiefs, when on tour, continue to receive tribute in kind. The interaction of such remnants of the traditional system with the bureaucratic norms of the present often places a considerable strain on the political system. What was once a deference gift to a chief today is regarded as a bribe.

The expenditure of public resources to achieve desired social ends was a recognized activity in traditional Bunyoro but today such undertakings have become highly specialized. In the past the child was educated in the home. For example, a son of a pastoral Muhima underwent a strenuous education to enable him to take his place within the complex cattle culture. But the modern social problems with which the child must be prepared to cope are quite different. Education is now the responsibility of the specialized government departments and religious missions. Although still influenced by the competing missions, the schools now receive nearly all their revenue from government. In Bunyoro the education system offers a twelve-year course leading up to the School Certificate, or a six-year course which entitles the student to the Primary School Leaving Certificate. There are about eighty primary schools in Bunyoro receiving assistance from the local government. But only slightly more than half provide a full six-year primary education. The primary school enrollment is about 10,000 children. However, in 1961 only 1,000 children sat for the Primary Leaving Examination and only 525 passed. There are eleven junior secondary and one senior secondary schools in Bunyoro. The enrollment of the senior secondary school is about 100 students. As late as 1957 only three Bunyoro students were enrolled at Makerere College and in the same year there were only three hundred-odd school teachers in the entire district. The central government grant for primary teachers' salaries in 1962 was £62,354, a sum slightly in excess of total tax revenue. It is apparent that the provision of the first few years of education is within the means of most parents. But to give a child the equivalent of an American junior high school education is economically prohibitive for all but a handful of parents. This, in part, explains the continued low standard of public administration and the problems of securing leadership oriented to the values of modern bureaucratic local government.

The Ministry of Community Development, in conjunction with the local government, has sought through the provision of adult literacy classes to narrow the disturbing gap which exists between the relatively educated youth and his illiterate and superstitious parents. At best, however, the adult literacy expenditures in Bunyoro are but a feeble effort. For 1956-57 the local government appropriated £50 to pay the salaries of "literary supervisors" and it was not until 1961 that a full-scale literacy campaign was launched, but even then only four hundred people actually purchased the literacy kits and registered for courses.

A cash economy and modern expectations have necessitated expenditures of funds for the maintenance of the integrative symbols of the tribe. Such expenditures are indicative of the problems inherent in transition from a traditional kingdom to a modern local government. Appropriations are regularly made to build and repair facilities to store and preserve the regalia of the realm and to purchase special emblems and flags. Although government has become more specialized and has assumed new functions, other nonpolitical associations are also evolving in answer to the problems posed by new conditions. For example, the public corporation, including local and central government investment, is a device currently employed to solve specific agricultural problems. In Bunyoro the "cattle ranching scheme" is an organization of this nature.

Before the introduction of a cash crop economy, subsistence agriculture and herding prevailed and a surplus in kind sufficient to meet the tribute demands of the chiefs was generally available. The highly organized distribution of tribute served as the major means of allocating resources, although trade in a few specialized products was also carried on. In answer to the distribution problems posed by a cash crop economy the government has sponsored the development of cooperative societies.[74] However, the cooperative movement in Bunyoro has not been spontaneous but rather has been encouraged and nurtured by the central government. The Bunyoro cooperatives are not beset with problems of multitribal hostility and suspicion as is the case in Bukedi; nor is the idea of large-scale non-kinship forms of organization alien to them as it is to the Iteso. Nonetheless the Bunyoro cooperative movement has not been an unqualified success and many of the societies exist in name only.

Occupational specialization has contributed to the establishment of a number of modern organizations like the Hoima and Masindi social welfare associations. These associations cater largely to the educated African civil servants (both central and local) resident in the headquarter towns; however, the peasants continue to prefer their own private-enterprise beer clubs.

The Bunyoro local government introduced an education tax of five shillings in 1953 and a graduated tax up to one hundred shillings in 1954. By 1963 the education tax had reached ten shillings and the graduated tax two hundred shillings. It was intended initially that the parish councils should assess their respective taxpayers according to capacity to pay. However, it was soon apparent that a council of neighbors and peers is reluctant to assess its friends and relatives above the minimum rate. In the first year of graduation, the councils assessed only 4,634 of the nearly 30,000 taxpayers above the standard rate, and only 128 taxpayers were rendered liable to the maximum. Only twenty-three persons were assessed the maximum of two hundred shillings. The 1962 assessment ranged from twenty-two shillings in grade one to two hundred shillings in grade nine. Fewer than two hundred persons paid a tax of one hundred shillings or more.[75] Even more distressing in terms of revenue is the fact that the total number of registered taxpayers is considerably less than the adult male population. The total number of taxpayers estimated for 1962 was 31,474, whereas the 1959 census shows an adult male population of more than 42,000. To counter this problem the parish council was replaced as assessing agent in 1956 by the sub-county council, the county chief, and a delegation from the county council, and by 1962 assessment for all practical purposes had reverted almost completely to a committee of chiefs.

In common with most local governments the world over, the Rukurato of Bunyoro-Kitara derives its revenue from three major sources: local taxation, central government grants, and other sources. Although local taxation has increased from approximately three thousand pounds in 1940 to sixty thousand in 1962, it has not kept pace with the increase on grant-in-aid revenue. Estimated per capita cash income over the past decade has grown at a rapid rate. Before 1950 total local and central taxes consumed almost all of the average Munyoro's cash income. By 1960 it is estimated that per capita cash income in Bunyoro was nearly 260 shillings or about one thousand shillings per taxpayer.[76] However, it should not be assumed from the relatively low rate of increase in tax revenue as compared with available incomes that local taxes could or should be significantly higher. The Munyoro's standard of expectation has risen probably more rapidly than his income and money is now required for many purposes other than the payment of taxes.

Taxes collected by the lower chiefs, who issue receipts provided by the sub-county chief, has been developed into a fine art. The village and parish chiefs know exactly where and when every taxpayer is likely to receive his cash income and make it their business to be at the right place at the right time. Cases have been noted of chiefs putting up roadblocks and stopping passing trucks and buses in order to check the tax receipts of the passengers. In addition to tax revenue and Protectorate government grants-in-aid, the Bunyoro local government derives significant recurrent revenue from a variety of minor sources. Peasants selling produce in an authorized market are charged a small license fee; prisoners are put to work making bricks which are sold on the market; a small fee is charged for registering marriages; royalties are paid for forest products, beer licenses, and permits, and income is received from the sale of licenses to traders and hawkers.

Bunyoro local government expenditures have increased nearly tenfold over the past decade, while locally derived revenue has increased only about half as much. In 1962 government grants accounted for nearly half of total expenditures, whereas in 1940 they made up less than 10 per cent. The salaries, travel and other allowances and pensions of chiefs, officials, and staff account for more than 70 per cent of total expenditures.[77] The local government treasury serves as a loan agency for officials and chiefs. County chiefs and other senior officials borrow money to buy automobiles, sub-county chiefs for motorcycles, and clerks and lesser employees for bicycles.

The rapid rate of increased local expenditure is being financed more and more by central government grants, loans, and from other nonlocally derived sources. A continuation of a policy of transferring public services to the local governments will likely lead to a further widening of the gap between locally derived revenue and total expenditure which in turn will require additional central government assistance.

The somewhat cumbersome and expensive local government machine that has evolved as a product of mixing the principles of indirect rule with twentieth-century English local government, consumes considerably more fuel than is locally produced. If this system is to achieve the ends for which its English model was designed, it must look to external sources for nearly all of its requisite resources. The only justification for transferring services from a relatively efficient central government to the Bunyoro local government is a political one —a purpose, however, which might well be justified.

In Uganda, today, the most important question in connexion with the life of the people is whether their development in consonance with British ideas is in their own interest.

H. B. THOMAS and ROBERT SCOTT, *Uganda*

CHAPTER FIVE

Teso: Change and Progress

The old men of Bunyoro-Kitara gather about the beer pot and sing songs venerating centuries of imperial glory, and upon request will recount with great emotion the genealogies of their divine rulers back to the mythical days of the Bachwezi. A system of hereditary divine kingship organized on a hierarchical territorial basis of necessity is legitimized by a carefully preserved history. The Munyoro lives and thinks much of his life in the past. The tombs of his rulers and kin are preserved and venerated. This legitimacy is expressed in the super-ordinate-subordinate relationship that characterizes the status conscious social organization. The Munyoro peasant lazily riding his bicycle to market or to the beer shop will come to an abrupt halt, dismount, sink to his knees and pay homage should he meet his chief along the road. A hardly audible tinkling of a tiny bell will bring the Bunyoro-Kitara Rukurato to immediate order.

A contrast of the Banyoro with the people of Teso is striking and revealing. The Itesot is little concerned with extensive tribal genealogies.[1] He dates a consciousness of tribal identity only with the coming of the European.[2] Regarded by many as the most progressive tribe in Uganda, the Iteso have swiftly abandoned much of their traditional social organization and have been relatively quick to accommodate themselves to new forms of association. Unlike the Banyoro, the more numerous Iteso never possessed a centralized territorial political system and, judged by Western standards, existed in a state of near anarchy. Nor do the Iteso possess a highly developed and extensive clan system as do their Nilotic neighbors to the north. Traditionally, Teso society was organized about an overlapping configuration of limited kinship association, small-scale territorial allegiance and age-grade organization. The major solidarity unit was probably a little larger than an extended family.

Outwardly, the formal local authority in Teso today is similar to Uganda's other districts. The differences in conditioning factors and traditional social system, however, have resulted in significant variations in the manner in which the local political system actually operates.

The Iteso peasant contemplating his chief perceives something quite different than does his Banyoro neighbor. This is vividly borne out by

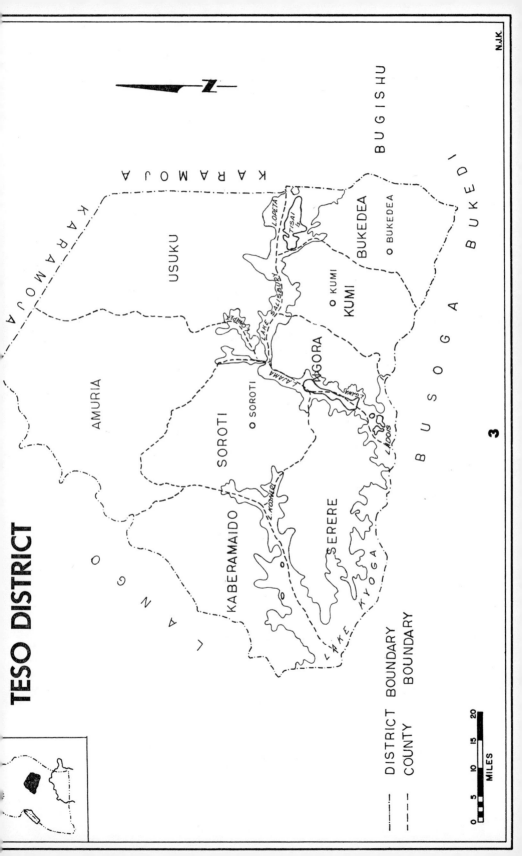

TESO DISTRICT

KARAMOJA

KARAMOJA

USUKU

AMURIA

LANGO

KABERAMAIDO

SOROTI

o SOROTI

NGORA

KUMI

o KUMI

BUKEDEA

o BUKEDEA

BUGISHU

SERERE

L. OPETA

TISAI

LAKE SALISBURY

L.OPETA

L. BISINA

R. OKERE

L. KYOGA

R. KOHWEDI

L.ODOS

BUSOGA

BUKEDI

LAKE KYOGA

DISTRICT BOUNDARY

COUNTY BOUNDARY

0 5 10 15 20

MILES

N.J.K.

3

N

an incident noted upon arrival in Teso. While attending a session of a sub-county court the proceedings were interrupted by gales of laughter and excitement. Everyone, including the court assessor and chiefs, ran outside. Approaching the court house was a young Itesot, his waist encircled by a stout rope, with free ends held firmly by a bloody and dirty village chief, assisted by a number of local government police and clan leaders.[3] This young Itesot was also bloody; his clothes were torn and covered with mud. He had failed to pay his taxes on time and the village chief, acting upon instructions from above, had sought to arrest him. In the process of arrest the chief insisted that the hands of the young Itesot be bound behind his back. The tax defaulter agreed to being tied around the waist and to being led to court, but in no case was he willing to suffer the indignity of having his hands bound. The chief insisted; the peasant resisted. The young Itesot arrived in court bound only about the waist, his head bloody but unbowed. The crowd which always loiters about the sub-county headquarters when court is in session found this event most hilarious and the independent behavior of the reluctant prisoner was cheered while the village chief was ridiculed.[4]

Until 1958 Teso District was considered by the British administration to be a model area, both with respect to progress made in agriculture and animal care and in the operation of the local government system. The multi-tier council system which is characteristic of Uganda local government had its origins in Teso, and, in the opinion of many, has succeeded best there.

The purpose of this chapter is to view certain aspects of Teso environment and social organization and to seek to relate the unique aspects of the social structure and environment to aspects of the transition of the local political system.

THE SETTING

Teso, located in east-central Uganda, is slightly larger than most districts. The distance from the District Headquarters at Soroti, sited nearly in the center of the district, to the district boundaries is approximately thirty-five to forty miles. The vegetation is that classified as short grass savannah. The rainfall of fifty-two inches is seasonal, with a pronounced dry season extending from about mid-October to mid-March. Teso lies within the complex drainage system of Lakes Kyoga and Salisbury and the Mpologoma River. With an average altitude slightly less than that of Lake Victoria, much of the country consists of low, gently rising promontories dissected by a complex of swamps, rivers, lakes and streams.[5] The terrain is spared the monotony of undulating grasslands and spongy swamps by the dramatic and often starkly beautiful rocky granite outcrops which suddenly rise, as much as six hundred feet, above the surrounding countryside. Many of these spectacular outcrops play a part in native superstition and are symbols of territorial identity and association.

It can be seen from Figure 3 that Teso District is neatly bisected by the Kyoga-Salisbury drainage system. The barrier posed by these lakes and swamps played an important part in determining the manner in which Teso was settled. A legacy of this topography persists to this day in the intense rivalry which characterizes the relationships of the Iteso south and north of this water barrier.

Settlement Patterns

Teso, with a population of approximately 460,000, is one of the most homogeneous districts in Uganda. The Iteso, Uganda's second largest tribe, were in the process of migration when the British occupation commenced. As a consequence, there exist sizable pockets of Iteso in Bukedi and Bugishu Districts to the south, as well as in the Nyanza Province of Kenya.

The Iteso believe that their forefathers lived far to the east and north in what is likely modern-day Abyssinia. From there, some three to four hundred years ago, they migrated gradually east and south, establishing themselves in what is now Karamoja District. It is thought that a part of the tribe, sometime about the turn of the seventeenth century, broke off from the main stem and began to move out of Karamoja into what is now Teso. The Iteso maintain that the word Karamajong means the "old men who stayed behind." Whether this gradual and sporadic migration was dictated by economic necessity or was the consequence of military defeat and pressure from the north and east is a matter of conjecture. It is safe to assume, however, that the Iteso who moved out of Karamoja were not unlike the Karamajong of today. They wore few if any clothes and depended for food on their large herds of cattle.

As they moved eastward, the migrating Iteso found a relatively unoccupied, well watered, and fertile land which heralded the end of their nomadic culture. Although Teso today exports more cattle than any district in Uganda, the average Itesot derives his major income and subsistence primarily from agriculture. Little tradition remains of the cattle culture that must have prevailed less than three hundred years ago. This is in sharp contrast to the Banyoro, who also have made the transition from cattle herding to sedentary agriculture. The lore and custom of the Banyoro continue to revolve about cattle as if the countryside was full of lowing herds rather than with fields of millet, cassava, and tobacco. The legitimacy of Bunyoro's political system necessitates the preservation of these long outmoded traditions. Unencumbered with such a legitimizing tradition, the Iteso have rapidly modified their indigenous culture. It is difficult to believe that today's relatively wealthy Teso farmer possessed of a plow and team of bullocks, and deriving a substantial income from agriculture, only a few generations ago resembled the present-day nomadic Karamajong. Today, little more than language and similar clan names testify to this common origin.

The manner in which the Teso migration took place is important to an understanding of the present-day political system. At the time of the migration, the Teso age-grade organization was probably at its zenith. Cattle were herded by members of a given age-set. The young men, bound together by age-grade initiation, inhabited temporary cattle camps on the outer fringes of the area of tribal settlement. A member of the age-set, in his efforts to retrieve straying cattle, likely moved westward into unoccupied territory. One can imagine the wandering herder, happy with his discovery of vacant and fertile land and with great elation, returning to his companions to tell them of his find. Frequently the greater part of the age-set would move en bloc to the new land and gradually stake its claim to specific portions of the new country. As plenty of land was available and no outside threat existed, the initial holdings were large and scattered. This area of settlement was termed "etem" and roughly coincided with an area bounded by swamps or other natural features. These migrating Nilo-Hamitic peoples also possessed a form of kinship association which overlapped age-grade organization. The newly formed etems were composed of men from a variety of clans. It is thought that in time the initial settler or patriarch of a section of the new etem gathered about himself, through reproduction and through recruitment of his relatives, a sizable community. Thus, members of the community or subsection of the etem were all members of the same kinship group. In this manner a nucleus differentiated from the remainder of the etem was established, and the etem evolved into an association of constituent kinship hamlets. This pattern, particularly in Usuku County, the area of initial settlement, is attested to today by the persistence in the smallest of the local governmental divisions (irony) of eight or nine clearly defined hamlets (ireria) which are primarily inhabited by members of a single clan.

Migration from Usuku into the remainder of Teso District took a somewhat different pattern. Evidence suggests that the Iteso, upon their arrival in relatively fertile Teso District, were quick to turn to agriculture as a means of subsistence. The clan leader (apolon ka ateker) in each clan hamlet tended to be the major local authority figure and had power over the allocation of land. These clan leaders or kinship group elders of a given etem met together to discuss and arbitrate intra-etem problems. The third element of Teso social organization, the age-set, was also integrated into this complex social system, for it was the young man of a given etem who shared the age-set initiation ceremonies. Whenever the population of an etem exceeded available land, the deprived age-set, composed of members of various clans and hamlets, migrated outward and established a new etem. The continuation of this process over a period of two centuries, and to a certain extent even after British rule, has led to the firm occupation of the entire district by the Iteso.

From the map of Teso District (Figure 3) it can be seen that the southern counties of Ngora, Kumi, and Bukedea are separated from the northern and western counties by the Salisbury and Kyoga lake system. The inhabitants of these two areas are primarily descendants of two distinct migratory groups which, through time, have developed separate dialects. To this have been added a number of modern-day distinctions which together with the above have led to bitter local political factionalism.

Observers of the Iteso early in this century remarked upon the tendency of the people to live in relatively large communities of up to 100 huts surrounded by defensive barriers.[6] It was also reported that a "village headman held sway over each village and that several communities were grouped together to form a larger unit under a minor chief or headman."[7] Soon after the available land was occupied, the Iteso came into contact with neighboring tribes. The ensuing conflict led the Iteso to build large fortified villages. The residential stability which followed a transition from herding to cultivation also contributed to the establishment of permanent villages. There is some evidence that the Iteso, in response to problems of order and integration resulting from residential proximity and permanency, began to develop relatively specialized and larger scale political institutions. The communal and ritual functions of the nomadic age-set association gave way gradually to an organization based upon residential proximity and shared territory. However, this embryonic political system was nipped in the bud, for Teso migrations had hardly slowed before British hegemony was established.

It is paradoxical that Pax Britannica served to frustrate the natural development of what might have evolved into a chieftainship-type hierarchy in Teso. British rule removed the necessity for large fortified villages and relatively extensive political organization. The Iteso peasant no longer required a territorial headman or chief to maintain community order or to organize the defenses of the large village. The authority of indigenous "chiefs" declined as the peasants moved their families into the bush. Today, the large compact villages are completely gone and the major residential unit is the family homestead. In a survey carried out in two villages in Usuku County—the area from which the Iteso fanned out into the district—it was discovered that the 351 homestead areas contained 1,022 houses.[8] In Usuku village, the site of the local government sub-county headquarters, the number of houses per homestead is 2.7. But in the village of Okoco, which is subject to periodic raiding from Karamoja, the homesteads are larger (3.2 houses per homestead) and are more thoroughly fenced for defensive purposes.

Present-day Teso, for purposes of local and central government administration, is divided into eight counties, forty-nine sub-counties, 195 parishes and 399 villages.[9]

The typical Iteso peasant, with his wives and unmarried children, makes his home within a circular compound circumscribed by a hedge of lilac trees or similar shrubbery. The house of the head of the family is larger than the others and is sited near the center of a grass-free well-swept compound. The compound may also contain smaller houses for wives and children, a number of granaries for storing the family food supply and, if the head of the house complies with the District Council bylaws, a separate kitchen and latrine; the cattle kraal is located some distance from the enclosure.

The Iteso family takes its main meal of a finger millet porridge (atop) at sundown. A light morning meal consists of the remnants of the previous evening's dinner of baked sweet potatoes or cassava root plus beer. Although the Iteso are still noted for their large herds of cattle, surprisingly little meat is eaten.

The British administration has long viewed the Iteso with pride. Accustomed to the frustration of attempting to introduce new social, political, and agricultural practices into their African territories, they were delighted with the readiness of the Iteso to accommodate themselves to rapid change. Nonetheless, the impact of Europeans on the Iteso significantly altered the latter's already rapidly changing social and political system. A summary of this impact is important to an understanding of the Teso political system of today.[10]

The Impact of the Europeans

Reference has already been made to Semei Kakunguru, the famous Baganda General and administrator. It is necessary that we refer again to this remarkable person for he was largely responsible for the subjugation of the Iteso and their subsequent unification into a single district. In 1896 the term "Teso" was unknown and the British referred to the tribesmen of the Kyoga-Salisbury lake region as "Bukedi" (the naked ones). At that time the Iteso were probably in the last stages of their gradual occupation of what is now Teso District. They possessed little social or political organization other than the extended family (ekek), the age-set (aturi) and the etem.

Kakunguru established his first fort in Teso in 1896 and began his conquest of the Iteso in earnest at about the turn of the century. J. C. D. Lawrance sums up the pattern of conquest and administration:

> It was everywhere the same; first an armed expedition would be made from an established fort to a new area; the pretexts were often obscure, sometimes a request for help from a warring faction, or sometimes a threat of attack by local inhabitants; after skirmishes or pitched battles a new fort would be established and a garrison of armed Baganda installed. This garrison would then extend its influence over the surrounding countryside by establishing armed posts or minor forts. When local opposition had been overcome the region would be proclaimed a saza (county) and the smaller areas controlled by outlying posts would be defined as gombololas (sub-counties). Baganda chiefs were appointed down to the muruka (parish) level.[11]

Impressed with the efficiency and order of the Buganda system of government, the early British district officers assumed that its application to Teso would not only facilitate administration but also would contribute to the political development of the Iteso. Lawrance concludes: ". . . his [Kakunguru's] brief rule resulted in lasting benefits to the district. When he started his great work . . . he found warfare and anarchy; when he left Teso in 1904 the district was peaceful with an ordered government on the Buganda model, with a hierarchy of officials owing allegiance to a central power."[12]

Admittedly Kakunguru built roads and bridges, levied taxes and generally established a system of order which by Western standards would be regarded as political progress. However, as Lawrance notes in passing, Kakunguru suppressed "any organization which might run contrary to his system" and contrary to Kakunguru's system were the Iteso age-grades.[13] The suppression of the age-grades destroyed one of the three foundation stones of the Teso traditional social and political order. The age-set was intricately associated with the major territorial political unit, termed "etem." As the spatial community (etem) was dependent upon the age-sets and kinship associations, Kakunguru's disruption of this institution had repercussions throughout the entire socio-political system.

The administrative units established by Kakunguru were staffed with his Baganda followers who requisitioned Teso cattle, women, and labor at will. The excesses and cruelty of Baganda domination are vividly recalled by many Iteso even today, with the result that suspicion and fear of the Baganda is a factor in current politics.

Thanks first to Kakunguru's organization and then to British administrative necessity, the Iteso have become conscious of themselves as a single people inhabiting a clearly demarcated territory.

TESO SOCIETY

Kinship Association

Much confusion and disagreement exists as to whether the Teso ateker is truly a clan in the anthropological sense. A detailed analysis of the clan system in Teso is not projected and for our purposes it is sufficient to note that the people of Teso perceive of themselves as belonging to extensive kinship groups termed "ateker." The total number of atekerin (plural of ateker) in Teso is unknown, but probably numbers well over 130. The Teso clan, unlike those in the Bantu and Nilotic areas, does not claim a common, founding ancestor or a common set of taboos. Nor is the Teso ateker an exogamous unit. Members of the same ateker are distributed throughout Teso, though there is a slight tendency for the members of a given clan to concentrate in certain areas.

The clan as an aspect of kinship organization is relatively unimportant in modern Teso. Although some taboos are preserved and regulate the ceremonies of childbirth and death, they play little part in either inheritance regulation or in the allocation of land. The clan leader is termed "apolon ka ateker" but his authority and influence extend only over the members of the clan who live in close proximity to himself and who share his taboos. The ekek (extended family) is of more importance as a kinship unit in Teso than is the ateker. The members of a given ekek include those who claim a common and known ancestor no more than three generations removed. The leader (loepolokit) of the ekek is selected by its male adult members and with few exceptions is the eldest member of the extended family. The ekek continues to play a vital role in Teso social organization and is instrumental in regulating inheritance, dowry, marriage, and, until recently, land allocation as well.

A typical Iteso village (or, in pre-British days, etem) consists of about eight or nine hamlets. The majority of the inhabitants of a hamlet belong to the same clan. The hamlet itself tends to be divided into clusters of three or four homes sharing a common ekek. Thus, in the first instance, the individual is held responsible to the ekek through the instrumentality of the loepolokit. Kinship integration on a somewhat larger scale is supplied by the sharing of a common ateker and its taboos. The senior loepolokit is, in turn, the apolon ka ateker of the hamlet. If there exist a number of hamlets of the same ateker the hierarchy of clan leaders (apolon ka ateker) extends higher and might embrace all the members of a given ateker in the village or possibly even the parish.

Two widely different villages in Usuku County were intensively surveyed in 1956. Village A is the site of the sub-county headquarters and is in close proximity to Katakwi (the county headquarters), a relatively large township. Village B lies close to the Karamoja border and has experienced little alien influence. In Village A, 204 heads of homesteads were interviewed and in Village B, 147. The clan affiliation of villages A and B are shown in Table 5.

It will be noted that the clan clusters reflect the tendency of the village to consist of six to nine clan hamlets and for a few clans to predominate.

TABLE 5
CLAN AFFILIATION IN TWO TESO VILLAGES

Clan Name	CLAN AFFILIATION		Total
	Village A	Village B	
Imalera	36	36	72
Isuguro	31	4	35
Igetoma	24	15	39
Ikarekalata	10		10
Isupatok	10		10
Ikorungany	6		6
Isureta	3	43	46
Eusukoit		23	23
Esuretait		13	13
Imugenya		13	13
Ilalei		10	10
Emodoit		7	7
Ikomolo		6	6
Other	26	23	49
Not Stated	1	9	10
Total	147	202	349

SOURCE: Author's survey, 1956.

Territorial Association

Territorial authority is rarely absent as a basis of social organization. In the societies characterized by predominantly kinship style associations, territorial organization is frequently assumed as a diffuse aspect of clan membership. In Teso, however, territorial organization played an important part in the traditional system. To the Iteso, etem meant a meeting place where the elders of the area gathered to discuss and decide upon common problems.[14] If there ever existed a really sovereign unit in traditional Teso, it was probably the etem. The etem coincided with the natural features of the landscape, and members of a single etem, though not living in concentrated villages, distinguished themselves from the people on the other side of the river, swamp, or forest. The constituent age-grades, which served as the basis of Teso military and hunting organization, were recruited and initiated from a single etem. In conjunction with the age-set system, the etem organization served to integrate the multiple kinship segments resident in a naturally isolated unit.

Within the etem a type of special purpose ad hoc authority predominated. Specific individuals, partly through heredity and partly as a result of demonstrated capacity, were recognized leaders with respect to certain activities, e.g., war, conference, adjudication, hunting.

Age-Set Association

The complex Teso system of age-sets is not treated in detail here. However, as it played a major role in traditional Teso social and political organization, certain of its relevant features must be noted.[15] It is difficult to assess precisely the role that the age-set organization played in the political system of traditional Teso. Although little more than a half century has passed since Kakunguru crossed to the east side of Lake Kyoga and wreaked havoc on the Iteso and their social institutions, it is by and large only the old men who today regard the age-grade or its related ceremonies as important. As some of the surrounding Nilo-Hamitic tribes continue to make use of age-grades (including the neighboring Karamajong), we can venture some assumptions about the part it played in nineteenth-century Teso.

The age-grade association which cut horizontally across the society was grafted upon the kinship system which integrated the society vertically. The Iteso age-grade system (asapan) consisted of eight rotational age-sets (aturi). Approximately every three years the young men of the etem, having reached the age of puberty, were carefully tutored by a senior age-set and duly initiated into the realm of the men of the etem.

The social responsibilities of the Iteso were not rationally divided on the basis of age-sets, but the supernatural aspects of the system did tend to attribute specific duties and powers to certain age-sets. Lawrance writes that the whole sphere of natural existence was methodically divided between the eight age-sets so that each set had religious or ritual powers over a series of associated objects of activities.[16]

Each age-set was supernaturally related to important aspects of Iteso life. As it was believed to have extraordinary control over its respective natural phenomena, a given age-set was looked to for guidance with respect to its particular area of competence. It was this supposed sensitivity to certain situations or natural elements, rather than an empirically recognized authority, that gave each age-set considerable influence over related aspects of social behavior. For example, the Flood age-set was believed to have extraordinary influence over water, fish and cattle; and in effect, did exercise considerable authority in this area. Before a person set off to fish he would consult with a member of the Flood age-set and would accept the advice of this person. In a like fashion the Warthogs were in a special relationship to leopards and rabbits; the Elephant age-set had supernatural influence with respect to fire, firewood, trees and vegetables, while the Antelopes stood in a special relationship to land and sheep.

An early Teso District Commissioner, who had devoted considerable attention to Teso social organization, viewed with dismay the passing of the age-set system and urged that it be revised and employed to curb the drift toward normlessness:

> If it is organized under European supervision as a mixture of dancing, drill, club life and rural education, it should not clash with the teaching of government or mission schools and should provide a degree of discipline which the rustic youth of Teso so obviously lack. . . . If a peasant has nothing else but the cotton cycle, drink and fornication to pass his time, he is apt to grow troublesome.[17]

Wright was among the very few to recognize the critical relationship of the defunct age-sets to the maintenance of Teso integration and order. And his proposal that the system be revived and incorporated into the local government organization was, in effect, an attempt to apply the principles of indirect rule to a small-scale diffuse society. The imported system of Baganda chiefs and courts did provide an extensive administration, but as this perceptive District Commissioner was quick to see:

> Litigation in the native courts provides a distraction as do the weekly ritual exercises of church, but *integration* of his life in a social discipline, in which he is *controlled* by his seniors and in turn controls his juniors is missing. Such reintegration should . . . be a deliberate policy not with an idea of anarchism but in the best democratic tradition.[18]

Teso Villages Today

Ultimately, the success of a system of modern local government will depend on its comprehension and support it receives from the mass of peasants. The grass roots characteristics of the Iteso and the day-by-day operation of the local political system were investigated by selecting one sub-county for intensive study. Usuku sub-county is one of the largest and most sparsely settled in Teso and is considered by the Iteso to be the area of initial settlement; and the term Iteso, among the older residents of the district, refers only to the inhabitants of Usuku.[19]

The population of Usuku etem (sub-county) is approximately 11,000.[20] The sub-county is divided into four parishes: Usuku parish, which in turn is composed of the villages of Usuku and Okaritok; Adachar and Okocho villages make up Adachar parish; Aketa parish is divided into Aketa, Omukuny and Obwobwo villages; the remaining parish Akum consists of Akum and Okelewko villages.

The countryside is a maze of swamps and seasonal rivers. But after a time even a stranger becomes conscious of the pattern of highlands separated by intervening swamps, and even at night the traveller can determine the village boundaries by the lonely song of the swamp frogs.

Two villages in Usuku etem were singled out for our survey. The residents of Usuku—the first village studied—have experienced relatively more external influences as a consequence of their proximity to Katakwi, the county headquarters. Katakwi is but a half hour's bicycle ride and there are to be found the great majority of the county's eighty-seven Asian merchants and their families. More important still is the location in Katakwi of the local government maternity clinic, dispensary, county administrative offices, and the county jail. Katakwi has a main street replete with a variety of dukas (galvanized roofed stores), peddlers, loiterers, and bicycle repairmen. Usuku village, on the other hand, has no main street and in the Western sense does not even exist. All that is to be seen from the road is the Lukiko Hall which, between meetings of the sub-county council, serves as the court of first instance. At one end of the building is the lockup and at the other, the chief's office. When the court or council is meeting, the area is filled with litigants, witnesses, the curious and the bored, while on less exciting days only a few askaris (local government police) and prisoners are to be seen.

To its inhabitants Usuku, like other villages, is a distinctive political and social community. The swamp and today the road, which serve as the village boundary, are recognized by everyone. The highlands are covered with a maze of twisting paths connecting one homestead to another; rarely is a neighbor's house visible. These paths appear to be in constant use as the women of Usuku go to and fro carrying water and firewood while the men bicycle on less arduous tasks from one homestead to another. The Usuku villager is in frequent contact with European influence for the modern local government and court are on his very doorstep. Even more important is the location of a large Roman Catholic Mission and school in his village.

Okocho, on the other hand, is probably as far removed from external influence as any village in Teso. Many of Okocho's women, in marked contrast to their more stylish neighbors in Usuku who purchase their frocks from Katakwi Indian dukas, wear few clothes, dressing as they did a half century ago. Some general characteristics of Teso villages as well as the variations between Usuku and Okocho are shown in Table 6.

TABLE 6
EDUCATION AND POLYGAMY IN TWO TESO VILLAGES

| | | LEVEL OF EDUCATION | | | | | NO. OF WIVES | | | | |
Village	Sample Size	None	1-4 Years	Full Prim.	Sec. or Higher	Not Stated	1	2	3	3+	None
Usuku	204	162	11	15	11	5	146	26	10	8	14
Okocho	147	126	9	12	0	0	103	30	4	4	6
Total	351	288	20	27	11	5	249	56	14	12	20

SOURCE: Author's survey, 1956.

In Okocho all but five of the 147 heads of households sampled were peasant farmers. Of the five who were not, two were chiefs, two policemen, and one a teacher. In Usuku, however, twenty-eight of the 204 heads of households had occupations other than farming. Included in this group were seven teachers, seven traders, three chiefs, six unskilled laborers, and three artisans.

The relative effect of the influence of the nearby Catholic Mission can be seen in the difference in education level between the two villages. (See Table 6.) This influence is also notable in the religious affiliation of the respective villages. (See Table 7.)

TABLE 7
RELIGIOUS AFFILIATION IN TWO TESO VILLAGES

| | USUKU | | OKOCHO | | TOTALS | |
	Number	Per cent	Number	Per cent	Number	Per cent
Catholic	125	62	20	14	145	42
Protestant	12	5	69	47	81	23
Muslim	0		1		1	
Pagan	60	30	57	39	117	33
Not Stated	7	3	0		7	2
Totals	204	100	147	100	351	100

SOURCE: Author's survey, 1956.

In our survey we made an effort to gauge the extent to which the average villager is cognizant of the existence and functioning of the modern local political system at various levels. The findings indicate that in outlying villages such as Okocho there is little concern or knowledge about the modern local government system; important interpersonal and intergroup problems threatening community order or integration occur almost solely within the context of the village and it is by and large the village chief and clan leaders who monopolize authority and possess legitimate status. Although the Itesot does not regard his chief with the humility and awe characteristic of the Banyoro, he generally obeys him and has come to accept his presence and authority as an inevitable part of the local scene.

The county chief, though seldom seen and residing a considerable distance from Okocho village, is known by nearly everyone, while very little is known about Teso-wide political figures. In Usuku village, lying in the shadow of the sub-county headquarters with its attendant court house politicians, nearly two-thirds of the villagers surveyed knew the name of their District Council representative, whereas in Okocho 64 of the 147 respondents either did not know that such a representative existed or were unable to suggest a name.

The secretary-generalship is the highest executive position in the Teso local government. Only twenty-six of the 147 respondents in Okocho knew the Secretary-General, while in Usuku slightly more than half of the respondents correctly identified him.

It may seem surprising that the residents of Okocho and Usuku were more familiar with Mr. Obwangor, Teso's representative to the Uganda Legislative Council than they were with Mr. Ogaino, the Secretary-General. However, this is explained by the fact that Mr. Obwangor (now Minister of Regional Administrations) is a native of Usuku whose success in the political world is viewed with considerable pride by the people of Usuku County.

When the heads of homesteads in the two villages were asked whom they considered to be the leader of the Iteso people, more than half replied that there "is no leader of the Iteso people," while nearly everyone who nominated a leader attributed this role to an important parochial person. This tends to support the thesis advanced that the traditional political system is an important factor conditioning the degree and nature of the institutionalization of the new local government system. Traditionally, there never was a leader of all the Iteso people and, despite the fact that the new local government system provides for Teso-wide authority roles, the vast majority of the Iteso have not as yet accepted the legitimacy of these roles. The tendency to identify local figures as Teso leaders also supports this proposition.

More Recent Forms of Association

Although Teso, in contrast to other Uganda districts, is tribally homogeneous, it too is plagued with its own style of factionalism. The people do not perceive of themselves simply as Iteso. Those living in the present-day counties of Ngora and Kumi regard themselves as Ingoratok. The Ikokolemu are the people of Soroti while Isera refers to the residents of Serere. The Iteso inhabiting Bukedea and Pallisa (in Bukedi District) are termed Ikedea. The 49,000 people living in Kaberamaido County speak a language more akin to that in neighboring Lango and do not regard themselves as Iteso. Only the people of Usuku are properly called Iteso. These distinctions can be traced to the early migratory routes which were dictated largely by the physical environment.

It is hardly to be expected that the Iteso would move in the space of a single generation from the intimate parochial political system of the etem, age-set, and lineage to one requiring districtwide loyalty and cognition. Nor has Teso District been spared the religious factionalism that characterizes nearly all of Uganda. The intense solidarity surrounding church affiliation is likely an attempt by the Iteso to reestablish horizontal units of social integration to replace the age-grades. This is suggested by the fact that symbolic membership and the unity of association appear more important to the Itesot than the spiritual aspect of church membership. The Catholic and Protestant missions in Teso have long competed to monopolize the business of salvation and the contest frequently took the form of attempting to attract the children of influential chiefs and other dignitaries into the respective mission schools. In 1912 a Catholic priest complained to the District Commissioner that a certain chief

> gave his two children to be educated by us in Catholic faith in our mission station. However, after two years the children returned home for Christmas and did not return to the Catholic Mission but were brought unwillingly more or less forcibly into the CMS [Protestant] station at Ngora.[21]

Personality and Political Life

Itesot life style differs significantly from that of the Munyoro. Absent in his everyday expression and behavior in contrast to the Munyoro are terms and symbols of superordination and subordination. The Iteso are basically an equalitarian people. The Iteso wife, for example, is a person in her own right and frequently challenges the authority of her husband. Charges of marital assault in Teso are not always brought by the wife against the husband and Iteso women are known for their vigorous independence.

Essays written by Teso secondary school students were studied for perceptions of Iteso character and values.[22] As the following excerpts will show, the findings reveal a concern primarily with climate and nourishment, death and violence, money and sex: The Iteso is "generous and tall." He has a "feeling of sharing anything he gets with each other." "Many people when they see that life is not enjoyable on their side commit suicide." "Hatred also causes death of my people . . . when a person sees that he or she is hated by his or her brother or brothers . . . the only thing to do is to find a possible reason for dying." "The Teso kill each other directly or indirectly by spearing and poison, mostly because of jealousy." "The greatest number of people directly killed from now, November to January, because the days between these two months are the days when they are rich with beer. For they drink and drink until at last they become real animals, because they lose all their human sense and cause incessive fights." "There is nothing which can't please an Itesot but beer, for he seems to be a man born in beer."

An Itesot's assessment of Europeans, extracted from a student essay, indicates the transition in cultural perceptions:

> Another belief of theirs is that Europeans are half-way Gods and half-way men, for so many wonders have been displayed—for instance the flying of an airplane, radios, phones and other working machines, and strongly believe in the saying that Africans are cutters of wood, drawers of water, appointed by God to serve the white man. For how ever educated a dark skinned man is he can never do any wonders at all, neither can he invent any wonderful thing like the European.

Asked to write their impressions of the city and faraway districts, the students spoke of "being beaten by other people," the problem of different "languages and tribes." It is interesting to note that the students tended to view the city and Buganda as inequalitarian and quite unlike their own country. "For the rich and the educated the city is bliss," while for the poor and "heathen" it is a veritable hell. The city does have its attractions for it means "good houses and no flies," "clean clothes," "regular meals," "never have to go to bed without food," and a variety of "beer" and "music."

Another boy indicates how intricately the senses are interrelated in a diffuse and subsistence type social system:

> Dear George . . . I have also to inform you that the girl that I

promised to marry has broken her promise and has married a butcher. The reason why she married the butcher is because she wanted to have meat throughout her life.[23]

Another student wrote that "most people dance only because they want to show off because in Teso the best dancers are really loved by women and most of them fight because everyone of them wants to be loved most."

The violence and disorder which seem to increase in intensity in proportion to the "progress" of the district is attributed, by most administrators, to excessive drinking. The District Council has for many years been encouraged to pass prohibitive bylaws and taxes on beer brewing and dispensing. As beer drinking and violence are but symptoms of a more profound social disintegration, it is unlikely that prohibitive ordinances will significantly alter the situation.

The lapsing of the age-set and the corollary etem organization in large part have tended to render the Itesot peasant relatively normless. He shuns communal work unless a full beer pot awaits the completion of his labors. The local government council and chieftainship system is reluctantly accepted, but has not effectively replaced the cohesion lost through the disintegration of indigenous institutions.

The modern local political system is based primarily upon the English model which has evolved over the centuries in response to problems of integration and order that have emerged as a consequence of the environment and a gradually changing social system. Problems of sanitation in the United Kingdom are important for they are perceived as a threat to community order and integration. Local councils operating through functional committees have evolved to cope with such problems. However, the presence of undesirable conditions in a given community is largely a subjective matter, even though there seems to exist a human tendency to assume that all peoples regard identical situations in a like matter. Iteso committees and the District Council, urged on by English community development officers, have passed ordinances to cope with what are thought to be serious housing or hygiene conditions threatening the maintenance of life and property. But much as one may be inclined to identify local problems for the Iteso, they are not necessarily similarly perceived by the peasants. The modern system of local government in this respect is a cumbersome and efficient nutcracker designed to crack a nut for which a taste is yet to be developed.

THE LOCAL POLITICAL SYSTEM

Indirect Rule Indirectly Applied

In Bunyoro-Kitara the British found a developed political system which closely resembled that of Buganda. Baganda chiefs were employed in Bunyoro not because local chiefs were unavailable, but because most of the Bunyoro chiefs, having supported Kabalega, were *persona non grata*. But if the chiefly hierarchy was to prevail in Teso District there was no alternative to employing Baganda chiefs. The British assumed *de facto* authority in 1909 after Kakunguru was relieved of his authority, and in 1912 Teso was proclaimed a district in the East Province of the Uganda Protectorate. However, it was not until 1916 that the entire district was brought under effective administration.

As early as 1917 an attempt was made to replace the Baganda agents with locally trained Iteso chiefs.[24] The district administrators were reluctant to replace trusted and efficient Baganda with truculent and unstable Iteso and only pressure from the central government secretariat led to the gradual transition. Although a number of lower Iteso chiefs were subsequently appointed, it was not until 1920 that the first Iteso county chief was named.[25] The rapid appointment of Teso chiefs during the late 1920's substantiated the fears of English administrators. The 1930 Annual Report notes that "punishment of petty chiefs ran into hundreds of cases in the native courts."[26]

Although Teso had been proclaimed a district in 1912, no pan-tribal organization existed demanding its administration as a unified district, and the five counties initially were treated as separate compartments. Each county had its own chiefly council composed of the sub-county chiefs chaired by the Baganda county chief or agent who was "placed in charge of the chiefs to instruct them in the proper methods of conduct and to control the people."[27] This assembly of chiefs was termed a county lukiko and its primary function was judicial. However, the county lukiko had its own funds derived largely from court fees and fines which were employed for limited public works.

The trend toward districtwide as opposed to county administration commenced in 1918 with the holding of the first biannual baraza (meeting) of all the county and sub-county chiefs in Teso District.[28] Early Iteso chiefs had no traditional basis for the exercise of authority and often secured their positions through association with the Baganda intruders. They proved to be even less concerned with the welfare or consent of their countrymen than had the Baganda, who at least were disciplined by their knowledge of the system and their longer association with the English. The substitution of Iteso for Baganda chiefs did not render an alien local political system indigenous, but merely replaced foreign administrators with local quislings, for no Iteso paramount ruler existed to insure the accountability of Iteso chiefs. They ruled autocratically, were checked only by the infrequent visits of British officers and by the natural reluctance of the Iteso to submit to autocratic rule.[29]

The first quarter-century of European and Baganda administration completed the disintegration of the indigenous socio-political system and substituted a system of direct rule through the agency of first an imported, and later a locally recruited, hierarchy of civil servant chiefs ruling without local consensus or traditional legitimacy. The 1933 Annual Report states that;

> A county chief is a complete tyrant and dictator. His court's sentence is *his* sentence. His lukiko's recommendations are his recommendations. The court thus given to him is a loaded rifle in the hands of an uninhibited untrained and often malicious child.[30]

The Baganda chiefs enforced their rule with the aid of armed followers. This lesson was quickly learned by their Iteso understudies who also surrounded themselves with armed camp followers, whom they rewarded with the spoils of office. In a special report in 1934 the District Commissioner of Lango, who had served in Teso until that year, commented on the state of affairs.

> Each county is packed with relatives of the county chief. The majority of native administration officials [sub-chiefs] are in fact nominated by his Lukiko, i.e., by him. Ipso-facto the courts are also thus packed. . . . At least half the cases of misappropriation and violence on peasants which come to notice . . . are personally perpetrated on them by their own chiefs, these have become a new rich caste apart.[31]

During the 1930's a number of British administrators in the Eastern Province sought to alter the local political system to render the autocratic chiefs responsible, in some degree, to the people. After nearly thirty years of direct rule through Baganda agents and local quislings, Teso's District Commissioner, F. R. Kennedy reexamined the traditional system in search of indigenous institutions capable of being turned into an efficient check on the irresponsible chiefs. The age-set organization was completely defunct and largely forgotten as was the corollary etem system. Only remnants of the peculiar Teso kinship system remained. But this had never played an important political role. It may be that Kennedy regarded the Teso clan system as comparable to that existing in the neighboring Bantu or Nilotic tribes, for he concluded that it would serve admirably as the basis of a tier of councils paralleling the chiefly hierarchy. In 1937 he instituted local councils at the county, sub-county, and parish level and reconstituted the chiefly District Lukiko. The total of seats for each level of council was fixed and a given number were reserved for "clan leaders." However, the available seats at the lowest level bore no resemblance to the number or distribution of traditional clan leaders. As already noted, a clan leader (apolon ka ateker) exercised influence in nearly every sub-section of a village. The number of eligible clan leaders, therefore, greatly exceeded the total council seats allocated.

Faced with the problem of selecting a limited number of clan leaders to sit on these councils, the Iteso evolved a hybrid political structure based in part upon kinship and in part upon a combination of the traditional and the superimposed area organization. The ingenious structure, which evolved in response to a set of problems resulting from changed conditions, went largely unnoticed by the British administration.

In his 1937 report, Kennedy proudly concluded that:

> As was anticipated, the bulk of the elected members have been recruited from the ranks of the so-called clan or kinship group leaders. . . . The authority of these clan leaders who were suppressed by the Baganda when they first entered Teso under Kakunguru, and whose existence and potentialities had for years been ignored, have now been sufficiently renewed to enable them to once more become a vital force in the tribe.[32]

The chiefs resented the intrusion of this new representative institution which was clearly intended to act as a check on their powers. In practice, however, they had little cause for concern, for the so-called "clan leaders" were would-be chiefs and disinclined to threaten the system that promised them future power and riches.

Prior to the 1937 reforms the largely defunct clan leader was influential only over his neighbors who shared a common clan name and taboos, and had no authority over a neighbor of a different clan. In response to requests for a limited number of clan leaders to sit upon the new councils, the chiefs, who had an interest at stake and who already had their lieutenants in the villages, combined with the real clan leaders to recruit individuals termed "apolon ka ateker" to fill these new council seats. In some cases the men selected were in fact clan leaders but many were merely important or wealthy men, or simply friends of the chief. Their authority and influence were no longer based upon kinship but solely upon area. They became, in effect, area headmen or sub-chiefs who perceived of themselves as an integral, though unofficial, part of the chiefly hierarchy. Today, in each hamlet a man termed "apolon ka ateker" exercises authority, sanctioned by the official village chief, over all Iteso residents in the hamlet. The importance of these little known petty chiefs cannot be overemphasized. They are the real link between government and the people. In more recent years, with the exclusion of clan leaders from the councils, and with the later adoption of a system of direct elections, the role of clan leader *qua* petty chief and local councillor no longer inevitably coincided. Nevertheless the hierarchy of unofficial clan leaders paralleling the official chiefly hierarchy persists and continues to play a most important role in the over-all Teso local political system.

The senior village clan leader is entitled "apolon ka ateker irony" and parallels in influence the government village chief. Possessed of a higher degree of local consent than the official chief, the village clan leader is a power in his own right. However, he depends for his ultimate authority upon the official coercion available only to the official chief. The official chief, on the other hand, relies upon the clan leader to effect his orders, which he in turn has received through the official hierarchy. As neither authority figure could effectively operate alone, they are interdependent. This unofficial system exists up to the county level. At the parish and sub-county level the role of the clan leader is particularly important. He is generally relatively wealthy with numerous wives and children and is often an ex-government chief.

The parish, sub-county, and county chiefs are government civil servants subject to transfer from one post to another. A new chief from a distant part of Teso, speaking a strange dialect, is greeted with suspicion and hostility by the localites. Furthermore, an alien chief possesses no knowledge of local uniqueness, does not know who the potential troublemakers are, what his junior chiefs are like, the nature of local customs which he must adjudicate or who the community power holders are. He does not know who is a witch doctor and who is not, or who and where the rainmakers are located, or who has tenure and on what basis over which land. However, successful administration necessitates just such knowledge. Thus, the chief is dependent upon his unofficial counterpart and together they administer the area. Sound administration at each level depends in large part upon the maintenance of a smooth working relationship between the official chief and his unofficial counterpart. The unofficial apolon ka ateker depends, in the last analysis, upon the authority of the official chief. However, the official chief relies upon his apolon ka ateker at each level for the information and influence necessary to ensure the consent of the population to his commands. The people in a local community in turn rely upon the unofficial clan leader to intervene and to present their case whenever a situation arises which conflicts with the rigid external authority system represented by the official chief. The official chief relies upon the clan leader to translate bureaucratic rules and regulations to the people in such a way that his orders are understood and obedience is ensured. Furthermore, the institution of the apolon ka ateker serves to give a broad range of power and freedom to the official chief who, as a bureaucratic civil servant, is often restricted by universal terms of reference and behavior. Occasions arise when it is imperative for good administration that the chief act outside the limits of his official role. To accomplish this he works through his parallel clan leader who, unfettered by ordinances, acts for the chief. Whenever a vacancy in the informal hierarchy exists at the sub-county or county level, the parallel chief calls a meeting of all official chiefs and unofficial clan leaders lower in the hierarchy than the vacancy to be filled. At the meeting the assembled leaders select a replacement.

In Usuku village there are approximately fourteen clan leaders each responsible to the village chief for the maintenance of order and integration within a defined part of the village. Each clan leader is responsible for about ten to fifteen homesteads. The senior village clan leader is selected by an informal gathering of parish councillors, clan leaders and the village chief. He in turn recruits, with local consent, his sub-village clan leaders. Nearly all civil disputes and a number of criminal cases are tried by this informal hierarchy before reaching the official sub-county court.

This hybrid political structure evolved in answer to radically changed social and environmental conditions. The traditional political system proved incapable of supplying the organized means for satisfactorily handling the functions resulting from the combination of old and new problems. Neither the imported Baganda nor the 1937 council system was capable of coping with local problems and there evolved to meet this situation an informal structure, related in part to traditional organization and in part to the new and imposed system.

The non-kinship based clan system which evolved in response to local government reforms in the 1930's has continued to alter its form through the years. Today's modern apolon ka ateker is elected by the people in his hamlet subject to the approval of the village chief. Many of these unofficial leaders are former chiefs and more familiar with the bureaucracy with which they must deal, than some of the official chiefs. In 1959 approximately two hundred representatives of this modern clan system gathered in Soroti, the district headquarters, for their first districtwide convention. Mr. Akileng, prosperous trader from Usuku, and a former chief, was elected president of what was significantly termed the Teso Parents and Elders Association. Rather than declining in importance, this unofficial authority system appears to be growing in significance, in part because its very flexibility has enabled it to better accommodate and adapt itself to the growing influence of political parties, than have the chiefs. The influence and status of chiefs has perceptively declined since independence. Some spokesmen maintain that the hierarchy of unofficial clan leaders is of greater importance and with little difficulty could effectively replace the chiefs. The central committee of the clan system decided in 1961 that each adult Itesot should be assessed twenty-five (East African) cents to cover administrative costs.[33] It is not surprising that the local influence of the clan leader should be directed toward partisan politics. In 1962 the District Council, alarmed by this trend, noted that "politics is entering into clan leaders." The council also deplored the growing tendency for "village chiefs to use clan leaders to execute their duties."[34] In the same year the Teso District Commissioner found it necessary to address the clan leaders to advise them to act within the established political system and not to assume local authority."[35]

Teso was one of the first to adopt the 1955 District Council Ordinance described in Chapter Three.[36] As a consequence, the African (District) local government, with its bylaws, senior officials, committees and greater financial autonomy, has rapidly assumed a dominant position within the local political system. The role of the District Commissioner, district and county teams, the chiefs, the clan leaders, and the missions, is becoming less important as the stature and specialized political authority of the modern local government increases.

The Iteso chief today often finds himself in an ambivalent position, which in some respects, resembles that of the Bunyoro chiefs. The Secretary-General, council chairman, Treasurer, and Chief Judge, along with a number of multi-committee members are gradually assuming the power formerly shared by the county chiefs, indigenous authority figures, and the District Commissioner. Today, all routine communications from the chiefs pass through the Secretary-General. If the subject is of concern to a central government department, copies also go to the relevant central government department head.

Possessed of no indigenous legitimacy, the position of the Teso chief is more precarious than that of his Bunyoro counterpart. The authority of the Bunyoro chief is accepted as a part of Bunyoro culture. An individual chief's authority, but not the institution of chieftainship, may be challenged by would-be claimants to the position. The authority of the Iteso chief is only partially legitimized as a product of but thirty short years of experience. The identification of chieftainship with the British overlords was a constant source of irritation. The rapid turnover of chiefs in Teso not only reflected the void of capable and experienced candidates, but also the active reluctance of the Itesot to submit to chiefly rule. In Bunyoro the chiefs and officials at all levels in the local government hierarchy tend to dominate the councils. This contrasts with the situation in Teso where the council members have constantly exercised considerably greater influence. Individualism and a sense of equality, which tends to generally associate with democratic institutions, is a part of the genius of the Iteso, and the independent nature of the District Council is in sharp contrast to the Great Rukurato of Bunyoro.

The Teso District Council, in the face of the opposition of the chiefs, officials, and the British administration, has long sought to retain to itself the power of recruiting chiefs. The committee system in Teso was long viewed by the elected councillors as the personal vehicle of the chiefs, officials, and of a few strong men—which of course it was. At the initial session of the first council elected under the 1955 Ordinance, the councillors resolved that they, and not an appointments committee, should recommend chiefly candidates to the central government. At the insistence of the council, Teso was for a time the only district in Uganda in which all of the senior officials (Secretary-General, Treasurer and Chief Judge) were elected by the council.

The *esprit de corps* which characterizes the chiefly hierarchy in Bunyoro is not much in evidence in Teso where, in order to ensure the fickle consent of his subjects, a senior chief will on occasion cut the ground from under one of his own subordinates. A county chief in Teso does not speak of "my sub-county chief," but rather of *the* sub-county chief of X area.

Functions and Functionaries

The Teso political system in operation consists of a number of overlapping and interrelated roles. As the system changes, the relationship of the roles, and thus the source of authority, is correspondingly altered. The hierarchy of local government officials, chiefs, and political party leaders tends to dominate the local scene. However, the parallel unofficial hierarchy of clan leaders is of considerable significance. The District Commissioner and other central government officers are still a major source of local authority though the influence of the former is rapidly declining. Although the traditional institutions have been largely replaced by the modern local government system and by the informal clan leader hierarchy, a number of influential traditional roles persist. Thus, the role of the clan leader, the witch doctor, and the rainmaker are still of some importance.

The relative contribution of the various roles to the over-all local political system is in a constant state of flux. Transition from one developmental state to another is reflected in the altered significance of these roles.

Chiefs

The development of the Teso chiefly hierarchy from its origins in the period of Baganda domination was described above. The Iteso chief who gradually replaced the Baganda agent was charged under the Native Authority Ordinance of 1919 with the "duty . . . to maintain order in the area within which he has jurisdiction and for such purpose he shall have and exercise the jurisdiction and powers which he may otherwise enjoy by virtue of any law or native customs for the time being in force."[37] The power to employ assistants (or henchmen) to arrest, to seize property, to judge cases, to fine and imprison, to issue orders, to require compulsory labor and to forbid movement, were granted to individuals who, prior to their appointment, possessed no authority or responsibility; one's neighbor and equal suddenly became his master. Within the limitations posed by a distant District Commissioner, and the influence of the unofficial clan leaders who were often in league with him, the chief ruled as an autocrat. Efficient tax collection and the maintenance of a reasonable level of order ensured his tenure and popularity with the administration.

The county chiefs were early appointed by the central government although it was customary for the District Commissioner to first obtain nominations by the District Council. In the early 1930's it became customary for the sub-county councils, composed almost entirely of chiefs and would-be chiefs, to recommend candidates for parish and village chieftainships. In 1947, a District Council resolution stipulating that parish and village chiefs be elected by the peasants was executed. However, in 1949 the District Council, composed largely of chiefs and clan leaders and would-be chiefs became suspicious of the implication of this democratic institution and voted to abandon direct election of the lower chiefs. It was subsequently decided that the village and parish chiefs were to be recommended by the sub-county and county councils, respectively. After 1949 the Standing Committee of the District Council was asked to recommend candidates for appointment as county chief.[38]

Under the District Council's Ordinance of 1955, the power of the District Commissioner was limited solely to the disapproval of an unsuitable chiefly appointment. It was the intention of the ordinance that the District Council should assume responsibility for the appointment and disciplining of chiefs. In February, 1956, the first council elected under the 1955 Ordinance was returned with a majority for the Northern Iseratok of fifty-three seats to the thirty-five obtained by the Southern Ingoratok. All went reasonably well until the middle of 1957. It was at this point that Mr. Inyonin, a southerner and long-time Treasurer, decided to resign from the Teso local government. He took this action largely because he was aware that as a southerner it was unlikely that he would be reelected to the post which he had occupied for more than twenty years. The Treasurer of the local government, under the 1955 Ordinance, was an ex-officio member of the Appointments Committee. The consequence of Inyonin's resignation and replacement was that the Appointments Committee came to be completely dominated by members of the northern faction. This majority was promptly used to appoint Mr. Egweu, a Protectorate government education officer and a northerner, Treasurer. The committee continued to use its majority to secure the appointment of two additional chieftainships for its faction. As Secretary-General Ogaino's term of office grew to a close, it was evident to the southern faction that the northerners would use their majority to appoint a northerner to this most important office as well. The northerners inferred that they would nominate Mr. Egweu for the post and that, on his elevation, the treasury position would be filled by another northern nominee. The southerners were convinced the northerners were determined to dominate every sphere of local government activity. The only course left open to them in these circumstances was to paralyze the functioning of the District Council by boycotting its meetings.

A harassed District Commissioner was able to bring the two factions together briefly for a District Council meeting in January, 1958, at which time it was agreed that the Appointments Committee be retired. But it proved impossible to obtain the council's approval for the composition of a new committee. It was suggested that the reconstituted committee consist of two members from each faction presided over by the Chief Judge. Although the Chief Judge was a northerner his impartiality was respected by both factions. The northerners refused to vote on this compromise and walked out of the council. The chairman of the council adjourned the meeting before a vote had been completed and subsequently used the majority at his disposal to defeat this proposal and to substitute his own. His alternative was that the Appointments Committee should be composed of one representative from each county. As this stacked the committee in favor of the northerners five to three, the southerners refused to serve and effectively boycotted subsequent council meetings. The Teso local government—the showcase of democracy and efficient administration in Uganda—began to come apart at the seams. The Governor appointed a Commission of

Inquiry to investigate the situation and to recommend policy changes. Once more events in Teso were to shape local government development throughout Uganda, for it was evident to all that the crux of the problem revolved about the political composition of the Appointments Committee. As some District Commissioners had predicted in 1955, to permit the District Council to elect the Appointments Committee would prove to be the weak link in an otherwise admirable reform. "There is only one possible conclusion to be arrived at in respect to the Appointments Committee and that is that the manner of appointing its members and its method of working must be completely revised."[39]

In a subsistence society the psychic and material rewards of public office are high indeed and the struggles to achieve positions as chief or local government official tend to be fierce. This, when added to the Ingoratok-Iseratok feud, which in large part was deliberately aggravated to give advantage to the political ambitions of the leaders of the respective factions, brought the executive and administrative posts of Secretary-General and Treasurer into the very thick of partisan politics. The Commission of Inquiry recommended that the secretary-generalship be removed from politics and made a purely civil service position. It was further recommended that the post be filled by a senior Itesot chosen from the eight county chiefs or from the central government civil service and that the selection be made by an appointments board responsible not to the Teso District Council but to the Governor of Uganda. It was also stipulated that the holder of the office would not be eligible to succeed himself at the expiration of his five-year term. On the other hand, it was recognized that the chairmanship of the council was a political post and the Commission recommended that it be reserved for a nonofficial member of the council.

The breakdown of local government in Teso plus less serious problems of a similar nature in other districts led in 1958 to the amendment of the 1955 District Council's ordinance. The major purpose of this amendment was to do away with the politically nominated Appointments Committee and to replace it with a seven-member board appointed by the Governor, subsequently the Minister for regional Administrations. The seven members would be appointed from a panel of ten names to be submitted by the District Council to the Governor. Upon nomination, those members who were District Councillors would be required to resign from the council. The right to appoint the chairman of the Appointments Committee was reserved to the Governor. The 1958 amendment stipulated that the District Appointments Board should assume responsibility for the appointment of all grades of staff in the district, while the 1962 Ordinance transferred nearly every aspect of local control or initiative over staff to the central government. Nearly every session of the Teso District Council since 1958 and the withdrawal of control over local appointments, has led to a resolution condemning the "nonpolitical" appointments board and demanding in the name of democracy, precedence, justice, and tradition that the council's powers in this respect be restored.

Party affiliation has largely replaced north-south factionalism in the politics of staff recruitment and appointment. It should be recalled, however, that the major schisms in regard to religion, north versus south, and political party, within modern Teso are interrelated with the south tending to be predominantly Catholic and Democratic and the north Protestant and UPC.

Conflict surrounding the composition of the Appointments Committee which in 1958 brought about a crisis in Teso local government, again rose to plague Uganda's most progressive local authority in 1963. The passage of the 1962 Local Administration Ordinance required the reconstitution of existing Appointments Boards. This, in conjunction with the resignation in 1962 of Mr. Egweu as Secretary-General and the resulting vacancy temporarily filled by the Assistant Secretary-General, triggered a revival of the struggle for the major offices. In September 1962 a UPC delegation of councillors (nearly all northerners and Protestants) met the Minister for Regional Administrations to petition him to dissolve the existing Appointments Board, which it will be recalled was constituted in 1958 of two northern, two southern members and a nonpartisan former Chief Judge as Chairman. The UPC councillors with a thirty-seven to twenty-two majority on the council had already carried a resolution condemning the Appointments Board and demanding its resignation on the basis that it no longer complied with the existing legislation.[40] The council also passed a resolution accusing the board of a series of bad appointments, most of which were said to have been made to favor friends and relatives.

The long latent conflict between the Kuman-speaking people of Kaberamaido County and the rest of Teso erupted at about this time and thereby interjected still another point of faction. Mr. Egweu, a Kuman and Secretary-General from 1958 to 1962, was accused of deliberately influencing the recruitment and promotion of fellow Kuman. As the Assistant Secretary-General, Mr. Ewiu, was also Kuman, Catholic, and a suspected supporter of the Democratic Party, the UPC majority was incensed with the Appointments Board's decision to elevate him to fill the vacancy of Secretary-General. The council resolved that Mr. Egweu "indulges a great deal in politics and movements which do not augur well for the peaceful administration of the district; he has now transferred all Itemwana chiefs who are Kuman to their area and this we believe is the cause of disturbances now arising in Kaberamaido County."[41]

The UPC-dominated council, over the opposition of the Democratic minority, demanded that the Appointments Board be dissolved and that its most recent appointments, including that of Mr. Ewiu to be Secretary-General, be rescinded. In a fashion which is becoming typical in Uganda, a delegation of the Democratic Party councillors travelled to the national capital to protest the position of the earlier UPC deputation. The situation was further complicated by the fact that Mr. Obwangor, who holds the all-important Ministry of Regional Administrations, is himself an Itesot and former Chairman of the Teso District Council.[42] As Mr. Obwangor was long recognized as the leader of the Teso UPC, and in common with other Uganda ministers determined to maintain control over his constituency, it is not surprising that he em-

TABLE 8
Survey of Teso County and Sub-County Chiefs, 1956 and 1963

	County Chief 1956	County Chief 1963	Sub-County Chief 1956	Sub-County Chief 1963	Total 1956	Total 1963
Number in sample	8	8	43	48	51	56
Religion						
Protestant	5	3	32	31	37	34
Catholic	3	5	9	13	12	18
Unknown	0	0	2	4	2	4
Area of residence and service						
Same	0	2	9	11	9	13
Different	8	6	31	37	39	43
Unknown	0	0	3	0	3	0
Occupational background						
Chiefly hierarchy	8	6	33	38	41	44
Clerk	3	4	21	19	24	23
Teacher	0	2	7	4	7	6
Police	0	1	2	2	2	3
Other	2	0	5	4	7	4
Education						
Primary	5	6	22	39	27	45
Secondary	0	1	14	7	14	8
Specialized	1	1	5	2	6	3
University	1	0	0	0	1	0
Unknown	1	0	2	0	3	0
Average age	53	50	45	48	46	49

Source: Author's survey, 1956 and 1963.

ployed his extraordinary powers to further the position of his own party generally and his personal political power specifically.[43] The Minister largely ignored the joint slate of twelve candidates put forth by the leaders of the two parties and designated that the reconstituted board should be composed of four members and a chairman.[44] All members and the chairman appointed by him in March 1963 are members of UPC; three members are from Usuku—the Minister's own county—and only one from the south. The Appointments Board Chairman, a resident of Amuria, is also Teso UPC chairman and a northerner. A religious balance was maintained, however, with two Catholics, two Protestants and a Muslim.[45]

County and sub-county chiefs in Teso, unlike those in Bunyoro, were never regarded as indigenous local leaders but rather as agents of the central government posted at the convenience of the District Commissioner. (See Table 8.) Of the fifty-one county and sub-county chiefs, only seven sub-county chiefs in 1957 were serving in their county of permanent residence.

Thus, there has been a relatively greater tendency to transfer chiefs in Teso than in Bunyoro where traditional associations are common. In 1956 only seven of Teso's forty-three sub-county chiefs were serving in their home counties. (See Table 8.) In line with a policy of breaking down traditional parochialism, the central government has long sought to further the nonpartisan civil service status of chiefs and urged their transfer on the basis of seniority and experience. In 1959, thirty-one of the forty-seven sub-county chiefs were natives of the Iseratok northern counties and only sixteen from the three southern Ingoratok counties. Six southern sub-county chiefs were serving in the north and five northerners in the south. However, in 1963 more sub-county chiefs (11) were serving within their home counties than in 1956. Of the thirty-three northern-born chiefs only five are serving in southern counties. It would appear that a reversal of an earlier policy of chiefs placement, rather than a decline in sectional rivalry, has contributed to the current abatement of hostility.

The Protestant Mission Schools in Ngora for many years supplied Teso with its chiefs. This concentration of early education in the hands of the Protestants, plus the general tendency of British administrators to appoint Protestants, in large part explains the predominance of Protestant chiefs in Teso. It is interesting to note that four of the county chiefs in 1956 were Ingoratok and four Iseratok, whereas in 1963, reflecting the growing power of the northerners, the balance had shifted to five to three. This ratio is carefully watched by the leaders of the respective factions and if one area has a majority of the chieftainships its members feel disgraced and fear that the advantage will be used further to discredit them.

Traditional Roles

The Emurwon is an Iteso witch doctor—a diviner and a specialist in the art of cursing. Although there is a tendency for the role to be hereditary, it is more often assigned to a person who is physically or mentally deformed. The role of the Emurwon has adapted itself to new conditions and, in conjunction with the unofficial clan system described above, acts to adapt the universalistic local government system to specific local Iteso problems, as the following illustration demonstrates.

The number of cattle required as bride price in traditional Teso was unlimited and was determined by agreement between the parents of the suitors. The introduction of money and a cash crop economy, as well as the influence of the missions, has led to periodic attempts to fix the number of bride price cattle. In 1958 in accordance with District Council resolutions, the bride price was limited to fifteen cows. However, this regulation was rarely observed and the bride price continued to vary with supply and demand. In cases of marital separation, the court can only order the return of the fifteen "official" cows.[46] But if local stability is to be maintained, it is imperative that all the cows be returned so that the family of the groom will be in a position to arrange for a wife to replace the departed mate. A number of cases were studied wherein the father of the separated woman returned only the fifteen "Lukiko cows." Under the provision of the local government system, no method existed whereby the additional cows could be retrieved. The solution that has evolved involves an adaptation in the role of the Emurwon. The victimized man, or his family, visits the Emurwon and requests that the father of the runaway wife be cursed. At a specific time, a cursing ceremony is performed which involves the sacrifice of livestock over a special ant hill. The Emurwon's curse not only purports to threaten the health and possessions of the father of the departed wife, but his entire extended family as well. Word of the cursing soon spreads throughout the village and, if the possessor of the cattle at issue does not, on his own volition, return the extra cows, his relatives, concerned for their health and wealth, pressure him into doing so.[47] In 1959 the District Council completed the circle by repealing a resolution of 1947 which precluded the courts from awarding the return of illegal dowry.[48] Similar cases involving debt litigation that could not be taken before the official court system were also noted.

The official local government system, in its effort to solve certain

local problems, often creates new problems or leaves a number of traditional problems without an organized means of effective solution. In
order to guard against local disintegration or disorder, the traditional
role of Emurwon persists as a necessary carryover providing a channel
for the resolution of disruptive conflicts.

Relationship of Central and Local Government Roles

In Bunyoro-Kitara the District Commissioner was never a completely free agent for he ruled *indirectly* through the traditional political system. The Iteso had no Omukama and the District Commissioner
ruled directly, employing in the process a hierarchy of assistants,
termed chiefs, to carry out his orders. Today, the District Commissioner has lost most of his many powers and has been relegated to the
role of advisor to the local government and coordinator of central
government activities. In Bunyoro the chiefs were accountable to the
Omukama as well as to the District Commissioner. Thus, introduction
of a system of accountability to a councillor-committee system and to
a centralized local government officialdom in Bunyoro was not perceived as a radical departure, for everything was still done in the name
of the Omukama. Furthermore, the office of the Katikiro was indigenous and well understood. In Teso, on the other hand, the transfer of
accountability from the District Commissioner to a centralized Teso-
wide native officialdom was not simply a variation on a familiar theme,
but rather something entirely new and different.

The Teso local government had long been regarded as the most
effective in Uganda and was frequently employed as an example of
the successful implementation of the British system. Despite the 1958
crisis, the evidence tends to support this evaluation. But a closer examination suggests that the resemblance may be superficial and that the
system in practice follows more closely the letter than it does the spirit
of the English model. In part, this is attributable to the fact that Teso
is a relatively homogeneous district and, though characterized by
north-south friction, does not suffer as intensely from factionalism as
do the multitribal districts.

Furthermore, the absence of a tradition of centralized rule has left
a legacy in Teso of direct rather than indirect rule. Thus the relationship of chiefs and local government officials to the District Commissioner has long been that of employee to employer and despite the official change in the locus of authority the relationship tends to remain
substantially the same.

The relative effectiveness of Teso local government is attributable
in large part to the long tenure of three or four very capable Iteso
administrators. To these men, who began their careers as employees

of the District Commissioner, the emergence of a local government was not perceived as a drastic change, for by and large they continued to take their cue from the District boma across the street; even though they had become technically responsible to an elected District Council. For example, Mr. Inyonin, who served as Teso local government Treasurer from 1944 to 1958, began his public career in 1929 as a clerk in the central government Medical Department in Soroti.[49] In 1934-35 he worked in the District Commissioner's office as an advisor on "native affairs" and from 1936-39 as a special clerk to the District Commissioner. In 1944 he became the first Treasurer of the Teso Local Authority; in 1947 he was selected as the first African Chairman of the Teso District Council and in 1949 the Treasurer under the Local Government Ordinance of that year. Until 1956, when Teso District adopted the provisions of the District Administration (District Councils) Ordinance of 1955, the Treasurer was, in effect, the District Commissioner's accountant for Local Authority funds. After 1956 he was elected by, and in theory received his orders from, the council. However, it is too much to expect that a technician after nearly thirty years as an employee of the British administration would suddenly perceive of himself as an official of a local government institution responsible to an amorphous and largely illiterate council. The path from the Treasurer's to the District Commissioner's office is worn deep by years of daily visits in search of advice and guidance. And it is easy for a Treasurer to allow a District Commissioner to make the major decisions. A habitual preference for a given manner of organization is not radically altered by changes in the formal system but tends to accommodate itself to new procedures. Independence and the substitution of African for British district officers has altered this pattern only slightly.

The Councils

Teso was the first district in Uganda to develop a representative council system. Concerned with the autocratic rule of the nonindigenous chiefs the British administration, beginning in 1937, established a hierarchy of councils upon which a majority of seats were initially reserved for "clan elders." An analysis of Teso county councils in 1950 reflected their conservative composition. Of the 143 elected county councillors fifty were chiefs and nearly as many were clan leaders.[50] Thus, more than 75 per cent of the over-all membership (elected, appointed, and ex-officio) of the county councils consisted of chiefs, ex-chiefs, and would-be chiefs. Since the District Council, until 1956, was recruited almost entirely from the county councils, it followed that it too was conservative and represented the interest of the ruling elite rather than those of the peasants.

This early council system seemed to work efficiently and rapidly became a model for the rest of the Protectorate. Lower councils met relatively regularly and, aside from the perennial Ingoratok-Iseratok factionalism, the District Council functioned to the admiration of most British administrators. It could hardly have been otherwise, for although the councils in theory were composed of a majority of representative members voicing the interests of the people over against those of the chiefs, they were in practice more akin to a conference of chiefs working in close harmony with their employer—the British district administration.

However, the District Administration (District Councils) Ordinance of 1955, as applied to Teso, led to some profound changes in the recruitment and organization of the councils.[51] The Teso constitutional regulations of 1956 make no provision for clan leaders but rather substituted a direct election for the former method of election upward through a tier of lower councils. Under this tier system the lower chiefs had not found it difficult to obtain lower council seats for their friends and unofficial colleagues, the clan leaders—and in this manner had successfully determined the composition of the District Council. However, the eighty-eight-member council, which first sat in 1956, was composed of only twelve ex-officio members (the Secretary-General, Treasurer, the Chief Judge, eight county chiefs and Teso's representatives to the Uganda Legislative Council), twenty appointed members (ten each by the District Commissioner and the District Council), and fifty-six directly elected members. Since independence and the 1962 District Administrations Ordinance, the democratic element has been further enhanced and party politics have emerged as a major factor. The first council elected under the terms of the 1962 legislation is composed of sixty-three members directly elected from as many single members constituencies plus seven members especially selected by the elected councillors. No seats in the new council are reserved for clan leaders, chiefs or officials. The interjection of a predominantly democratic element has rendered council meetings more rowdy; and there gradually became manifest the latent but basic antagonism between the illiterate peasants and the educated elite (which has always existed but been successfully suppressed heretofore) as well as the conflict between the Iseratok and the Ingoratok.

Despite direct elections, the composition of the District Council does not accurately mirror the occupational profile of the Iteso. The Teso farmers, as in Bunyoro, make up a large majority of the population and though they are relatively better represented in Teso than in Bunyoro, they still accounted for only 18.2 per cent of the total District Council membership in 1956 and only slightly more in 1963.

The occupational composition of the council has changed only slightly since 1956 and the first directly elected assembly. Traders and shopkeepers were about equally represented then as now but there is a slightly larger percentage of teachers in the current council. Farmers, which make up the largest category, account for about one-fifth of the members in 1963 as well as in 1956. But whereas nineteen members of the 1956 council were ex-chiefs, the more democratic 1963 council counted only ten former chiefs among its members. A new category of occupation—professional party organizers, unheard of in 1956—is now of considerable importance. Fourteen of the sixty-three elected members in the 1963 council are party officials at the district branch or sub-branch level.

The average Iteso District Councillor as of 1963 is twice as likely to be Protestant than Catholic, is relatively wealthy, and has had considerably more education than his constituents. More than a third of the councillors have had six years or more of education and sixteen claim junior or senior secondary school level. Compared to the first elected councillors of 1956, the post-independence representatives are younger—generally in their late thirties and likely to be involved in party politics, the Co-operative Movement and the Teso African Traders Association.

Although the tier system of local councils had its origin in Teso, the lower councils have had a checkered history. There have been numerous and sporadic attempts to develop the parish, sub-county, and county councils into viable institutions, but with relatively little success. Considering the fact that the powers devolved on the District Council until 1962 were extremely limited, it is not surprising that there was little inclination to transfer functions or authority to the lower councils.

The current local government reforms call for the reestablishment of directly elected lower councils. The districts have been encouraged to eliminate either the sub-county or parish council but there is a natural reluctance to do so. The Teso District Council, in 1963, passed a bylaw to "Establish Local Councils," at the county, sub-county, and parish levels. However, after considerable debate the only functions that the District Council was willing to devolve on the lower councils were grazing control and improvement of agriculture.

Who Guards the Guardians?

No single aspect of the Teso local political system can be viewed separately. The council system, the chiefly hierarchy, the central government administrators, religious, area, and party factions, vestiges of traditional culture and the fabricated clan leader system, are all interrelated, sometimes mutually reinforcing and at other times working in contradiction. The Iteso, of course, do not sharply distinguish between these various forces and structures, but tend to perceive of these inter-relationships and institutional complexes as a single integrated system which requires that certain things be done and others be prohibited.

The many institutions which together constitute the system possess legitimacy in the eyes of the Iteso, though the degree and basis of their acceptance vary considerably. The development of districtwide political and administrative institutions which followed the assumption of authority by the British at the turn of the century heralded the demise of the small-scale, diffuse indigenous political system and the development of a hierarchy of chiefs patterned after the Buganda system. But as early as 1926, district officials noted the difficulties involved in attempting to superimpose a hierarchy of appointed chiefs over the Iteso. Iteso chiefs, enjoying the privilege of authority without the necessity of winning consent, jealously guarded their prerogatives and as the 1926 Annual Report noted, "the widespread exploitation of the peasants by the chiefs [was] very unpopular with the masses of the latter."[52]

Possessed of no traditional legitimacy, and often recruited from the less scrupulous ranks of the Iteso, the "chiefs" rapidly evolved into an autocratic ruling class. A District Commissioner, writing in 1926, observed that "there seems to be hardly any difference in intelligence between the most reprobate peasants and the best of chiefs." He commented at greater length: "There has been no ruling class in the county in the past and the majority of the chiefs approximate in reality more nearly to petty officials of the clerk type than to real chiefs or elders of the people who could by precedent and example ensure the proper progress of the race. . . . The imposition of Baganda ideals . . . have not been either complete or very suitable to the national genius of Teso."[53] The system of chiefs, though tolerated, has never won the full acceptance of the populace.

The sub-county chief in the Usuku area in 1957, for example, was not highly regarded by the local people largely because his home was not in that region. He received only grudging obedience from his subjects and lower chiefs, and even this was in deference to his power to apply judicial sanctions. Aware of the manner in which he was regarded, he worried constantly about his lack of status and he literally feared for his and his family's safety. Nor were his fears unfounded, for in 1955 his subjects burned his official house to the ground; he no doubt also was aware of the fact that in the past more than one Usuku chief had been poisoned. As a visible scapegoat, the local people held him personally responsible for the initiation of the district graduated tax and other unpleasant innovations. This particular sub-county chief's troubles were compounded by his failure to establish effective working rapport with his unofficial counterpart—the apolon ka ateker. Furthermore, the county chief at that time, ever suspicious of a potential rival, sought to discredit him in the eyes of the District Commissioner and Secretary-General. Although he was supported by the district administration and to a lesser extent by the officialdom of the local government, his failure to secure either voluntarily or through compulsion the consent of his subjects rendered his rule ineffective. After developing a severe case of ulcers, he was transferred to another and distant sub-county where he could try again to win friends and to influence people.

The time when chiefs could rule by force alone has passed, and today a varying degree of local consent is required. But as the institution of an extensive area-based, all-purpose, local authority runs counter to traditional Iteso values, this consent is difficult to secure. The lot of an Iteso chief is not an easy one. The council system, which was designed to check his arbitrary rule but which initially he was able to control, now effectively challenges his powers. The District Commissioner, who formerly acted as the chief's coercive agent, now often forsakes the chief in favor of the council, the majority party, or the local government officials. Complaints to the District Commissioner or party leaders concerning chiefly misconduct are on the increase and are likely to receive a more favorable audience from an administration currently committed to developing local government on the British model, than are the denials of the chiefs.

The peasant today is painfully conscious of a bewildering number of authority figures in his village, all of whom possess some degree of legitimacy. The rapid changes which have occurred, particularly since 1957, radically altered the existing pattern of influence and obligation. The chiefs in particular have suffered an enormous loss in power and status, while the district councillors have become progressively more influential and are identified with national political parties. The interjection of party politics into local government has placed new strains on the major officials. This extremely fluid situation has encouraged ambitious councillors and politicians to usurp authority of chiefs and local officials alike. District Council chairmen have been inclined to act as the executive officer of the local government; in one instance the chairman assumed authority of arrest as well. The councillors in their home constituencies have challenged the authority of chiefs on a number of occasions. Matters reached such a stage by 1958 that circulars prepared by the Secretary-General and the District Commissioner were sent to all councillors and chiefs. "There should be no clash between chiefs and councillors if their respective functions are understood . . . the Chief is appointed to carry out lawful duties and orders of his superiors efficiently even if these might be unpopular. The councillor is elected to represent the people of his area, not as a kind of advocate to attack the chief, or to appear as rival of the chief. . . ."[54]

Chiefs and clan leaders until 1956 dominated the District Council; but by 1962 no chiefs and only two (higher) ex-chiefs were members of the council. It is not without significance, however, that the two ex-chiefs are respectively Teso leaders of the UPC and the DP. The county UPC and DP leaders today often possess greater prestige and influence than the chiefs. For example, the UPC leader in Usuku County has secondary level education, is a district councillor, wealthy trader and a member of the powerful Teso Land Board. The branch chairman in Soroti is a District Council member, former chief, and large cattle trader. The revised and directly elected lower councils which took place late in 1963, are chaired, not by the chiefs as in the past, but by the respective branch majority party leaders.

In the Teso District, with its heritage of decentralized, diffuse rule, the District Officer, regardless of the diminution of his power, continues to exercise considerable influence and elicits significant local support. Nevertheless, his role is a difficult one. The chiefs and officials often prefer to allow him to continue to assume major responsibility, particularly for unpopular administrative decisions. The temptation for a District Commissioner to ignore an inefficient local government system and act unilaterally is often difficult to resist. To move from the role of all-powerful benevolent autocrat to constitutional advisor in the span of a few years demands an extraordinary endowment of patience and faith.

Few European district officers held informal talks with the chief in an effort to build up his security or prestige. And this well established superior-subordinate pattern set an example for the "proper" attitude between African and African within the local political system. This attitude, though not so pronounced in the outlying areas, characterizes the relationships at the local government headquarters where officials and senior clerks often treat their subordinates and messengers more harshly and rudely than they were treated by the British.

What is extraordinary is not the inability or reluctance of the British and more recently the African field officers to implement with perfection an alien system of local government, but rather the degree to which they have been relatively successful and sincere in their efforts under extremely adverse conditions. Not only was the European district officer tempted to get on with the job and do things himself quicker and better, but he was also hampered by the attitudes and activities of government departmental officers who rarely shared his dedication to the task of developing modern and democratic local political institutions. The agricultural, veterinary, community development, and other officers are primarily concerned with accomplishing set technical tasks and frequently are oblivious to the importance of working through the local government. To further complicate matters, most African officers and assistants today are not natives of their area of service. Baganda officials are distrusted and frequently accused of attempting to assume the role of their forefathers who perhaps served with Kakunguru.

A rapid transition from a traditional to a modern local political system, involving as it invariably does the transfer of accountability and consent for socially binding decisions from one institution to another, upon occasion gives rise to stresses which may take the form of temporary disintegration or disorder. For example, the British administration and educated African elite have long been convinced that hygiene is a serious local problem in Teso—so serious in fact that they have manipulated the District Council into passing a series of relevant bylaws and resolutions. However, these regulations sometimes conflict with many clan taboos that are still binding. It is compulsory, for instance, that each head of household dig a latrine adjoining his homestead. But some Iteso believe that a pregnant woman must not be allowed to urinate outside of the family compound. Other Iteso, refusing to dig or use latrines for fear that evil spirits abide within deep, dark holes, are arrested by the chiefs and subsequently fined. Whenever local customs are particularly contrary to universal regulations, the chief, if he is to secure a requisite level of local consent, must himself deviate from the ideal, which in turn places him in a difficult position.

A comparable situation concerning marriage dowries has long posed a similar problem. As early as 1947 the Teso Native Authority was "encouraged" to regulate the number of cows that could be paid as dowry. But as already noted, the various regulations and amendments were rarely observed. Subsequent litigation over desertion or death of a wife was complicated by the fact that in nearly every case more cows changed hands than were authorized. One month after independence the District Council, free of alien influence, voted that the bride price was a matter to be arranged by the parents and not by the District Council. This position was taken despite arguments that because few young men could pay the going price of twenty to forty head of cattle the marriage of young girls was delayed with a consequent increase in illegitimacy. The majority position, however, was that the council had learned that dowry "reduction has provided a market for witch doctors and bylaws never succeeded anyway for people continued to pay the number of cattle that was demanded and in case of divorce parents of brides were only willing to refund the recognized five head of cattle and the rest were got under the threat of murder."[55]

Other Western ideals, sometimes in response to British pressure, have been given legal sanction by the modern local government system. For example, the customary privilege of beating one's wife has been compromised, but "ever since the beating of women was forbidden, signs have not been lacking that the authority of husbands has steadily been growing less," with a corresponding increase in cases of adultery and other forms of local disintegration.[56]

Area and Consent

The traditionally parochial Iteso have only recently developed a sense of "belonging" to areas larger than the customary etem. The political and administrative district which generally coincides with the area of tribal residence is now accepted and Teso nationalism, on occasion, rises to the emotional level of Bunyoro and the other ancient Bantu kingdoms. Teso nationalism today has spread beyond the frontiers of Uganda. Demands are frequently made that the Iteso in Kenya be incorporated with their brethren in Uganda. In 1961 Raiti, a Kenyan Itesot, addressed the Teso District Council to inform the councillors about the aims and purposes of the Iteso Welfare Union of East Africa, one of the more important of which is to unite all Iteso. In July 1961 the Iteso Welfare Union cabled Mr. Ian Macleod, Secretary of State for the Colonies, expressing its disappointment that nothing had been done about the "Iteso tribesmen who are deliberately cut off from the rest of their brethren in Uganda."[57] Also indicative is the growing tendency to attempt to purge the Iteso language of foreign and particularly of Luganda words. In 1959 the General Purposes Committee resolved that thirty-five Teso towns be renamed according to traditional usage.[58]

Despite this shift in the level of political identification, the Iteso have retained a surprisingly high degree of local parochialism. The lower administrative units which often coincide approximately with the traditional etem, do not always regard the District Council with the respect and awe which is characteristic of the former kingdoms. The minutes of Teso lower councils are replete with motions resolving that a variety of powers be devolved to them and there is a frequent demand that the District Council should not act without the prior consent of the council representing the community affected by such action.

This legacy of parochialism is also reflected in the emotion surrounding the sitting of sub-county headquarters or proposals for the amalgamation of lower councils and areas. Lying at the heart of local parochialism and suspicion are the values that cluster about land uses and tenure, beautifully expressed by an Itesot in these words: "We very well know that chiefs get transferred and sometimes retire, . . . chiefs die, we the writers of this letter die, and the Iteso people also will die, but the land will remain just as God made it."[59]

There is little sense of civic obligation among the Iteso. English local government is characterized by the participation of thousands of unpaid councillors, who, with no thought of monetary compensation, devote considerable time in the public interest. Until a similar spirit prevails in Teso, it is unlikely that the Teso council system will ever approach its English model beyond superficial resemblance. The Teso councillors are inclined, at nearly every session, to vote themselves an increase in their attendance allowance—an action that would be quickly understood by many American state legislators. The English-trained administrator views this approach to public service with dismay. The average Teso councillor does not serve from a sense of civic duty nor does he think himself to be democratically accountable to his neighbors. He more likely sees his role as leading to an eventual chieftainship or official position with the local government; he enjoys the prestige and power that accompany council membership; and finds the meetings a pleasant distraction for which he also is relatively well paid.

Growing out of the *1953-55 Report of the East African Royal Commission* were proposals by the Uganda government for alterations in the system of land tenure.[60] Government efforts to convince the Iteso of the need for land tenure reforms as a consequence of increased population and low agricultural productivity were met with hostility that upon occasion bordered on violence.[61]

This issue of land tenure illustrates well the misunderstanding which often arises out of a conflict of values between ruler and ruled. The British rationally concluded that a rapidly increasing population and fragmentation of land would preclude the development of an agricultural system capable of supporting a modern economy. The solution proposed was one of limited private ownership and transferability of title with the apparent assumption that the value of land was primarily a factor of production. The Iteso, however, feel differently. There never was a shortage of land before the European came. Land is like air; without it one will die. To introduce a system whereby a man's sons may not inherit his land is like a father denying his sons the very air they must breathe to live. To divide the land into individual parcels which can be bought and sold is nearly as fantastic to the traditional Itesot as the sale of blocks of atmosphere would be to a European.

What else but a scheme to "steal our land" could such a proposal be? The British realized that their proposals would contribute to a concentration of landholding and to a growing class of landless persons. But the Itesot cannot perceive of a normal individual not holding and tilling some soil, however small it might be.

Part of the Iteso's suspicion of British intentions was more rationally based. They fear the influx of wealthy Asians and Baganda who, they thought, would trick them into selling their land. Much of this fear, however, runs deeper and draws its substance from the traditional social system. For example, some Iteso voiced the fear that individual title would force a man to live permanently on his holding and in many areas native custom is such that there is a genuine fear of residing on a plot where too many relatives have died or other misfortune has struck.

As late as June 1962 the District Council resolved against proposals for individual land title and demanded that their representatives take the issue to London for discussions at the forthcoming constitutional conference.[62]

The complexity of modern local government is beyond the comprehension of the parochial and uneducated lower councillors. Efforts to bring them into the picture frequently result in confusion and misplaced suspicion. The peasant who finds himself a member of a lower council is accustomed to being told what to do and is confused when his opinion is sought on what he considers to be a complicated and sometimes irrelevant issue. His view of government is simple, and he finds it impossible to distinguish between administrative levels, institutions, departments, and programs. He confuses the resettlement scheme in northern Amuria County with the Land Tenure Proposals or believes that the Land Tenure Proposals will lead to the District Land Board uprooting and redistributing the people at will.

The issue of a paramount chief (Ekaraban) for Teso has occupied the attention of nearly every council from the establishment of modern local government in 1956 to the present. Colonial administration consistently refused to authorize the establishment of this institution, maintaining that it had no basis in traditional Teso society and was sought out of envy for the Buganda system. The desire to emulate the kingdom districts is also evident in repeated demands for a ministerial form of government.

However, the motives underlying the persistent demand for a paramount chief are more complex than the obvious effort to emulate the Baganda. In part it is an attempt by a people newly conscious of their homogeneity to establish a symbol of tribal unity. It also is related to the emergence of the hierarchy of unofficial clan leaders discussed above. At the same time, many Iteso feared that self-government for Uganda would open the door to domination of Teso by the Baganda. A paramount chief, it was thought, would symbolize the strength of the Iteso people and give them a single ruler who could meet on equal terms with the Kabaka of Buganda or the Omukama of Bunyoro.

The 1961 London Constitutional Conference was attended by representatives from each district local government.[63] The Teso District Council instructed its delegates to demand that the new Constitution for an independent Uganda make provision for a head of state and that federal status for Teso be considered if for no other reason than "[since] the last London Conference some districts had been asking for a federal status which left Teso without anyone to remain with in the unitary government."[64] The District Council further instructed its delegates to support a second chamber to be indirectly elected from the district councils with hereditary rulers as ex-officio life members including, of course, the Ekaraban of Teso. At the same session a committee was appointed to meet with the Governor to obtain permission to establish the position of Ekaraban (head of state). Heading this delegation was the council chairman Mr. Obwangor who, a year later as Minister of Regional Administrations, was to find himself on the receiving end of similar delegations. As the 1962 Uganda Constitution authorized "the council of a district by resolution [to] make provision for establishing the office of constitutional head of that district" . . . agitation for an Ekaraban after independence was accelerated.[65] The constitution, however, also stipulated that the position must be supported by a two-thirds vote of the council and required the approval of the Governor-General (in practice, the Minister for Regional Administrations). At its first post-independence meeting the Teso District Council decided that an Ekaraban should be selected immediately. However, the Minister has refused to sanction the long sought for position on the basis that sufficient funds are neither available nor budgeted. There is some speculation, however, that the real reason is that the Minister, aware of the fickleness of national politics, would like to assure the position for himself.[66]

A major reliance on the committee system also contributed to a diffuse and unwieldly authority structure. The three most important committees in 1957 were Finance, General Purposes and Education. Of the total of forty-eight committee seats, twenty-one were filled by elected members of the council and twenty-seven by nonelected members. Nearly a third of the total major committee seats were held by six official members of the council. Twenty-eight of the sixty councillors held all of the forty-eight major committee seats. Of the remaining sixty councillors, ten sat on the two minor committees.[67] More than half of the councillors served on no committee, while only fourteen of the forty-nine elected councillors served on a major committee. The tendency of the elected members to regard the committees with suspicion and to refuse to accept or to support committee recommendations can be readily understood.

The 1962 Ordinance and the absence of party politics has had a democratizing influence on the committee system. Every councillor in 1963 was a member of at least one of fifteen committees. Most committees have eight members; this number is not without significance for until party affiliation replaced county constituency as the major decisive force, it was common to allocate a committee seat to each county. The UPC, which has a two to one majority in the council, holds 72 of the 104 committee seats. All committee chairmen, as one would expect, are UPC. Three UPC and one DP members hold three committee assignments. Fifteen councillors, of which only three are DP members, hold two seats. The chairmen of the Finance, Education, Health and Natural Resources are termed ministers. Committee seats and chairmanship are evenly distributed with a councillor from each county as chairman of a major committee.

Crime and Punishment

Before the Europeans and the Baganda modified the parochial Teso political system and extended the individual's range of obligations and responsibility, the Iteso were organized socially and politically into a multitude of semi-autonomous etems. Within a given etem the realm of permissible and prohibited behavior was well known. Disputes between etems were frequently settled by force for only a rudimentary code of inter-etem association existed. However, within their circumscribed area of daily association, the Iteso possessed a well developed system of insuring the security of life and health from antisocial behavior on the part of neighbors and kinfolk. In cases of murder and homicide, not only the killer, but his family as well, were held responsible. Compensation (blood money) payable to the family of the deceased was established through arbitration within the kinship-etem unit. In 1961 the District Council increased from five to ten head of cattle the blood money that a person is required to pay to the relatives of the person killed. For the first time liability for blood money was extended to women. Also indicative of the arrangements required of modern institutions was an agreement that blood money is to be paid by the local government to any of its employees killed while on the job.[68]

Teso local government courts are not empowered to hear cases of homicide and murder but may adjudicate questions of blood money which arise as a consequence of homicide. Compensation for assault, rape, and defilement follows a similar pattern. Through the agency of witchcraft, mystical and supernatural sanctions still persist in Teso. The following case is illustrative.[69]

Mr. A claimed that his brother Y had committed adultery with A's wife. Y denied this charge. In order to prove his innocence to neighbors and kinfolk, who had begun to ostracize him, Y resorted to witchcraft. On the night of June 11, he secretly threw a spear and a hatchet into a sacred tree in front of A's house. This was strong medicine, for everyone knew that if Y was guilty of the charge he would become ill and die. If, on the other hand, he was innocent, the spear and the hatchet thrown at night into the sacred tree would cast a spell upon his accuser, as well as upon his accuser's wives, children and livestock. The strength of this belief is such that Y's act immediately made it apparent to his neighbors, and to A as well, that he was innocent and had been wrongly accused. Seeing the spear and the hatchet in the tree, A realized that he had wrongly accused his brother and immediately went to the clan leader to report his folly and to ask the clan leader to call a clan court so that Y could be compensated and called on to remove the curse. The clan leader assembled a clan court meeting to be held under the symbolic tree. The village chief was notified of the time and place and was asked to come and preside. Testimony was given by witnesses for both A and Y. Two goats supplied by A were sacrificed at the base of the tree and the dung from the intestines spread by both A and Y in turn over the cut in the tree left when Y removed the spear and hatchet. The meat was eaten by the gathered throng. The issue was settled, A's life was saved, the conflict resolved and integration of the family and locality was maintained.

Responsibility for community misfortune, in the form of a severe and unusual loss of property or a series of inexplicable deaths, may be assigned to a wizard (ekacuban). An individual may be regarded as a wizard if he habitually acts in a manner which threatens the integration or security of the community. For example, the insane, whose presence in the village often poses a danger to others, may be considered as wizards. If death or other serious misfortune was attributed to an ekacuban, he was executed; today he is tried by the clan court. If found guilty by the official court system, which normally upholds the decision of the clan court, a convicted wizard is imprisoned and thereby removed from the community. Persons who deviate from local custom in a mystical or secretive fashion are also liable to be charged as wizards.

It is important to distinguish between a wizard, ekacuban, and a witch doctor, imurok. The first is an antisocial individual possessed of supernatural powers who probably has long been recognized as a threat to the community; and the political system, as noted above, is organized so as to remove this threat. The imurok, on the other hand, is a respected specialist and although his activities are today illegal he continues to play an important role in securing local conformity, particularly in cases where the official coercive system of the local government is ineffective. His services, for example, are sought to assist in collecting debts, and curing the sick.

The lowest member of this professional traditional hierarchy is the medicine man. He is usually a herbalist with an extensive knowledge of the curative properties of local plants. His position in Teso society is innocuous and his knowledge of native medicines should not be confused with the supernatural powers of the witch doctor.

It is possible for a medicine man or witch doctor who has attracted unusual notoriety to be regarded as a wizard. The greater his success, the more likely it is that he will be viewed with suspicion for fear that he may use his powers for evil. It is not unusual for a witch doctor to be brought before the court and charged as a wizard. Although the witch doctor will protest that he has only exercised his powers for the good of the community, the prosecution will likely enumerate a series of local misfortunes which are commonly ascribed to him. The legitimacy of a witch doctor in Teso society is dependent upon the popular conviction that his practices are well intended.

The rapid transition and disintegration of the traditional social system has confused the realm of permissive behavior. Proper behavior as determined by modern associations and standards is frequently viewed as deviation from traditional norms and there would appear to be a relationship between the relatively high incidence of violence in Teso and the rapid rate of social change. The traditional land tenure and inheritance customs, for example, have not successfully accommodated the change to cash crops agriculture, permanent buildings, and other hoardable wealth. Customary laws dealing with marriage dowry, divorce, child-rearing, and adultery often contradict Christian norms, modern obligations of women and youth and wage labor. A bumper cotton crop is almost invariably followed by an increase in crime and violence, for whereas beer was traditionally brewed and served only to community elders and rarely taken in excess, a cash economy has introduced the provision and sale of bottled Western beer. Heavy drinking normally occurs in large gatherings around the beer shops that have sprung up everywhere in Teso. Communal drinking often leads to argument and fights—usually over women. Flirtations are sometimes followed by ambush as a drunken husband seeks satisfaction for real or fancied adultery.[70] The high incidence of crime and violence in Teso has been attributed to a variety of factors ranging from the expedient one of national character to a high malarial rate with accompanying enlarged spleens which renders the Iteso more liable to fatal injury. The highly respected former Chief Judge of the Teso District Native Court concluded that:

> Teso's reputation for assault [is due] largely to a breakdown in social custom, which now countenances the presence of women at drinking parties and tolerates the brewing of beer for retail instead of for recognized and intimate social occasions such as the birth of twins, marriage and death ceremonies.[71]

Urged by the missions and the central government, the District Council through the years has passed numerous bylaws relating to beer brewing and consumption. With the exception of cattle herding, the Iteso are not institutionally inclined toward communal labor. When an Itesot requires additional help in cultivation or house building, he tells his neighbors that those who help will be rewarded with beer. The District Council in 1949, under considerable pressure from the District Commissioner, reluctantly resolved that brewing beer for repayment of labor in cultivation and house building without a permit from the chief was prohibited. The following year the council not only repealed this ordinance but resolved that the one shilling beer permit be abolished as well. At the same session, the council refused to support a tax on beer recommended by the District Commissioner.[72] The Iteso are not inclined to view excessive drinking, assault, and homicide as problems so serious as to require District Council bylaws. The council was persuaded to attach a prison sentence to such behavior, but imprisonment has never been an effective deterrent for, as a District Commissioner once concluded, "There is a sneaking sympathy with prisoners and little or no stigma is attached to a prison sentence."[73]

The process of separating the judiciary from the administration and integrating the native court system with Central Judiciary, begun in the late 1950's, is nearly completed. The national laws of evidence now apply to local courts which have been reorganized. The court of first instance presided over by a magistrate is at the sub-county level. The county courts have been abolished as has the role of the District Commissioner. Appeal now is to the District Court presided over by the Chief Judge and then directly to the Uganda High Court.

In Teso District there has been an average of one court case per year for every seven adult males since 1926. As nearly every court case involves at least two litigants it is likely that approximately one in every five adult Iteso males is involved in official court proceedings once every year.[74] But this is probably only a small part of total litigation for though it is impossible to know the number of disputes that are solved by unofficial clan courts, most observers estimate that for every official there are at least three unofficial cases.[75] The exceedingly high rate of litigation in Teso District is indicative of the low degree of institutionalization of modern norms and the conflict between new and traditional obligations.

In Bunyoro District, where the social system has experienced relatively less change, the incidence of adjudication is much lower. For example, in 1961 when in Teso District the native courts tried one of every ten adult male Iteso, the courts in Bunyoro tried only one in every nineteen adult male Banyoro. The rate of official adjudication in "progressive" Teso District is almost three times as high as in traditionally oriented Bunyoro. The difference is even more striking when it is noted that the Banyoro make relatively little use of unofficial clan courts.

The difference between the two tribes is more clearly revealed in a contrast of cases dealing with crimes of violence and disobedience to local laws. During 1961 one in every twenty adult Iteso males was involved in a criminal case. In the same year in Bunyoro, less than half as many persons were involved in litigation of a violent criminal nature. Nearly three thousand cases in 1961 of disobedience to local laws is further evidence that the Iteso have not completely institutionalized the alien Bantu chieftainship system.

The 1962 Ordinance authorizes the local government, subject to the approval of the Minister, to establish a police force. Unlike the para-police of the past, which were little more than messengers and bodyguards for the chiefs, the post-independence police force is under the direct control of the Secretary-General. The position of the chief is likely to deteriorate even further for the 1962 Ordinance authorizes the Minister, if he is satisfied that an adequate local police force exists, to remove responsibility for law and order from the chiefs and transfer it to the police.[76] The Teso local police force consists of one sergeant, eight corporals and 182 constables.

The flexibility of transitional social norms and the insecurity resulting from permissible variations in behavior are conducive to disorder and disintegration. If the Itesot regulates his behavior in accordance with that set of rules associated with the ever-changing imported social and political system, he runs the risk of deviating from his indigenous obligations. On the other hand, the older Itesot who clings tenaciously to surviving elements of the traditional system often is accused of deviating from the requirements laid down by the modern political system. Other individuals, unable to adjust to rapidly changing obligations, react by denying the legitimacy of all norms.

Revenue and Expenditure

It is difficult for non-Africans to fathom the values associated with land. In traditional Teso the land supplied all of the necessities of life and without land life itself was unthinkable. The fertility of the soil and of the people were perceived as an interrelated phenomenon. Probably the singlemost important function of the traditional political system was that of regulating the allocation, inheritance, and tenure of the land.

Land was held by the extended family group (ekek) and the senior male member of the family, in council with the heads of other families in the etem, exercised authority over the allocation of plots. Rights in land were acquired through inheritance, cultivation of vacant land, or through allocation by the ekek leader. Disputes concerning usufruct were traditionally settled by the clan leaders. Although the parish councils have assumed authority over land allocation, inheritance regulation still remains within the domain of the extended family. Land disputes today are first arbitrated by the clan leaders with appeal provided to the lower chiefs, the parish council and to the District Land Board.

Uganda's Constitution made provision for a central land commission and land boards for each district and federal state.[77] The District Land Board composed of a chairman, three members representing the farmers and one each representing traders, property owners, traditional interests and the administration. Control and management of township land is vested in this board. The allocation of rural land has changed only slightly and continues to be carried out by the parish council and chief. It is thought that eventually the authority of the Land Board will be extended over the entire district.

Before the arrival of the British, the council of etem clan leaders demarcated and reserved specified areas within the etem for communal grazing. Customary law dealing with grazing land has changed only slightly and pastures continue to be held in common.

As noted above, certain authority roles in traditional Teso were specialized and situational. Military leaders exercised authority only in time of war and were rewarded with a portion of the spoils. To the leaders of the hunt were reserved the choicer parts of the kill. The supernatural specialists, as noted above, were compensated in grain and livestock. The status of kinship and etem leader was largely acquired through age which, in turn, generally coincided with relative wealth expressed in number of cattle and wives.

When an Itesot dies, his eldest son inherits his land and possessions unless, in the opinion of the extended family, the son is unfit to assume the responsibilities of family head. The son also inherits his father's wives with the exception of his own mother who remains at the deceased's homestead maintaining her rights to her own gardens or who returns to the home of her brother or father.

A man's wives are an economic as well as a social asset and the regulation of marriage, dowry, divorce, and wife inheritance played an important part in the traditional allocation of resources in Teso. The dowry system placed a high premium upon female children, and the regulation of the allocation of children of divorced or deceased parents was an important factor in the economy.

The imposition of the Buganda hierarchy of territorial chiefs greatly altered traditional patterns. The maintenance of a cadre of full-time specialist chiefs required a regular and substantial allocation from local resources quite unlike anything the Iteso had been accustomed to. Regular taxation depended on a cash crop economy which in turn required large-scale administration, extensive roads and improved education. Not only was it necessary to develop political institutions commensurate with the enlarged area and scope of society, but also to devise a system of obtaining and allocating local resources to meet demands posed by these rapidly changing conditions.

It was customary in the kingdoms for the peasants to provide labor and food for their chiefs.[78] In Teso, however, no regular tribute was required prior to the imposition of the Buganda political system. The Iteso peasants were recruited in large numbers by Kakunguru to build a network of roads which subsequently contributed to the unification of the district. In 1919, the African Authority Ordinance formalized this method of obtaining resources:

> Any chief may, from time to time, issue orders to be obeyed by the Africans residing within the local limits of his jurisdiction . . . requiring all Africans between the ages of eighteen and forty-five who are physically fit, to work in the making or maintaining of any work of a public nature constructed or to be constructed or maintained for the benefit of the community.[79]

The chiefs were permitted to interpret liberally this provision of the ordinance, and chiefs' houses, gardens, and herds absorbed the greater part of compulsory labor (luwalo). All eligible males were initially required to work thirty days a year for the benefit of the community as the chief directed. The Nilo-Hamitic Iteso, unlike their Bantu and Nilotic neighbors, had never been required to perform manual labor for their leaders and found the system of luwalo extremely degrading and distasteful. To make matters worse, they were required to work an additional two days per month for the chief. The income the chief derived from cash crops cultivated by his subjects and the sale of their labor was regarded as proper compensation for his services. In 1934, chief's labor (but not luwalo) was abolished. In 1936 a total of 48,692 luwalo laborers were employed in Teso District, while 44,233 paid a ten-shilling commutation fee.[80] The manner in which local labor resources were allocated is shown in Table 9.

TABLE 9
COMPULSORY (LUWALO) LABOR, TESO DISTRICT

Roads and Rest Camps	17,348
Special Work	11,378
Tree Plantation	4,378
Grain Stores	3,941
Saza Headquarters	2,578
Court House	2,041
Chief's Houses	2,368
Government Messengers	1,907
Guards	1,516
Saza Messengers	726
Agriculture	511
TOTAL	48,692

SOURCE: Teso District Annual Report, 1936.

Beginning in the late 1930's the use of paid porters and other laborers began to replace luwalo. Although luwalo is no longer permitted, its legacy still lingers. The distaste the Itesot harbors for any form of servitude reinforced a predisposition to reject the imported system of territorial chiefs. In theory, all labor in Teso today is compensated for in cash. Nevertheless, prior to independence it was common, though illegal, for a sub-county chief to inform one of his parish chiefs that he needed forty men on a given day to weed his cotton. The parish chief would then order each of his village chiefs to recruit a proportionate number. They, in turn, would pass the burden on to their clan leaders. The peasants whose "voluntary services" were sought in this manner were, of course, entitled to refuse. However, to do so was not, in the long run, in their best interest.

In 1962 the District Council passed an ordinance providing for the provision of communal labor under carefully defined conditions.[81] Chiefs are authorized to call any ablebodied person to perform a variety of communal tasks including burying the dead, maintaining water supplies, clearing paths, and repairing schools and churches.

The modern local revenue system in Teso District is approximately the same as described for Bunyoro in Chapter Four. The graduated tax first implemented in 1955 is the major source of locally derived revenue. Assessment is made by a committee composed of the sub-county chief as chairman, a parish chief, and two persons elected by the sub-county council plus the parish chief of the parish being assessed. The ordinance requires that the Assessment Committee be assisted by an assessment officer who is to compute the individual's tax according to his wealth as determined by the committee. But for reasons of economy the District Council has not appointed special assessment officers and this function tends to be carried out by poll tax clerks in each sub-county. Possessed of little status and accustomed to taking orders from the chiefs, these clerks have done little to improve the assessment process.

Tax revenue in Teso District continues to provide the greater part of local revenue. Of a total estimated revenue of approximately £513,000 in the fiscal year 1962–63, the graduated local tax accounted for £300,000 or approximately 58 per cent of the total. But as the local government assumes new obligations, grants-in-aid play an increasingly important part in the local revenue picture. In 1940, grants-in-aid accounted for only £3,000 or about 7 per cent of total revenue. In 1956–57 grants-in-aid accounted for 29 per cent and in 1962–63, 30 per cent.

In Teso the relatively large proportion of local revenue secured through taxation contrasts with the situation in Bunyoro District. By 1954–55, grants-in-aid to Bunyoro were exceeding tax revenue and in 1961–62, per capita grants-in-aid (sixteen shillings) were considerably in excess of per capita local taxes (ten shillings).[82]

Despite the assumption of responsibility for new services, a large portion of total expenditure goes to cover the costs of administration. For example, personal emoluments account for nearly half of estimated expenditures for the fiscal year 1962–63.[83]

Excluding education costs, which are largely covered by central government grants, total salaries are nearly twice as large as all other expenditures. Attendance allowances for councillors represent a sizable expenditure and one which has tended to increase significantly through the years. The District Council has consistently sought to increase salaries and allowances and only the refusal of the Minister has precluded an even larger portion of the budget being allocated for this purpose. Despite the British, and more recently the African central government's, constant reminder that allowances are not salaries but compensation for travel and food, the Teso Councillor does not regard his services in this manner but expects to be paid for his labors just like a chief or any other government servant. Although the Minister informed the District Council in 1962 that increased allowances would not be approved, the council voted to include such a provision in the 1962/63 estimates. It was resolved that each councillor was to receive twenty shillings a day. In August 1962 at its first meeting the new councils moved that each member receive one hundred shillings monthly allowance.

Central control over local expenditures is particularly frustrating to the Teso District Council. As the Minister (their former chairman) can reject individual items in their estimates, attempts to provide for pet projects or to increase their own salaries are generally disallowed. For example, in 1962 the council approved estimates showing a £50,000 deficit which the Minister refused to accept. Instructed to balance projected increased expenditure for such positions as leader of the opposition, Ekaraban, and Ministers, the council proposed a series of minor licenses and fees which they anticipated would significantly increase revenues. Projected revenues were also to be increased by inflating the anticipated return for the sale of prison produce and similar public enterprises. These paper savings and increased revenues were then used to justify additional expenditure, primarily to cover increased allowances and new salaries.

Unlike the Bantu kingdoms to the south and west, Teso has been subject to British influence and administration only from 1910 to 1962 —a relatively short period. Though speaking a common language and sharing a relatively homogeneous culture, the Iteso have only recently developed a sense of tribal identity and solidarity. For in contrast to the Banyoro, the traditional Teso political system was diffuse; sovereignty, to the extent to which it can be said to have existed, was vested in a linkage of the extended family form of organization, a highly developed age-set association, and a small-scale territorial authority termed the etem.

Unable to perceive an indigenous political system worthy of recognition, the British imposed over what appeared to them to be a state of near anarchy, the Buganda hierarchical system of chiefs. Much of Teso's subsequent political history is a product of rebellion against, and adaptation to, a culturally alien political system.

Local government and politics as they have evolved in Teso are quite different from the Banyoro pattern described in the preceding chapter. A legacy of parochialism, a traditionally diffuse small-scale political system, and a heritage of rebellion against an alien order have rendered it difficult for the Iteso to submit to specialized and centralized authority. The relationship of culture and social systems to the nature of local problems, and to the structures that evolve in response to those problems is sharply posed in the contrast of the political systems of Bunyoro and Teso.

If, however, you come to your senses and decide to establish these Councils, I have one word of warning. Do not try to imitate the European system. What is one man's meat is another man's poison. Follow out and develop your own system and choose the leaders of the clan and the heads of your family groups, people whom you yourself look to as your leaders and spokesmen.

> Provincial Commissioner Eastern Province to
> Baraza Central District, May 22, 1941

The overwhelming impression we have gained from this evidence is that Bukedi is not ready for representative local government.

> *Report of the Commissioner of Inquiry into*
> *Disturbances in the Eastern Provinces,* 1960

CHAPTER SIX

Bukedi: From Tribes to Counties

TRIBES AND AREAS

Bukedi is the third and last district in this study of local political systems in Uganda. Bounded on the west and north by the Lake Kyoga drainage system, on the east by Mt. Elgon and its foothills, and on the south by Lake Victoria, Bukedi District resembles a funnel emptying southward into Lake Victoria. Into the mouth of the funnel during the seventeenth, eighteenth, and nineteenth centuries poured a complex variety of migratory tribes. The maneuverability of the migrant tribesmen was severely restricted by the geographical environment, which, in conjunction with a variety of other factors, contributed to the settlement of this area by a multitude of small, antagonistic tribal and ethnic groups.

Extending for sixty miles from north to south, rarely more than thirty-five miles from east to west and with a total area of only 1,753 square miles, Bukedi's 397,000 people are divided into seven distinct tribes. The Nilo-Hamitic Iteso, whose migratory pattern was traced in the preceding chapter, fought their way south into the area bounded by the Mpologomo River and the Elgon highlands. Today the Bukedi Iteso are in a majority in Pallisa and Tororo Counties. The Iteso of Pallisa and Tororo are separated from one another by two Bantu tribes —the Banyuli and the Bagwere. The Bagwere are closely related to the Bantu-speaking people of northern Busoga District and to the Banyoro. The Bunyuli tribe, on the other hand, is thought to have migrated from the southeast and claims an affinity with the Bantu Samia and Bagwe, which collectively inhabit the southernmost county of Bukedi District. The remaining county, West Budama, is populated almost exclusively by the Padhola, a relatively small, isolated Nilotic enclave left in the wake of the great Luo migration into what is now northern

BUKEDI DISTRICT

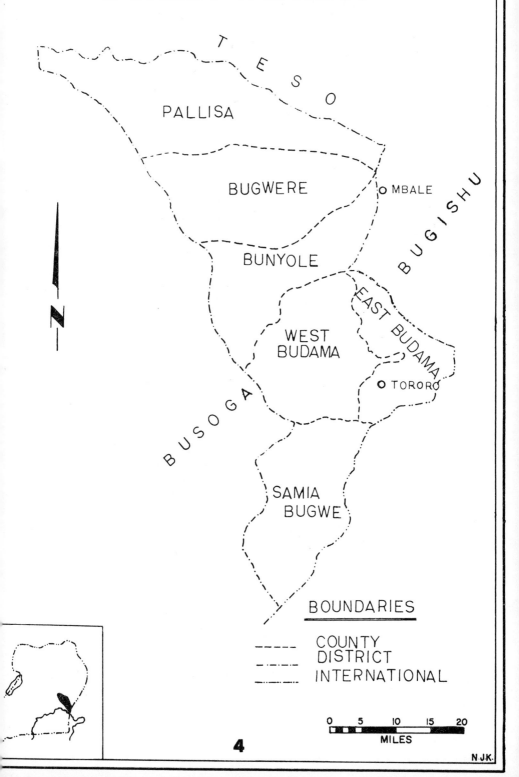

BOUNDARIES

- - - - - COUNTY
- · - · - DISTRICT
- · · - · · INTERNATIONAL

0   5   10   15   20
MILES

4

N.J.K.

Kenya. The heterogeneous construct of the district is summarized in Table 10.

The Bukedi tribes are small and, at the tribal extremities, tend to be intermixed. This area, possibly because of the confusing array of tribes, has received little detailed ethnographic study. It was obviously beyond the capacity of available resources to subject the six tribes inhabiting Bukedi District to intensive study. However, survey data was gathered which sought to identify those tribal variations particularly relevant to the comparative approach employed. For reasons noted below, the Nilotic Padhola were selected for relatively intensive study.

TABLE 10
ETHNIC COMPOSITION OF BUKEDI DISTRICT

County	Major Tribe	Major Ethnic Group	Population (thousands)	Square Miles
Pallisa	Teso	Nilo-Hamitic	76.2	401
Tororo	Teso	Nilo-Hamitic	53.8	171
Bunyole	Banyuli	Bantu	49.0	250
Samia-Bugwe	Samia-Bagwe	Bantu	64.9	286
Bugwere	Bagwere	Bantu	79.7	355
W. Budama	Japadhola	Nilotic	74.1	290
TOTAL			397.7	1,753

SOURCE: Uganda General African Census 1959.

The Bukedi-Iteso

The indigenous social and political system of the two Nilo-Hamitic Iteso groups in Bukedi District generally resembles that of the parent tribe in Teso District proper. However, the Iteso isolated in the south of Bukedi (East Budama), have been subjected to relatively more influence from their Bantu neighbors and have assimilated many non-Iteso customs.

The traditional political system of the Iteso inhabiting Pallisa County, however, follows very closely that of their fellow tribesmen to the north. Traditional authority was diffusely structured and shared by parochial area-based etem units, etem oriented age-grades, and by a small-scale kinship association. Although Pallisa is predominantly inhabited by Iteso, a sizable number of Bagwere also make their home in that county. Of Pallisa's population of 76,000, 45,000 are Iteso and 20,000 Bagwere. The Bagwere, a Bantu agricultural people, are quite different from the cattle-keeping Nilo-Hamitic Iteso and the relationship of these two tribes has long been characterized by suspicion and frequent conflict. The Bagwere have never reconciled themselves to the establishment of a distinct and predominantly Teso County.[1]

The Bukedi-Banyuli

The Banyuli, in contrast to the Iteso, based their traditional political system upon a large-scale clan organization. Although the Banyuli possessed neither a king nor a hierarchy of chiefs as did the Banyoro, their traditional political system in many respects was midway between that of the decentralized parochial Iteso and that of the centralized bureaucratic kingdom of Bunyoro-Kitara.

Among the Iteso the clan (ateker) is not an exogamous unit and the extended family (ekek) is the major kinship association. In contrast the Banyuli possess a myth of origin that revolves about a tribe-wide exogamous clan system.[2] Story and song proclaim that a man named Munyuli, had three sons by his wife Namunjuli. Subsequently the territory of the Banyuli was divided into three equal parts, under the suzerainty of Munyuli's three sons. Each of the three sons gave his name to a major Banyuli clan (Ndegwe, Muyagu and Ngalwe). As time went by, sub-clans split off from the three original parent groups. However, the initial status position of the three major clans persists and is important in current Bunyole politics. Today there are more than fifty clans in Bunyole, each possessed of a specialized traditional responsibility allocated initially by the parent clan. (For example, it is reported that Ngalwe gave the Baria clan permission to be in charge of rain.) The leaders of the respective major clans served as paramount chiefs over their three sections of the country. Today the hierarchy of clans, all of which have descended from one of the three major clans, is not clearly perceived by the young. The elders, however, maintain that the three major clans were, in effect, royal clans and that the clan leaders (or chiefs) possessed a veto over the recruitment of leaders in the subsidiary clans. Even today clan disputes often run the hierarchy of the tripartite clan system before being referred to the official government chiefs.

In common with most of the other tribes of the district, the Banyuli claim that at one time or another they held sway over nearly all of present-day Bukedi and Bugishu districts, and from time to time inflicted crushing defeats upon their neighbors. The Banyuli nostalgically recall military campaigns against the Nilo-Hamitic Iteso and maintain that it was their military victory that was responsible for the fragmentation of the Teso tribe. Only reluctantly do the Banyuli admit that the Nilotic Padhola defeated and then deprived them of the area now known as West Budama. Banyuli children are taught, at an early age, about the savagery and cunning of the Padhola to the south, and the Banyuli maintain that the Lunyuli origin of many Padhola place names testifies to their former dominance in West Budama.[3]

British rule, a cash economy, and other modern conditioning factors have affected the Banyuli as they have the Banyoro and Iteso. Today the clan groups are largely dispersed, although there still exists a noticeable concentration of certain clans within the regions traditionally associated with them. The recent unification of Bunyole into a modern administrative county necessitated the appointment of a single county chief which led to a revival of the struggle for preeminence between the three clans. Nonetheless, there was agreement that the county chief could only be recruited from one of the three original founder clans.

The Banyuli, in common with other Bantu tribes but in contrast to the Nilotic and Nilo-Hamitic peoples to the north, subsist largely on a diet of plantain (matoke). This basic cultural difference is a constant reminder that they are distinct from the neighboring, grain eating, Nilotic Padhola and Nilo-Hamitic Iteso.

The three major clan leaders (Omukulu) did not possess absolute authority over the sub-clan leaders (Omukulu Omotono) as was customary in Bunyoro. Nevertheless, a rudimentary hierarchy of authority based upon a coincidence of area and extensive kinship organization did exist. It is said by some Banyuli that the Omukulu could replace unsatisfactory sub-clan leaders. Questions of war and peace were decided by the Omukulu in council with the sub-clan leaders. The role of the Omukulu was hereditary and recruitment was in part supernaturally based. When an Omukulu died it was believed that God helped his sons to choose a successor. At the succession ceremony the son whom God had ordained to rule would fall into a trance recognizable as a sign of his selection. The major leaders also possessed regalia symbolic of their position and special stools are still held by the three major clan leaders.

The sub-clans not only provided tribute, but also performed sundry labors for their Omukulu. Princes who might be tempted to usurp their fathers' position were traditionally reared at a distance from the Omukulu's homestead, with the dominant clan in the area in each case being responsible for supplying the prince with the necessities of life. It is maintained by some Banyuli elders that the Omukulu was assisted by a Prime Minister (Omukungu) somewhat comparable to the Katikiro in Bunyoro. The Omukungu was chosen by the Omukulu only from that clan falling immediately below the major clan. The role of the Omukungu was primarily that of guarding the Omukulu and of assisting him in resolving interpersonal and intergroup conflicts.

Today the remnants of this partially specialized and semicentralized traditional political system still operate at the lower levels of the official local government system. For example, those who hold traditional authority as a member of this ancient hierarchy frequently serve as assistants to the officially appointed village chiefs in a fashion not unlike that of the Iteso apolon ka ateker described above.[4]

This description of the traditional Bunyole political system should not be regarded as definitive. It is much more complex than might be inferred. The purpose of this brief outline is to sketch some of the major aspects of the traditional political system of this small tribe in contrast to the Nilo-Hamitic Iteso already discussed, and with the Nilotic Padhola which follows.

VILLAGE POLITICS IN A NILOTIC TRIBE

West Budama County, the home of the Nilotic Padhola, was selected for more intensive research. A relatively close study of the Padhola is useful for it permits us to treat, in some detail, with the three major ethnic groups in East Africa—the Bantu Banyoro, the Nilo-Hamitic Iteso, and the Nilotic Padhola. The study of the Padhola was also undertaken in order to analyze more intensively the lower levels of the local government system.

Padholaland

West Budama County is a land of rolling plains, sloping from about 3,600 feet in the west to 4,000 feet in the east. The northwest region was apparently the area of initial Padhola settlement and is more fertile and better watered than the more recently settled southern and eastern portions of the county. This settlement pattern is not without significance and is an important factor in modern-day local politics and government, as we shall have occasion to note. The southern part of the region is relatively dry and heavily infested with tsetse fly; it is only in recent years that the expanding Padhola tribe, in search of arable land, has extended its domain into this hostile area. The eastern highlands spilling over into what is now Tororo, were wrested from the Iteso late in the nineteenth century and are still a major issue of contention between the two tribes.

The weird granite outcrops which characterize the Teso landscape are also to be seen in Padholaland. In common with the Iteso, the Padhola regard the more prominent rock formations as sacred shrines.

The People of Padholaland

The Padhola are an isolated migratory fragment of the virile Nilotic Luo peoples. In Uganda the Acholi, Alur, and possibly the Langi belong to this linguistic and cultural group as, of course, do the Luo proper in Kenya. Unlike the Banyoro, the Padhola do not recount an elaborate theory of supernatural origin. On the other hand, unlike the Iteso, they do hold and preserve a tribal history, partly mythical, but obviously founded in fact. This history, which explains the origins of the tribe and its migration into Budama, is supported, in general outline, by modern historical studies of the Luo migrations.[5] The semi-mythical story of how the Padhola arrived in West Budama is important and is summarized here because it significantly affects the current local political system.[6] All accounts agree that the tribe began its migration from northwest Uganda in what is probably present-day Acholi. The fact that the Acholi and Padhola languages are very similar and mutually understood would seem to support this view.

Tribal History

It is believed that during the fifteenth century two brothers, Adhola and Owiny, left Acholi land after a dispute with their chief and led their extended families southeastward. It is said that Nyajuria, the wife of Adhola, was pregnant at the time of this migration. After crossing the river Kitonde, she sat under a mvule tree sighing that, "the child in my womb is as heavy as the sky (polo) and I can go no farther."[7] It is believed by some that Nyajuria's son was therefore named Nyapolo and became the founder of the first of the major Padhola clans. All other clans are descended from the succeeding fifteen sons to which Nyajuria gave birth or from the sixteen sons of Adhola's second wife. When Adhola halted his migration southward to await the birth of his son, he advised his brother Owiny to continue southward and added that he, his family, and followers would rejoin Owiny later. The two fragments never joined and the Padhola believe that Owiny, moving on into Kenya, was the founder of the famous Lwoo, one of the largest tribes in Kenya.

The validity or prevalence of this myth is not as important as the fact that, soon after their settlement in eastern Uganda, the Padhola gave rise to an extraordinary patrilineal exogamous clan group (Nyapolo). It is probable that the members of the Nyapolo clan are more or less direct descendants of the original Lwoo settlers who, for one reason or another, arrested their migratory journey in Budama. The evidence suggests that this Nilotic enclave was hemmed in on all sides either by hostile non-Nilotic tribes or by unfertile land. Their very existence depended upon a capacity both to enlarge their domain and to absorb non-Padhola tribesmen into their midst. They were early faced with an attack by the far-ranging Masai to the east. The constant threat of attack inclined the Padhola to live in concentrated villages surrounded by deep trenches, the remnants of which are visible even today. After the Masai were driven eastward, the Padhola, feeling more secure, moved out of their fortified villages. Nevertheless, survival still depended upon the maintenance of a relatively unified tribal political-military system, for the Padhola were constantly engaged in battle by the Banyuli, the Iteso, the Gishu and the Baganda.

On the basis of clan analysis and evidence of cultural assimilation, it is apparent that the Padhola not only usually defeated their neighbors, but also incorporated into the Padhola tribe captured Iteso, Banyuli, and Bagwere, who subsequently assumed Padhola names, customs, and clan membership. In turn, of course, Padhola society came to assimilate aspects of the culture of these incorporated aliens.

The Padhola relationship with the Iteso is particularly interesting, and of more than passing significance even today. During the latter half of the nineteenth century, the Padhola, at the expense of the Iteso, sought to extend their domain eastward. In the course of the military operations, which ensued over a number of years, many isolated Iteso segments were gradually absorbed into the Padhola tribe, while other Iteso factions were driven across the Malwa River into Kenya. The Iteso, it must be recalled, did not possess a heritage of tribewide association or centralized authority and were probably highly susceptible to absorption by the better organized Padhola. Nevertheless, Teso warriors were highly regarded by the Padhola and, when their loyalty was assured through assimilation, were considered a valuable military asset. The most famous of the Iteso-turned-Padhola warriors, whose sons still play an important role in local politics, was named Oguti. Oguti's exploits and feats of military cunning are cherished in Tororo and West Budama alike. In West Budama, Oguti is revered as a Japadhola and a member of the Bendo clan; in Tororo he is remembered as an Itesot. At about the turn of the century, Oguti, a semiautonomous chief, held sway over much of southern Budama and had acquired an extraordinary degree of wealth and power. As a consequence of his successful raids upon the Iteso to the east, many of his followers were themselves assimilated Iteso carrying Padhola clan names, while others were true Padhola who came to him from a variety of clans eager to seek their fortune under his shield. Given sufficient time, it is possible that the Iteso would have been completely and irrevocably absorbed. However, the Pax Britannica, an imposed peace which has affected much of the present-day political system, enabled those Iteso who had not been assimilated but merely driven eastward, to return to the area now known as Tororo and to settle in a no-man's-land between the warring groups. This area was gradually occupied by Teso-etem and extended family groups, assimilated Padhola-Iteso and a few true Padhola. Although the majority of the inhabitants of this area were Iteso, Kakunguru as well as the subsequent British administration treated the territory as a part of Budama—the land of the Japadhola. As local chiefs replaced the Baganda agents, it was Padhola, and not Iteso, chiefs that filled the positions of authority. In 1946, after a complex decade of administrative changes, Budama was divided into two counties—East and West, and an Iteso chief was appointed over the former. The grant of county status to East Budama (subsequently renamed Tororo) implied British recognition of the Iteso in that area as a distinct tribal entity. The Padhola reacted violently and only the presence of a British administration prevented these Nilotic warriors from again driving the Iteso into Kenya.

Prior to the advent of Iteso ascendancy in Tororo, the assimilated Iteso disclaimed all reference to their Teso origins. However, once Tororo became a separate Iteso county they came to appreciate the material and political advantages coincident with their original tribal origin. Thus Padhola society has experienced the disaffection of a significant element of its population. The implications of this series of events have been disintegrative, threatening the very existence of the tribe. The repercussions of this conflict are felt not only in the appointment of chiefs and other formal authority holders, but within the kinship system, which had fictitiously absorbed the Iteso foreigners, as well. In the course of a survey carried out in West Budama, close to the Tororo frontier, many elders claimed Padhola clan membership whereas their sons insisted they belonged to Iteso clans.[8]

Many Padhola are wont to read into their history an unbroken line of paramount chiefs culminating in the rule of Majanga, who ended his days in a British prison. And evidence suggests that a decided trend toward centralized and partially specialized political authority was long under way amongst the Padhola. While they certainly never experienced a political system comparable in its complexity and centralization to that of Bunyoro, they did possess something considerably more sophisticated than the near anarchy of the Iteso.

Political Evolution

It is likely that the initial Lwoo settlers were divided into very few clans, which of necessity worked and fought in close harmony. It is generally agreed that one clan, Nyapolo, always possessed a special status. The early leaders of the Padhola tribe were most likely also leaders of this dominant clan. Thus some native historians state that the first Rwooth (paramount chief) was a man named Door, whom they associate with a war against the Bagishu of Mt. Elgon. A number of rulers are said to have followed Door and they too are associated with military campaigns against neighboring tribes. Although there are various and conflicting interpretations of the early political system, a sifting of the data suggests that after the Padhola fanned out from the core of initial settlement into relatively isolated and localized kinship groups, the remnants of their migratory centralized chieftainship largely disappeared. However, in contrast to the more diffuse social system of their neighbors, the Padhola retained a well-defined sense of tribal identity.

The myth of an unbroken line of paramount chiefs was reinforced by the emergence, at the turn of this century, of an extraordinary tribal leadership. It appears that at the time of the arrival of the British the Padhola were gradually moving toward a hierarchical pan-tribal, territorially based political system. The centralizing influence was the Nyapolo clan which had long been divided into two non-exogamous sub-sections (Ogule and Orangi). It was only fitting that this relatively recent supernaturally based paramount chieftaincy should have sprung from one of these two factions. Before relating the evolution of what appears to have been a transition from a diffuse to a more specific political system, it is necessary to note the nature of Padhola settlement, kinship organization and corresponding political system.

Kinship Structure

The basic kinship unit was the localized clan segment or lineage, which tended to dictate the pattern of residence. However, the sharing of a common myth of tribal origin, language and religion served to extend territorial consciousness over the entire tribal region. The migration of Padhola from the area of original settlement in the northwest of Budama was accompanied by the fragmentation of older clan clusters and the subsequent resettlement of the segments in the newer areas. This contrasts strikingly with the Iteso pattern in which the age-grade served as the primary unit of migration. The clan fragments that split off to move to new lands were often separated from the authority of the parent group by territory held by other clans. It is important to recall that the settlement of Budama by the Padhola occurred comparatively recently. An old member of the Koi Kantanti clan interviewed in the Kisoko area stated that he, along with five kinship mates, left Nagongera between 1876–86 and subsequently settled vacant land in the Kisoko area.[9] When other small clan segments arrived, the isolated Koi Kantanti, ever conscious of their vulnerable position, were more than pleased to share their land, while the intermarriages which followed and the resultant web of interdependencies served to bind the relatively isolated settlements together.

The localized Padhola clan segments were as autonomous as the localized multiclan Teso etem units in everyday affairs. However, the areal separation of clan groups did not lead, as it did in Teso, to the evolution of new clans. For on the contrary exogamy was retained and for certain purposes the entire clan, even though scattered throughout Budama, acted as a single unit.

Although each localized clan segment or lineage retains its own leader, the clan organization has adapted itself to the modern local government hierarchy which has rapidly become the dominant element in the Budama political system. Each clan today has a hierarchy of leaders which generally parallel the official administrative system of county, sub-county, parish, and village. It should be noted, however, that the exact area of a clan leader's authority does not necessarily coincide with the official local government territorial unit. Only the terminology and the concept of hierarchy have been adopted. Today each clan has a paramount leader who is recognized and known by all members of the clan. The leader of the largest or oldest localized segment was generally regarded as being in a superordinate position and deserving of obedience from the lesser leaders whenever communication or need gave rise to direct contact.

The Padhola maintenance of a large-scale clan system in spite of the dispersal of the localized segments (in contrast to the near anarchy which characterized the relationship between the localized groups in Teso) is most important. The existence of a limited number of exogamous clans consciously sharing a specific tribal area, worshiping the same gods, and holding a common myth of origin, are elements conducive to the evolution of a relatively centralized and specialized political system. There is no evidence that the Iteso ever combined on a tribewide basis for purposes of warfare or ceremony, whereas the outstanding military exploits of the generally outnumbered Padhola were attributable in large part to tribal unity and a capacity to wage war as a tribal entity.

Kinship and Territorial Clustering

Had the Padhola clans extended their holdings outward contiguously as did other Nilotic tribes, rather than in a leapfrog fashion, it is possible that they would have developed a relatively centralized and specialized political system much earlier, as did the related Acholi to the north. This view is supported by a contrast of local rule in the northwest area of initial settlement, where the extensive Nyapolo clan resides in large and contiguous segments, with the dispersed kinship pattern which characterizes the more newly settled areas in the south. With this thought in mind, the author, together with Aidan Southall of the East African Institute of Social Research, conducted a survey in two villages in West Budama—one in the more recently settled area joining the Tororo border, and another in the heart of the area of initial Padhola settlement. In the Senda and Katandi areas of original settlement, a survey of 361 homesteads revealed the presence of twenty-two clans or sub-clans which, for reasons of exogamy, are here viewed as distinct clans. (See Figure 5.) Of the total homestead heads, 261 belonged to one or another of the four sub-clans of Nyapolo. The clustering of homesteads on the basis of kinship is important when it is recalled that the clan and its localized segments traditionally served as the basis of the Padhola political system.[10] Of the 361 homesteads surveyed in this area of original settlement, twelve consisted of isolated residences whereas forty-nine households were located in small clusters of up to five homes. Forty-seven of the Padhola families in this area lived in intimate and sole proximity with from eight to sixteen of their fellow clansmen. However, the great majority of the homesteads surveyed (265) were located in clusters ranging from 37 to 114 homesteads.[11] The political implications of this kinship based residential pattern cannot be overestimated. The average population of the homestead (pecho) in the Senda area is 6.1 persons. Thus one finds areas with populations of 600 or more inhabited solely by people who share a common ancestor and taboos and who respect the authority of a single nearby individual who, in turn, is a living symbol of their association.

This relationship of space to authority is a factor in the local political system that should not be ignored. For those Padhola who reside in the large contiguous clan clusters, everyday government, which sanctions certain behavior and prohibits others, is the kinship organization and not the official local government system. Taxation is a ready reminder of the official system, but it pales into insignificance when contrasted to the authority of the clan over inheritance, bride price, witchcraft, etc. In any case the Japadhola does not make a sharp distinction between the official local government system and his kinship association and many believe that the clan leader and clan courts possess the power of official imprisonment. On occasion this is true, in effect, for the official chiefs, cognizant of their reliance on the pervasive authority system of the clan leaders, often will imprison individuals who are delivered up to them by the clan heads. Furthermore, clan courts regularly exact compensation in the form of money as well as cattle. Failure to abide by the decision of the clan court leads to litigation in the official local government court but the prior ruling of the clan court is rarely overturned.

Kinship organization was, and continues to be, a predominant element in the political system in those areas of extensive concentrated clan settlement. The consent of the clan elders and leaders in the Senda

NYA

NYAPOLO-OGULE-
CLAN

NYAPOLO-ORANGI-CLAN

LOL

5

SENDA VILLAGE

WEST   BUDAMA—UGANDA.

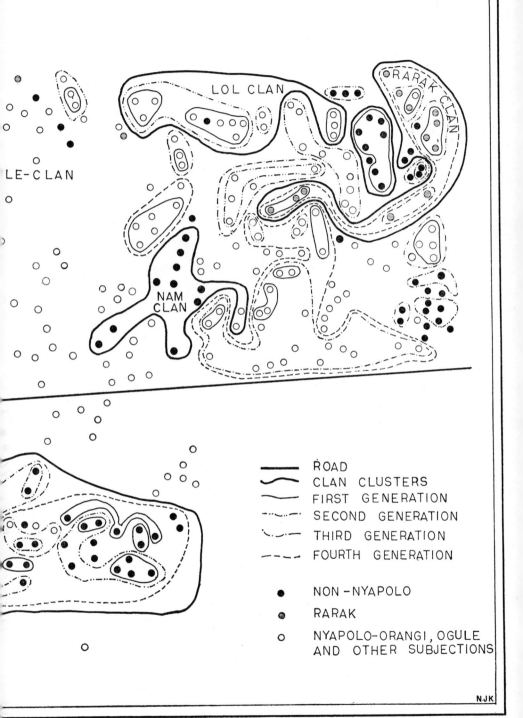

LOL CLAN

RARAK CLAN

LE-CLAN

NAM
CLAN

ROAD
CLAN CLUSTERS
FIRST GENERATION
SECOND GENERATION
THIRD GENERATION
FOURTH GENERATION

●   NON-NYAPOLO
⊜   RARAK
○   NYAPOLO-ORANGI, OGULE
    AND OTHER SUBJECTIONS

NJK

area is requisite to the effective carrying out of official local government policy. In the more recently settled areas, particularly in the regions where Padhola live side by side with absorbed Iteso, the settlement pattern is quite different. To contrast this difference, a similar survey was carried out in Kisoko, the West Budama county seat. A survey was made of the 259 homesteads which make up the village. In contrast to Senda it was found that only one clan cluster exceeded 25 homesteads. A comparison of the settlement patterns in Kisoko and Senda is shown in Table 11.

TABLE 11
CLAN CLUSTERS IN TWO WEST BUDAMA VILLAGES

Village	Total Home- steads	Per cent Isolated	Per cent in Clusters of				
			1–5	6–15	16–25	26–35	36+
Senda	361	3.3	10.2	13.0	0	0	73.1
Kisoko	259	20.6	19.7	25.0	0	24.7	0

SOURCE: Author's survey of Senda and Kisoko Villages, 1956.

As already noted, the interrelationship between the Teso etem (non-kinship based) segments was one of near-anarchy. However, there is a significant difference between the Teso segmentary etem and the pattern of settlement in the Padhola village of Kisoko. In Kisoko the number of exogamous clans is smaller than in the average Teso-etem. Furthermore, the dependence upon one's neighbors for defense, and the ties established through interclan marriage, as well as the emphasis upon tribal solidarity, served to extend Padhola loyalty (despite the absence of large clan clusters) over a much larger area than was true for the Iteso. In addition, the clans in Padholaland traditionally possessed reciprocal responsibilities. For example, the members of clan A might be responsible for the burial of the members of clan B. Intraclan disputes were handled by the localized clan head and elders, but interclan disputes were arbitrated by the leaders of a specified third clan. This system of arbitration was well institutionalized and coincided with the interclan arrangements for burial. Although the Padhola localized clan units, upon occasion, resorted to violence in order to settle their disputes, recourse to arms was rare and viewed with disfavor.

In Teso the kinship organization never played a dominant role in the political system and the age-grade association was ruthlessly destroyed by the Baganda. Thus the informal elements of the Teso political system requisite to the operation of the superimposed local government organization bear only slight resemblance to traditional institutions. In Budama, however, the kinship organization was not destroyed by the Baganda and has continued to maintain its virility through a process of gradual adaptation to meet changed conditions.

In earlier days the clan effectively structured and regularized the individual's relationship with other members of his kinship community and represented the community vis-à-vis neighboring societies. Today the modern local government system, characterized by its hierarchy of chiefs and councils, has interjected a new element into the sociopolitical system, and the clan, in order to successfully fulfill its traditional role, has had to vary its organization to cope with the new problems posed by local government. Traditionally, the clan leader was recruited solely upon a hereditary basis with each localized lineage possessing virtual independence. The centralization of the administrative machine, which accompanied the introduction of modern local government and administration and the premium now put upon modern education, has altered this recruitment principle. Today the major clans are hierarchically organized on a tribewide basis, for modern communications and the Pax Britannica have enabled a closer association. The clan leader today is elected at the funeral of his deceased predecessor. The drums and other paraphernalia which are associated with the respective clans continue to be handed down solely on a hereditary basis while the leadership is elected on the basis of education and other modern criteria. It is understandable that a degree of strain exists within many clans between the relatively young and educated clan leader and the hoary guardian of the traditional symbols of authority.

Many of the problems which the clan system traditionally provided for no longer exist, or have become relatively unimportant, e.g., warfare, witchcraft, criminal violence. However, some of the new problems and values are not adequately handled by the modern local government. It is the traditional clans that have gradually assumed responsibility for these new needs. For example, many Padhola clans today collect membership dues, issue receipts, grant assistance to destitute members, offer scholarships, and even build schools.

Political Transition, from Kinship to Area

Approximately two decades before the arrival of Kakunguru and the Baganda legions, there is evidence that a centralized political system began to evolve in Budama. As noted above, the Nyapola has always been perceived as somewhat superior to the other Padhola clans and was predisposed to assume tribal leadership. Furthermore, the Padhola had absorbed so many of their alien neighbors that, in addition to the Nyapolo, only two or three clans were primarily composed of relatively pure Padhola. Our survey of Budama established the

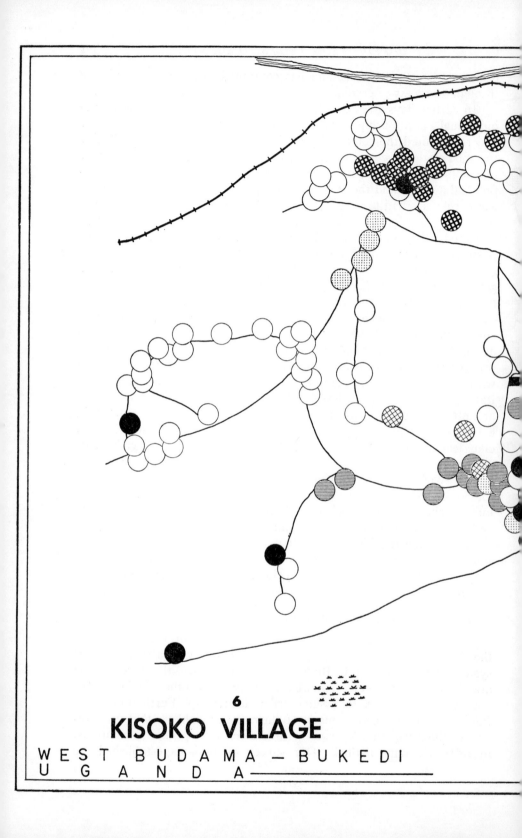

6

KISOKO VILLAGE
W E S T   B U D A M A — B U K E D I
U G A N D A

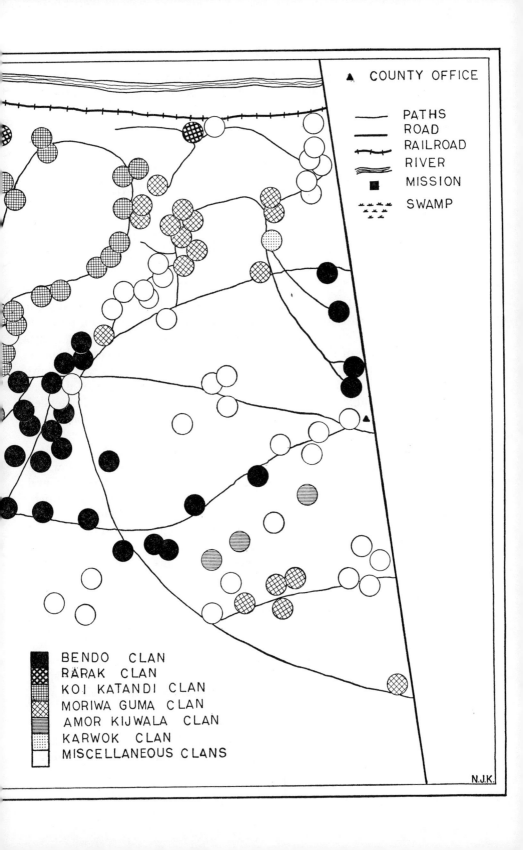

COUNTY OFFICE

PATHS
ROAD
RAILROAD
RIVER
MISSION
SWAMP

BENDO CLAN
RÄRAK CLAN
KOI KATANDI CLAN
MORIWA GUMA CLAN
AMOR KIJWALA CLAN
KARWOK CLAN
MISCELLANEOUS CLANS

N.J.K.

existence of approximately sixty clans which we divided into six categories. Only about half (see Table 12) were definitely ascertained to have had Padhola origin.[12]

TABLE 12
PADHOLA CLAN ORIGINS

Clan Origin		Number of Clans
Founder clan (Nyapolo)	1	(incl. 4 sub-clans)
Padhola	29	(incl. 11 sub-clans)
Assimilated Iteso	8	
Assimilated Bantu	6	
Foreign Iteso	6	
Foreign Bantu	5	
Total	55	

SOURCE: Author's survey, 1956.

As we noted earlier, from the time of their settlement in Bukedi District until late in the nineteenth century the Padhola had no territorial chiefs. Clan leaders exercised authority over individuals with the areal scope of their influence depending upon the extent and homogeneity of the clan cluster. Several of the elements of statehood, however, were potentially present. The Padhola did perceive of a tribe-wide territorial sovereignty and had effectively defended and extended their territory as a tribal unit. Although there existed no specialized political structure at the center possessed of a universal authority, there was a diffuse recognition of the preeminence of the Nyapolo clan. Furthermore, and in sharp contrast to the non-Nilotic tribes which completely encircled them, the Padhola shared a common religion and language. It seems evident that even before the arrival of the British, the segmented Padhola were moving toward a more centralized and specialized political system wherein the concept of territorially based political authority was gradually replacing kinship.

The catalytic agent in this evolutionary process emerged in the guise of a supernatural leader. Majanga, the leader of the Ogule section of the Nyapolo clan, was well on his way to establishing a unified Budama when the Baganda and British arrived upon the scene. The various accounts of the coming to power of Majanga are confusing, but it is generally agreed that the pattern for a paramount chieftaincy had begun to take shape at about the time of Obweke, whose son preceded Majanga as leader. Mbweke was a rainmaker whose spectacular performance, in conjunction with his able leadership in war, endowed him with extra-clan influence. He was succeeded by his son Akure who, failing to give evidence of supernatural ordination, was supplanted by Majanga, his young herd boy. Even as a youth Majanga reputedly gave evidence of his supernatural powers. He had the ability, for example, to predict events, and innumerable tales are told of his feats of divination. One of the more common myths amongst the Padhola justifying Majanga's authority, was his intimate association with Bura, the supernatural manifestation of the Padhola creator, Were.

It is said that on one occasion Majanga disappeared for a number of days. When he was found and asked where he had been and what he had done he related that he had been instructed to relocate the Bura shrine. Majanga claimed to be possessed by Bura, and was soon recognized as his interpreter and worldly representative. This, added to his Nyapolo clan membership, assisted him rapidly to achieve an extraordinary tribewide influence that cut across the heretofore independent localized kinship segments. At this time the Padhola were particularly hard-pressed by the Iteso, and Majanga added to his stature by leading his people to military victory. Thus his powers of divination derived from his association with the Padhola god, along with his success in leading the entire tribe against the Iteso, established for him a degree of authority over all of Budama.

Bura's temple, which is still in use today, lies in the depths of a peculiarly shaped amphitheaterlike granite outcrop within a dark and sacred forest. Each clan group built within this mystic temple its own shrine to Bura. Thus, as a spokesman of Bura, Majanga exercised influence over the leaders of all Padhola clans. In his ecclesiastical capacity he appointed assistants who came to exercise temporal as well as religious authority.

Majanga was at the height of his power at about the turn of the century. It is probable that Majanga's more powerful warrior chiefs, who had also come to exercise extra-clan authority, served as his lieutenants or military governors. Had Majanga's supernaturally oriented paramountcy been institutionalized, it would likely have evolved into an elaborate state system not unlike that of Bunyoro-Kitara. However, this must always remain in the area of conjecture, for in 1901 Kakunguru and his army arrived in Budama with the goal of adding the Padhola to his British-supported realm. Majanga led his warriors, armed with spears and shields, against Kakunguru's rifles; the massacre is still recalled in Budama. Though the Padhola, even according to Buganda reports, fought fiercely, it was evident that the rifle would triumph over the spear. Majanga was defeated and, failing to cooperate with his conquerors, was imprisoned in Jinja, where he died in 1905.

The Baganda, and later the British, recognized the embryonic preeminence of Majanga and appointed his sons and lesser relatives as the first Padhola chiefs.[13] Initially this served to reinforce the claim

to preeminence of both the Nyapolo in general and the direct descendents of Majanga in particular. Budama, which at that time included
Tororo as well, was organized as a saza (county) and divided into
gombololas (sub-counties), muruka (parishes), and pecho (villages).
To some extent the sub-counties coincided with the areas formerly
ruled by Majanga's lieutenants.

The Political Legacy

Majanga's mantle of leadership was handed on to his son Lwoo,
who, like his father, was unable to wear the yoke of Baganda and
British rule. He too was imprisoned in Jinja. Ria, the chief Baganda
agent, then attempted to break the hold that Majanga and the Nyapolo
clan had upon the major chieftainships by appointing one Sakakarhi,
a member of the Bendo clan. Faced with the threat to their preeminence, the Nyapolo took to arms and in the ensuing struggle the
Bendo pretender was killed.

Majanga's heirs and other quasi-traditional Padhola chiefs, associated as they were with the spirit of Bura, were unable to accommodate
themselves to the specialist and impartial role required of a government chief and often ran afoul of the law while fulfilling obligations
to their respective clan segments. Many were arrested and imprisoned
while others were discharged from their positions. Gradually the Nyapolo lost their positions of official authority and were replaced by
younger, nontraditionally oriented, non-Nyapolo chiefs. Thus, in current-day Padhola politics, there exists a disaffected and bitter element
which takes advantage of every opportunity to discredit the usurpers
and seeks to regain the authority and influence that Bura intended
the Nyapolo to possess.

In addition to the imported administrative system, the European's
religion has served to complicate the local scene. Bukedi generally and
West Budama in particular, in common with other regions of Uganda,
are sharply divided by religious differences and conflict that affect
almost every aspect of society and government. Early in 1960 serious
riots (described elsewhere) broke out in Bukedi. The official commission which investigated the situation reported that "the evidence has
been overwhelming that the bitter rivalry between the adherents of
the Protestant and Catholic churches, respectively, has actually promoted the disturbances into which we have inquired."[14] Catholic missionaries arrived in Budama soon after the establishment of British
rule and proceeded to convert the existing holders of authority to
Catholicism. Thus the Catholic faith rapidly assumed a dominant position in the northwest area of initial settlement. This also meant that
the Nyapolo, and consequently most of the early chiefs, became Catho-

lic. Thus the loss of power by the early Nyapolo chiefs also involved a transfer of authority from Catholics to Protestants. Budama politics today consists of a tangled web of rivalries and vendettas which interlace kinship and religion. A survey of the forty-five sub-county and parish chiefs established the fact that in 1957 only one Nyapolo held a chieftainship position. There are seven sub-counties in West Budama. One sub-county chieftainship was held by the county chief's brother (Koyo clan) and another by his brother-in-law. A survey of twenty-three of the fifty-six Budama village chiefs revealed that only five were Catholics—this despite the estimate that approximately 75 per cent of the population of West Budama is Catholic. It is interesting to note that, in a survey which included all sub-county and parish chiefs and a representative sample of the village chiefs, 100 per cent of the Catholic chiefs reported that their fathers had been chiefs whereas less than half of the Protestant chiefs were descendants of former chiefs.[15] The problem of chieftainship, compounded as it is by religion and clan, reached a climax in 1938 when the British decided the day had arrived to appoint for the first time a native county chief over all Budama. The issues were not limited to the claims of the royal clan and Catholicism, but also were complicated by the fact that Tororo, then an integral part of the county, was inhabited primarily by Iteso. The Iteso would no more accept a Japadhola (sing. Padhola) county chief than would the Padhola an Itesot. The Nyapolo and Catholics working hand in hand claimed, in the name of Majanga, a traditional right to the office. The British responded to this explosive situation by appointing Odinga as the first county chief of Budama. Odinga, the British felt, was a safe compromise as he was neither Iteso nor Padhola, but rather a Musamia, who for many years had served as a minor chief in Budama.

Though the Padhola could not agree upon a candidate from their own ranks, they were united to a man that the county chief must not be a non-Padhola. Long-neglected spears were sharpened and battle shields repaired. The Padhola were prepared to fight and stated that, if Odinga became county chief, he would rule over the single remaining Padhola warrior that survived Armageddon.[16] The Provincial Commissioner himself visited Budama and installed Odinga as chief. The Padhola responded by stoning the British officers and by damaging and stealing the Provincial Commissioner's car. The British finally capitulated and decided that the only solution was to divide Budama into predominantly Padhola and Iteso counties. Alasia Obel, a son of Majanga, was then appointed the first chief of West Budama County. The Protestant, anti-Nyapolo faction immediately began to agitate and maneuver to remove Obel, while Catholic, Protestant,

Nyapolo and non-Nyapolo Padhola alike maneuvered to deprive the Iteso of their separate county. It is these two issues, firmly rooted in the history of the tribe, that dominate Padhola politics today. The Padhola, in countless protests and resolutions, have expressed their sorrow and anger that "mere guests" (Iteso) in their country were given their land.

As a consequence of one of the many administrative reorganizations that must be taken into account in an analysis of Bukedi District, Andrea Obel, in 1943, was made a divisional chief of Budama, which included the former counties of Tororo, West Budama, Samia, and Bugwe. In 1944 Obel was charged with cattle theft and various other misdemeanors and, as one might have expected, his non-Nyapolo Protestant contenders were instrumental in his detection and prosecution. In 1947 the central government capitulated to incessant agitation for the recreation of tribal counties in place of the multitribal division. In that year the preeminence of the Nyapolo was broken with the appointment of A. Ofumbi, a Protestant and non-Nyapolo, as West Budama county chief. Ofumbi held office until his death in 1953, at which time he was replaced by Z. Ochieng, also a Protestant and a member of the Koyo clan.

The fortunes of the Nyapolo predominantly Catholic and consequently Democratic Party faction took a turn for the better in 1961. The 1960 riots dramatically demonstrated that the Protestant chiefs could command the support of but a small minority of Padhola while the Catholic majority was prepared to use force to alter the situation. The resignation, retirement and hospitalization of many chiefs led to an unusually large number of vacancies and new appointments, many of which were filled by Catholics. The dimensions of this political revolution are suggested by the fact that the non-Nyapolo Protestant county chief was replaced by Mr. P. C. Ofwono, grandson of Majanga, former member of Uganda's Legislative Council and recognized heir to Nyapolo and thus to Padhola leadership. Our survey of West Budama County Council in 1956 revealed that only nine of its thirty members were Catholic, and only four belonged to the Nyapolo clan. After the 1961 direct elections only three were Protestants, one Moslem and the remaining thirty-three were Catholic. Not only had the religious tables been turned, but the triumph of the Catholic faction meant victory for the Democratic Party as well. Of the thirty-five members of the county council in 1963 only three were UPC. West Budama's sub-county councils are also dominated by the Catholic-Democratic Party faction and only one sub-county (Igowla) has a UPC chairman.

Theoretically only the county chief (chairman) and up to 1961 his sub-county chiefs are ex-officio members of the County Council. However, our survey in 1956 revealed that fifteen of the thirty members were chiefs and three ex-chiefs. The revived fortunes of the Catholic faction as a consequence of direct elections dealt a serious blow to the prestige of the chiefs who were predominantly Protestant.

There is a tendency for members of the County Council to be clan leaders. Thus, nineteen members in 1956 stated that they were either clan leaders or officers in their clan associations. Aside from the chiefs, only two members of the 1956 West Budama County Council had more than a secondary education. It is interesting to note that of these two educated councillors, one was the treasurer of his clan and the other a clan secretary.

A major function of the County Council is to sift sub-county and parish council resolutions and pass them, along with its own recommendations, to the Bukedi District Council. As a consequence of the coincidence of tribe and county boundaries in Bukedi, the County Council exerts relatively greater influence in district politics than is true, for example, in Bunyoro or Teso. Therefore, few districtwide decisions of any significance are made without prior reference to the county councils.

Until 1961 the representative members of the Budama County Council were elected by the sub-county council members who, in turn, were elected by the parish council. The parish council was composed of the parish chief as chairman, village chiefs and one member elected by the adult males of the parish for each 100 taxpayers. If the Protestant county chief and his hierarchy of lesser chiefs were to succeed in perpetuating their dominance it was imperative that they control the direct elections to the parish council. In 1957 the Catholic-Nyapolo alliance was determined to reestablish its position in the tribe and thus in the county. The predominance of Catholics in West Budama would seem to have assured their success. However, the entrenched Protestants, through manipulation of the superimposed British-styled democratic machinery, were able to frustrate these attempts. Although direct elections to the parish council often resulted in the selection of many Catholics, their names were strangely omitted and those of Protestants substituted before the election returns were sent on to the sub-county and then to the county chief. It was not until the introduction of direct elections in 1961 that the political dominance of the non-Nyapolo faction was ended.

The Bukedi riots of 1960, which ostensibly were attributable to discontent over tax assessment, were particularly severe in West Budama where police activity and mob action resulted in four deaths and destruction of about 400 homes. It was apparent from the outset, however, that the environment of disorder and violence was employed to reactivate religious conflict. The Protestant chiefs were attacked by the long-embittered Catholic-Nyapolo clans. The Democratic Party in West Budama, as elsewhere in Uganda, is primarily supported by Catholics. Official complaints against the predominantly Protestant, non-Nyapolo chiefs in West Budama, which followed in the wake of the 1960 riots, were largely prepared and presented by the local leaders of the Democratic Party (who were also frequently lay leaders in the Catholic Church and Nyapolo clan). The Protestant, non-Nyapolo chiefs were not inclined to be lenient in assigning communal work in areas inhabited predominantly by Catholic-Nyapolo. A Democratic Party leader in Uganda prior to the 1960 riots was convicted of a plot "whereby peasants were put into a chief's plantation (garden) and then falsely represented as being forced workers."[17] The 1961 direct elections to the lower councils brought a Democratic Party– Catholic majority to six of the seven constituent sub-counties. More striking is the fact that all councillors in four of the seven sub-counties were DP–Catholic, and that only fourteen of the ninety-two sub-county councillors were Protestant or Muslim–UPC. Also of significance is the fact that Iyolwa, the only sub-county council with a UPC majority, is an area of recent settlement in the southeast part of the county and the home of a sizable non-Padhola minority.[18]

A conflict situation tended to develop whenever a chief, in order to ensure "good administration," and simultaneously secure his position, found it necessary to take an active part in determining the composition of the councils upon which his success and tenure in large part depended. The situation was further complicated by the inclination of deposed chiefs to seek retaliation through disruptive influence within the councils. The game is a complicated and personal one. Certainly neither the District Commissioner, the Bukedi Secretary-General, nor the Appointments Board could tolerate blatant and extreme divergence from the ideal pattern. However, the county chief was quite aware of this and the knowledge became part of his action frame of reference. The successful chief is the one who correctly assesses the extent of deviation allowed by his superiors while the unsuccessful chief is one who either miscalculates the degree of deviation permitted, and is reprimanded for interfering with the democratic process, or fails to deviate at all. It is worth noting that the techniques a chief employs to structure his hierarchical organization to suit his administrative needs are not solely limited to playing a blind hand in local elections and frustrating lower council resolutions.[19] For he also retains the prerogative of discrediting a lower chief who

has managed, despite the higher chief's best efforts, to secure a position within the hierarchy.

The many factors which serve to split Padhola society into factions are relevant only with respect to county-tribe politics, for when
Padhola-wide interests conflict with those of other tribe-counties in
Bukedi, the Padhola are highly unified. In the last analysis, predominant political orientation is to the tribe—as it is in every Bukedi
county. So important is the tribe-county in Bukedi that one tends
to contrast this level to the districts elsewhere in Uganda. Many of
the idiosyncrasies of the West Budama local political system described
above can be found in the other five counties as well. The emphasis
on the county in Bukedi alters significantly the usual relationship
between central and local government. Tribally homogeneous districts
like Teso associate with the central government through the agency
of their local government officials. According to this pattern, however,
the Padhola of Bukedi District would likely find their interests vis-à-vis
the central government represented by an Itesot or Munyuli. In Teso,
the Secretary-General almost surely will be an Itesot and the question
of alien domination does not arise. In Bukedi, however, the chances
of his being a Padhola are slim, and to many Padhola the presence
of a Mugwere Secretary-General or Itesot Treasurer means a serious
loss of face and a disproportionate share in the spoils of office.

The impact of this tribal diversity upon the development of local
government at the district level serves as the subject of the remainder
of this chapter.

VARIATIONS ON A BRITISH THEME

Outwardly local government organization and evolution in Bukedi
District generally resemble that outlined in Chapter Three. The
Bukedi District Council, for reasons that will be noted, did not adopt
the 1955 District Administration (District Councils) Ordinance until
1961 and therefore operated until that date under the Local Government Ordinance of 1949. As a consequence, many central government
services were not transferred to the District Local Authority; autonomy in fiscal affairs was relatively limited and the overt role of
the District Commissioner much more in evidence. Under the 1955
Ordinance the District Council would have been *the* Local Authority,
with the chiefs relegated to the status of Council employees.[20] However, under the 1949 ordinance "an African local government . . .
shall consist of chiefs, a district council and such other councils as
may be established."[21] Therefore, county chiefs sitting on the Bukedi

District Council continued to play an important part in district administration until 1963 and the implementation of the 1962 District Administrations Ordinance.

Bukedi Administrative History

Present-day local government problems in Bukedi cannot be understood without some knowledge of the administrative history of the area. The eastern region of Uganda posed a thorny problem for early British administrators. The philosophy of "indirect rule" hardly seemed applicable to this region, where a day's walk would take the district officer from one language and culture to another. Furthermore, little evidence was found to suggest that this confusing array of tribes possessed indigenous political institutions on a scale sufficiently large to support a minimum level of administrative efficiency. Kakunguru solved one of these problems by ruthlessly superimposing the Buganda chiefly hierarchy over the entire multitribal region. Subsequently, the British assumed authority, recognized the Buganda system and, in a sense, thereby applied the principle of indirect rule, twice removed.

The term Bukedi, which according to the Baganda means the land of naked people but which to the residents denotes a host of more flattering translations, has been in use since the early days of British rule in East Africa. We share the conclusions of the O'Conner Commission that "from 1909 on there has been a bewildering series of changes" in the Bukedi-Bugishu area.[22] The first Bukedi District was formed in 1902 and consisted of the present Bukedi District, excepting Samia-Bugwe but including present-day Bugishu, Teso, and Sebei districts. Teso achieved separate district status in 1909; in 1923 the old Bukedi District was split into three units—Bugishu, Bugwere, and Budama. Mbale Town, in 1925, was gazetted as the headquarters of Bugwere district, as today's Bukedi politicians are quick to note. In 1936 the district officers in the area began to agitate for reamalgamation of these small districts:

> I am of the opinion that the two districts—Bugwere and Bugishu —should be amalgamated en toto . . . and that the fusion of these two districts be regarded as the precursor of the eventual absorption of Budama.[23]

The movement toward centralization and development of district councils, which had gained momentum by 1936, led to a subsequent decision to reestablish and enlarge the old districts on the basis that improved communications and a decline in tribal parochialism warranted such a move. Thus, on February 19, 1936, a meeting was held to discuss a possible amalgamation.[24] The composition of this meeting is significant, for it reveals the British perception of the *loci* of local authority and their view as to the nature of local consent thought necessary to effect such a reorganization. In attendance were the District Commissioners of Bugwere, Bugishu, and Budama districts, the Provincial Commissioner of the Eastern Province, the County Chiefs of Budama, Mbale, Pallisa, Bukedea, Bugwere, Central Bugishu, and North Bugishu, and the Buganda native advisor of Bugishu. In 1937 Bugwere District (Bugwere, Pallisa, and Bunyole) and Bugishu District were amalgamated and termed the Central District. The headquarters for the combined unit was established at Mbale, which had previously served as the District Headquarters Bugwere.[25] At this time Budama District existed in name only and Baganda agents were in charge of the locally autonomous counties of Budama, Samia-Bugwe, and Bunyole.[26]

In 1940 the boundaries of Bugwere sub-district of the combined Mbale District were changed with the transfer of Bukedea County to Teso, from where it had come in 1924. The following year Budama District was merged with Mbale District to form a new Central District. However, three distinct native authority units—Bugishu, Bugwere, and Budama were maintained. The year 1941 was also marked by further reduction of the old Bugwere District. Mbale, which had traditionally been the senior county in Bugwere District, was dismembered, with one sub-county and two parishes being transferred to the old Bugishu District, and Mbale Township becoming a sort of federal area independent of both native authorities.[27] With only a pause for breath, the British administration in 1942 joined the native authorities of Bugwere and Budama and termed the amalgamation Bukedi sub-district.

In 1943, as a wartime necessity to economize upon staff and resources, Bukedi sub-district was divided into two divisions. The county, as a unit of local authority, and county chieftainship were abolished. Budaka division was composed of the former counties of Pallisa and Bunyole plus the remnants of Bugwere District. This shuffle was resisted by the Pallisa Iteso and the Banyuli but was seen by the Bagwere, who succeeded in having the name of their dominant clan—Budaka—applied to the division, as advantageous and saw in this reconstitution a return to their former preeminence in the northern part of the district. The southern counties of Tororo, West Budama, and Samia-Bugwe were termed Tororo Division, with the divisional headquarters located in the important rail center of the same name.

Mr. Obel, son of Majanga, who had served but four years as Budama's first permanent native chief, was made Tororo divisional chief and charged with the responsibility of ruling over four tribes speaking three languages. The situation in Budaka division was no less complex with Mr. E. Kageni, the former Bagwere chief of Pallisa County, now ruling over three tribes and three languages. The amalgamations had hardly been completed before mutterings of rebellion were heard in Tororo Division. Riots broke out in Bunyole, where a man favoring the amalgamation was beaten to death at a meeting held by an English officer.[28] The unrest in Bunyole led to a commission of inquiry, which promised a plebiscite in 1946.[29] In that year Bunyole was given back its county status. This led to repercussions elsewhere in Bukedi with only the Padhola in control of Tororo Division and the Bagwere in charge of Budaka Division supporting the maintenance of the status quo. Reluctantly, the British were forced to consider a return to the county-tribe organizational scheme. Though generally applauded, the reestablishment of the counties also brought to a head a number of other problems. The Bagwere fought to keep the Pallisa Iteso from achieving county status and having their own chiefs. In a like manner the Padhola attempted to preclude the Tororo Iteso from securing separate county status. The emotion and violence which surrounded this issue in West Budama was noted in the foregoing. In Tororo the Iteso refused to accept two minor Padhola chiefs and threatened one Padhola chief with violence if he did not resign. As a consequence of this intrigue a number of Iteso were arrested and tried. Only British control kept the two tribes from resuming their ancient feud.

In 1953 a decision was made to divide Mbale district into the separate districts of Bukedi and Bugishu.[30] Bugishu in contrast to Bukedi, was populated by only two homogeneous tribes and it was felt that its spectacular post-war economic and political progress in conjunction with a high population density warranted separate district status.[31] The Bagwere did not like sharing the mantle of leadership with the Bagishu and resented their presence in Mbale Town— the former administrative capital of the old Budaka-Bugwere division. The transfer of much of Mbale County to Bugishu had never set well with the Bagwere and they very much disliked the fact that Bukedi District headquarters, though technically lying in neither district, was surrounded by territory now belonging to Bugishu. It was the hope of the Bagwere that the division of Mbale District would lead to the return of Mbale Township as the headquarters of a new Bukedi which they felt they could dominate.

The status of Mbale Township has evolved into a major controversy. Although the Bagwere are particularly concerned about the "return of Mbale," the crusade has been adopted, more or less, by all the tribes of Bukedi and is a rare unifying factor in this multitribal district. The local government headquarters building, which formerly housed the offices of the combined district, in 1949 was enlarged and partitioned into separate wings. Although the building is in Mbale Township, it is necessary for Bakedi councillors and officials to suffer the humiliation of crossing a narrow section of Bugishu soil to reach their capital. The thin partition separating Bugishu from Bukedi local government offices has become an insurmountable barrier and the focus of high emotion. The controversy with Bugishu over Mbale Township and over the jointly held local government headquarters has had a unifying effect. When faced with the claims of Bugishu, tribal factionalism tends to give way to distinct solidarity. This fades rapidly, however, whenever purely internal Bukedi problems are discussed. The Bukedi District Council has exhausted every known tactic, with the exception of bodily eviction, in its attempt to rid the headquarters area of the Bagishu.

Before the turn of the century the territory around Mbale Town was a no-man's-land, and battleground for the Iteso, Bagwere, Bagishu, and Masai. Kakunguru's arrival on the scene and the establishment of his headquarters at what he subsequently named Mbale, brought peace and settlement to this no-man's-land but also laid the groundwork for a generation of controversy.[32]

In 1950 the Protectorate government sought to reduce the growing tension by giving each district freehold title to its portion of the headquarters land in Mbale. The Bagishu, fearing that this would give Bukedi's presence in territory surrounded by Bugishu legal status, forcibly prohibited the necessary survey. The Munster Commission in 1961 recommended that an independent Uganda government establish a Boundary Commission to which problems such as the dispute over Mbale could be referred.[33]

The Uganda Constitution of 1962 took notice of the dispute and exempted the frontiers of Bukedi, Bugishu, and Mbale from the general provisions requiring local consensus for boundary alterations.[34] The Uganda National Assembly in March 1962 empowered the Governor to establish a commission to investigate the boundary problem. The O'Conner Commission, after lengthy hearings, issued its controversial report in June, 1962. It recommended that the boundaries be altered so that the Bakedi would have access to Mbale Town "through their own district and not subject to interference by the Bagishu" and that Mbale remain a municipality within the municipalities ordinance and therefore under the authority of neither district. As the greater part of Mbale lies within Bugishu District, it was recommended that former crown land be turned over to the Bugishu District Land Board which would immediately lease the land to Mbale for ninety-nine years. Whereas Bugishu District Head-quarters should remain in Mbale, the Commission recommended that Bukedi local government headquarters be moved elsewhere and preferably to Tororo as soon as possible because "there will never be peace in Mbale while both the Bukedi and the Bagishu have the head-quarters of their local administrations at Maluku."[35] Because the Commission correctly recognized that any attempt to move the administrative headquarters of Bukedi from Mbale to Tororo would drastically alter the tribal balance of power in the favor of the southern counties of Tororo and Budama, and would be resisted stubbornly by Bugwere, it suggested consideration of the possibility of two administrations—one for the south in Tororo and the other for the north in Budaka Bugwere.[36]

There is a constant danger that an incident will trigger intertribal fighting on a large scale. In September, 1962, a group of Bugishu tribesmen stopped the car of Mr. Kirya, the Bukedi Secretary-General. He was attacked and forced to flee for his life. Had he been wounded or killed it is conceivable that Mbale would have become the scene of a bloody intertribal war. In May, 1963, Mr. Kirya was found dead under strange circumstances.[37]

The perpetual reshuffling of the complex tribal areas in the Bukedi region has left a legacy of suspicion, of heightened intertribal antagonism and of general confusion. Each proposed administrative change was viewed in the context of tribal advantage or disadvantage. The many reorganizations noted above often involved the transfer of administrative staff with a consequent absence of continuity. This confusion is well illustrated in a speech by the acting District Commissioner, Mbale, before a meeting of the District Council.

> Mr. Lindsell District Commissioner has gone to England on leave and for a short time I shall perform the duties of the District Commissioner, Mbale, but as you know I am to be the District Commissioner of Bukedi and Mr. Lindsell, on his return, will be District Commissioner, Bugishu.[38]

The 1960 Bukedi district report draws attention to the fact that despite the devastating riots of that year only three of the fourteen officers posted to the district in 1960 remained throughout the year and two of these were on notice to transfer.

Tribal Balance of Power

The decisional mechanism of the Bukedi local government, until 1961, was based upon the 1949 ordinance. The coincidence of tribal residence and county boundaries, however, has significantly altered the actual workings of this system. In nearly every district in Uganda, the district administration and local government proved reluctant to delegate effective authority to the county level. In Bukedi, however, the District Council, committees, and officials, are inclined to shirk their responsibility and tend to refer even trivial matters to the county councils. As the county councils, until 1962, were indirectly elected and heavily influenced by the county chiefs, the effect of this delegation of decision was to render the Bukedi county chiefs probably more powerful and under less restraint in certain matters than anywhere in Uganda.

One report observed that "the part played by the District Council in directing the work of the chiefs is to all practical purposes unknown."[39]

The 1960 Bukedi riots were, in effect, a rebellion against the authority of the chiefs and reflected a continuing disinclination of these diffuse tribes to submit to chiefly rule. The relationships of the chiefs to the councils in most of Bukedi has rarely been harmonious. The chiefs have tended to ignore or to manipulate the councils, or the councillors have been inclined to perceive of themselves in opposition to, rather than as advisory to, the chiefs.

Each tribe is constantly on guard against entrenchment of personnel of another tribe in positions of authority. The Padhola, in common with the other tribes, for example, resisted central government appointment of the judiciary for fear that it might lead to a monopoly of judicial positions by one tribe, or even worse, that a non-Padhola might be appointed County Judge in Budama. The three major local government positions—Secretary-General, Treasurer, and Chief Judge—are vigorously sought after by each tribe.[40] The equitable division of these major roles, along with their assistantships and the position of representative to the Uganda National Assembly, is most important in maintaining a minimum of district integration.[41] This tribal consciousness was carried to the extent that the District Council in 1954 resolved that all three of the major officials were to sign local government documents.[42]

We have had frequent cause to comment upon the dominant role played by the district council committee structure in the local government system under development in Uganda. Although the situation existing in Bukedi is similar, the tribal-county solidarity pattern has served to alter the manner in which committee control is exercised.

Committee System and Tribal Solidarity

Because Bukedi did not fall under the terms of the 1955 Ordinance until 1961, the District Commissioner was authorized to appoint the committees.[43] In practice, however, the Council was long permitted to select its own committees. The major committee seats are carefully allocated to preserve a county balance of power, for the members tend more to regard themselves as delegates of their respective tribes than as an executive committee of the District Council. Since 1960 political party affiliation has tended to play a more important role, and to some extent has cut across lines of tribal solidarity. For example, the minority Democratic Party has been allocated two of the eight seats on the major committees. More significant still is the fact that in 1961 the District Council resolved that the UPC majority should sit on one side of the aisle and the DP minority on the other. This is in marked contrast to the earlier practice of sitting by tribe-county constituency. The three major committees, now that appointments are in the hands of an independent board, are Finance, General Purposes and Education. In 1960, before the implementation of the 1955 Ordinance, the Standing Committee was composed of three county chiefs, one representative member for each county, the Secretary-General, Bukedi representative on the Uganda Legislative Council and the District Commissioner as chairman. The composition of the Finance Committee was basically the same, with the three county chiefs not on the Standing Committee having reserved seats on the Finance Committee.

On considering the Wallis Report recommendation that county chiefs be precluded from council membership, the District Council in 1954 voted fifty-nine to three that chiefs should sit on the councils.[44] It was further resolved that the system of indirect elections (whereby the control of the chiefs over the council hierarchy was assured) should be retained.[45] The Wallis Report recommended that the tier of councils be condensed through the elimination of the county level. This, of course, struck at the very heart of the Bukedi system and was rejected unanimously.[46]

> It was agreed that the county councils cannot be abolished, because they are the tribal government and as such they are the great councils in each county . . . even before the Europeans came each county had its tribal leaders. . . .[47]

Lower councils generally and county councils in particular have relatively greater significance in Bukedi than elsewhere in Uganda. In 1961 the lower council system was drastically revised. The most important change involved the direct election of one representative member from each parish in the county, and the substitution of a representative member in place of the chief as chairman of the county council. A survey of county council members completed in 1963 shows

the variation in occupational patterns between the predominantly
Protestant UPC northern counties and the DP Catholic southern
counties (see Table 13).

TABLE 13

OCCUPATION AND PARTY AFFILIATION

BUKEDI DISTRICT COUNTY COUNCILLORS

	UPC	DP	Farmers	Teachers	Traders	Other	Total
Pallisa	34	10	29	8	5	2	44
Bunyole	19	3	13	2	5	2	22
Budaka-Bugwere	25	9	19	6	9		34
Tororo	4	16	8	11	1		20
W. Budama	3	32	18	12	3	2	35
Samia-Bugwe*	17	9	5	13	9		26
TOTAL	102	79	92	52	32	6	181

* 6 UPC members nominated; 5 traders nominated, Chief ex-officio and party
not known.

SOURCE: Author's survey, 1963.

The educational and occupational level of county councils in
Bukedi is significantly higher than in Teso or Bunyoro. This difference is largely accounted for by the relative importance attached to
Bukedi county councils and the keen competition for seats. The
county councils are not content with passing resolutions on local needs
to be submitted to the district council. The Bukedi Secretary-General
in 1962 found it necessary to seek the assistance of the District Commissioner in order effectively to prohibit the county councils from
involving themselves in district politics. "In all cases the councils
seem to be usurping the functions of the chief ordering people what
to do and what not to do."[48] In one sub-county the council passed a
resolution instructing people not to pay taxes until the sub-county
buildings destroyed during the rioting were rebuilt by the district
local government. "Chiefs are inevitably finding so many odds against
them in the field with all the folk poisoned against them and petty
politicians that there is already marked deterioration about the whole
administrative machinery. . . ."[49]

Local government in Bukedi, despite a uniform application of the
British model, has evolved into something considerably different from
that in Teso or Bunyoro. The multitribal composition coinciding with
county boundaries is undoubtedly the crucial variable in the development of this unique decisional structure.

After the Commission of Inquiry into the 1960 Bukedi riots, local
government was considerably altered. The two major changes involved the establishment of an Appointments Board, similar to that

described for Teso in the preceding chapter, and the adoption of the 1955 Ordinance. This was followed early in 1961 by the first direct elections to the reconstituted council. That such constitutional changes were not without influence on the political behavior of men is suggested by the tendency in the election for political parties to compete with tribes as a major focus of political solidarity. We must recall, however, that party is not indifferent to traditional divisions and often reflects existing deep-seated loyalties. The Democratic Party won a narrow one-seat majority in the Council election. However, this was overturned when the official members of the Council (chiefs and officials), nearly all Protestant and anti-Democratic (Catholic) Party, threw their support to the UPC thereby providing a UPC majority sufficient to fill the six nominated Council seats with UPC supporters. Thus the first directly elected Council to sit under the 1955 Ordinance got off to an unfortunate start, for the slim DP majority was effectively cancelled by the influence in the Council of the county chiefs and other officials. When the Council met in March, 1961, twenty Democratic Party councillors boycotted the session and thereby precluded a quorum. The Council was unable to act and local government came to a standstill, as it had in Teso for similar reasons. The central government dissolved the Council, ordered new elections and amended the local constitution so as to eliminate the county chiefs from membership. The UPC fared better in August winning 23 of the 41 seats, the Democratic Party captured 17 and the remaining seat went to an independent. Exactly half of the old councillors won reelection. As the quorum was reduced from 36 to 20, the UPC emerged as a viable majority party. The twenty-three UPC councillors were elected from Pallisa (6), Budaka Bugwere (8), Bunyole (5) and Samia Bugwe (4). West Budama and Tororo elected no UPC candidates and together returned 12 of the Democratic Party's 17 members.[50] It is not surprising that the northern counties tend to dominate the major committees. For example, West Budama has no representation on the Finance Committee, while Budaka Bugwere has two; Tororo is without representation on the General Purposes Committee while Pallisa, Bunyole and Budaka Bugwere each have two members.

This party–religious–tribal domination of the council in conjunction with the O'Conner Report's suggestion that the southern counties have a separate headquarters in Tororo has given added impetus to the perennial movement for a return to a separate Budama or Tororo district to be composed of West Budama, Tororo, and Samia Bugwe.[51]

The County-Tribe and Recruitment

The recruitment of councillors, officials, chiefs, and even minor staff is carried out primarily with reference to tribal solidarity. Until 1961 District Council representative members were elected by the county councils. The tribal composition of the pre-1961 and the 1963 District Councils is shown in Table 14.

TABLE 14

COUNTY-TRIBE REPRESENTATION, BUKEDI DISTRICT COUNCIL, 1956 AND 1963

(excluding ex-officio, nominated and specially elected)

		Representatives	
County	Tribe	1956	1963
West Budama	Padhola	16	7
Pallisa	Iteso	18	9
Bugwere	Bagwere	17	9
Bunyole	Banyuli	12	5
Samia-Bugwe	Basamia-Bagwe	10	6
Tororo	Iteso	10	5
TOTAL		83	41

SOURCE: Author's survey, 1956 and 1963.

Recruitment of the major officials has long entailed tribal competition, log-rolling, and more recently party and religious conflict as well. Prior to the reconstitution of the local government in 1961, the Secretary-General was elected from among the ex-officio members of the council. Thus only county chiefs, the Treasurer and the Chief Judge were eligible for the highest post. This practice, in conjunction with tribal-county sentiment, gave rise to a thorny administrative problem. If a Secretary-General was not reelected but was succeeded by another county chief, the only vacancy available for the ex-Secretary-General was as chief of the county vacated by the newly elected Secretary-General. Obviously the successful candidate was rarely of the same tribe as the defeated one; therefore, if a given tribe successfully elected its county chief as Secretary-General, it left itself open to being saddled with a county chief from an alien tribe. This situation actually arose in the 1956 election when Mr. Mudanye, the Secretary-General and a Munyuli, was defeated by the Treasurer, Mr. Kirya. The vacancy in the treasury was filled by Mr. Otim, the Iteso county chief of Pallisa. The district could ill afford the loss of the services of Mudanye, a university graduate with a quarter-century of administrative experience. The Appointments Committee, however, sought to get rid of Mudanye by pensioning him off. But, so long as Bukedi did not fall under the terms of the 1955 Ordinance, the District Commissioner retained the prerogative of appointing chiefs.

Mudanye was appointed to fill the chieftaincy vacancy in Pallisa County left by the selection of County Chief Otim as Treasurer. The reaction in Pallisa was as anticipated; Mudanye's life was threatened. To suffer the indignity of a foreign chief was too high a price for the Iteso to pay for the prize of the treasurership. The tension was considerably lessened when Mudanye was subsequently selected Chief Judge. The Pallisa Iteso again demonstrated their antipathy to alien chiefs in 1961 when they took advantage of the riot situation to kill a Bagwere chief serving in their county.

The British administration long sought to break through the enigma of tribal parochialism, but centuries of conflict and bloodletting, plus the confusion of two decades of incessant administrative reorganization, when combined with a confluence of political party and religious affiliation have left a legacy of distrust and suspicion. It is difficult to know whether tribal nationalism is as strongly entrenched among the peasants as it obviously is among the political activists. The indirectly elected councils, the chiefs and the officials, both for personal reasons and in the interests of tribal solidarity, were long able to frustrate the implementation of the democratic 1955 reforms which might have enabled the people themselves to temper the parochialism of their chiefs.

The issue of relative status of chiefs and officials which is present in every district in Uganda is particularly pronounced in Bukedi. In 1954 the council resolved that a special chair be made for the Council Chairman and that others "not exactly the same" be prepared for the Treasurer and Secretary-General.[52] The District Commissioner, possibly reflecting upon English practice, refused to approve of this resolution, maintaining that a special chair for the chairman alone was all that was required. The council did not accept this point of view and re-resolved chairs for all the officials, for to have granted a special chair only to the chairman would have acted to enhance the prestige of the tribe he represented.

A fundamental tenet of the British system of local government depends on the recruitment of staff on the universalistic criteria of training and demonstrated capability. This standard is not accepted by the African local governments, but in districts such as Teso and Bunyoro, where the district coincides with the tribal entity, the failure to adapt to the British model has not resulted in as serious a departure from the norm as in Bukedi, where the presence of seven tribes in six counties has seriously narrowed the area from which acceptable candidates can be recruited.

The establishment of an Appointments Board relatively free from partisan and tribal parties has made it increasingly difficult for the council to ensure tribal equity in public employment. In 1962 alarmed over the consequences of appointments on other than a tribal basis, the council resolved to request the central government to name an independent commission to look into appointments. It was argued that "some counties have no employees at their headquarters, most particularly in senior posts."[53]

Later in the same year the council requested the central government to dissolve the Appointments Board on the grounds that "it is biased and full of corruption."[54]

The predominantly DP and Catholic counties in South Bukedi maintain that they are discriminated against by the UPC, Protestant Northern majority. In December 1962 DP-Catholic leaders in West Budama petitioned for the reestablishment of a separate Budama District on the basis that "most of the administrative posts in the district administration are filled by the Bagwere and the Banyuli . . . [and that] forty-five per cent of the total revenue was spent on the county of Budaka Bugwere. . . ."[55]

Levels of Legitimacy

We have had occasion to note variations in the pattern of solidarity between the Bukedi tribes. Padhola kinship, with its strong sense of tribal solidarity, was contrasted with the disjointed Iteso age-grade and etem system. The levels of loyalty to which Bukedi tribesmen give their consent can effectively be portrayed in graphic form. A high intensity of consent can generally be associated with the lower administrative levels of the tribal-government system. Thus if concentric circles from small to large (see Figure 7) are taken to refer to extended family, clan, tribe, county, district, and state, and degree of solidarity is indicated by the intensity of the shading, the emerging pattern for the Iteso and Padhola is considerably different.

The solidarity of the Padhola tends to focus on the clan and tribe and—because of the coincidence of tribe and county—on the county as well. The Itesot's major loyalty is owed more to his extended family and etem group; and, as a consequence of the coincidence of the tribal and district boundaries—plus a newly discovered sense of tribal homogeneity—to the district as well. The concentric circles and density shading can also be likened to perceptions of relative legitimacy. In Bukedi, the county with its own council and language is viewed as more deserving of local consent than the district. In similar vein, county representatives to the District Council until 1961 sat in tribal blocs and still are inclined to act as tribal delegates.

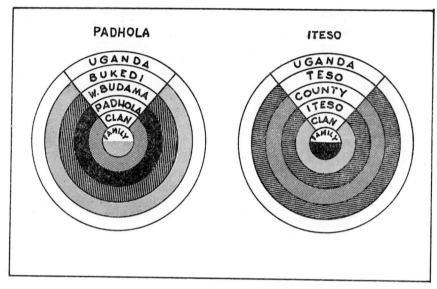

FIGURE 7
Iteso and Padhola Level and Intensity of Solidarity Contrasted

Nearly all issues that affect a given county-tribe are referred to that county council for prior discussion and comment. There is also a tendency to refer matters of districtwide significance to all county councils. On questions involving customary law, which are often recast and incorporated into district council bylaws, the necessity for prior county-tribe consent is even more apparent. The issue of limitations on bride price, for example, is clearly related to the culture of a given tribe and has required district bylaws setting out detailed regulations for each county.

The general legitimacy of the district level is accepted whenever all tribes of the district consider themselves threatened as a collectivity. Thus the tribes of Bukedi are relatively united in the conflict with Bugishu over Mbale. However, the preeminence of tribe-county solidarity, even in the face of an issue affecting the entire district, is suggested by the tendency of certain political factions in the southern counties, and particularly in West Budama and Samia Bugwe to sabotage Bukedi's case for control over Mbale. In 1962 Councillor Hamato from Bunyole warned the Council that a special committee report on Bukedi's reaction to the O'Conner Report had been deliberately leaked to the Bagishu. He noted that in "other countries" anyone betraying his county received the death sentence.[56] Another member accused Mr. Orach, the Bukedi Democratic Party leader and representative for West Budama, of betraying Bukedi secrets to the enemy. In reply Orach said that if no apology was forthcoming he was "going to fight for a separation of the District into two and for the formation of Tororo District."[57] On another occasion Mr. Orach, in a petition to the central government, "reminded the Minister that they the people of South Bukedi had no stakes in Mbale which they were forced to accept as their administrative center." Orach and his fellow petitioners emphasized that the quarrel over Mbale was essentially an intertribal struggle between the Bagishu and the Bagwere.[58] Bukedi District Council resolutions and motions directed against other Eastern Province districts or the Uganda government provide a needed context for districtwide consent in a region otherwise characterized by internal factionalism.

The District Council has long regarded itself as relatively more autonomous vis-à-vis the central government than have most other Uganda districts, despite the more severe limitations posed by the maintenance in Bukedi until 1961 of the 1949 Local Government Ordinance. For example, in reviewing the Wallis recommendations, the council in 1954 voted against the term "Bukedi" Local Authority and moved to substitute "Mbale-Bukedi Government."[59] This of course was not only an attempt to strike the designation "local" but to lay claim to the disputed city and surrounding region of Mbale as well. Assuming the guise of a semi-sovereign entity, the District Council in 1955 moved to "file a writ in the high court" challenging a central government decision.[60] It was further resolved that a deputation be sent to meet with the Governor and that expenditure from the Bukedi treasury for the purposes of meeting legal costs be authorized. In 1962, despite the intertribal problems it no doubt would raise, the District Council went on record supporting a ceremonial head (W'Egwanga) for Bukedi District. On another occasion the District Council assumed responsibility for discussing the issue of multiracial government in Uganda and unanimously appointed a subcommittee to prepare a memoranda for the Colonial Secretary. In an attempt to force the Colonial government to solve the Mbale impasse before Uganda achieved its independence, the District Council in 1961 prepared a petition for the Governor which stated that "it will amount to high treason to the land, customs, and people of Bukedi for Her Majesty's Government to relinquish its powers before handing back that disputed area to the people of Bukedi."[61]

Accountability at all levels for major local government decisions in Bukedi, before 1961, tended to rest with the chiefly hierarchy. Since the Bukedi riots, the rapid decline in the influence of the chiefs and the democratization of the councils, accountability has shifted only slightly from the tribe-county to the level of the district. For the county political party organizations, closely allied with the major religious factions, have largely supplanted the influence of the chiefs. Tribal heterogeneity and a delicate balance of tribal factions has precluded the evolution of a more centralized democratic system of accountability, despite the traditional inclination of most Bukedi tribes toward democratic procedures. And political activity, which is dominant at the district level in Bunyoro and Teso, occurs primarily at the county level in Bukedi.

Law and Order

The prominent role of customary law throughout Uganda has furthered the development of district nationalism in relatively homogeneous Teso and Bunyoro. In Bukedi, as in other districts, customary law is tribal law, and the bulk of adjudication and litigation still depends on indigenous custom. However, extreme variations in tribal customary law in Bukedi have prohibited the evolution of a unified districtwide code. Sanctions concerning land tenure, bride price, and inheritance, for example, vary from tribe to tribe. It is most important therefore that a knowledgeable local person assume the duties of adjudication at the county-tribe level. Not only do institutionalized norms vary between tribes, but procedural values are also different. Among the Pallisa Iteso, for example, guilt and punishment were traditionally determined by a form of jury. In Teso District this has evolved into the use of jurors as opposed to assessors. The judge-chief in Teso was required to pass judgment only after consulting the views of nonofficial court members. Among the Bagwere, on the other hand, and to a lesser extent among the Padhola, the powers of adjudication were traditionally exercised by a single individual.

The close proximity and border area intermingling of different tribes and languages produce considerable friction and serve to keep old feuds alive. The likelihood of conflict is enhanced by the attendance at beer clubs and dances of young men and women from more than one tribe. Faced with a problem of increasing disorder, the Provincial Commissioner of the Eastern Province, as early as 1931, wrote to the District Commissioners, in a vein reminiscent of America's Wild West, suggesting that:

> if orders do not already exist to that effect would it not be possible to make a standing order that at any organised beer party or dance all spears and sticks have to be stacked at a place to be decided by the chief with the view of reducing the casualties which occur in the heat of the moment and so often result in death.[62]

The Iteso of Pallisa County—like their brothers to the north, and for reasons noted in the previous chapter—are known throughout Uganda for their record of violence and homicide, while the crafty and politically minded Bagwere are inclined more toward conspiracy and character defamation. In 1962 there were 760 cases of assault in Bukedi. The Iteso of Pallisa, though making up only 19 per cent of the district's population, accounted for nearly 30 per cent of such crimes. In 1952 there were thirty-five homicides in Bukedi but the Pallisa-Teso accounted for twenty and their fellow Iteso tribesmen in Tororo for four more. In 1953 the homicide rate in Bukedi fell to ten but the Iteso of Pallisa maintained their record by accounting for nine of the ten.[63]

The region roughly coinciding with present-day Bukedi District was long recognized by the British as extremely volatile, violence-prone, and most difficult to administer. Bukedi with its welter of tribes and customs has witnessed periodic outbursts of violence and destruction and the 1960 riots were particularly extensive. Although the spark that ignited the widespread rioting and pillage of January, 1960, involved intensive criticism of the arbitrary levels of tax assessment, the breakdown of law and order was immediately employed as a pretext for the resumption of numerous tribal, clan, religious, and territorial conflicts that have so long characterized this complex region. Not only were the people traditionally unaccustomed to a system of chiefly hierarchy, but the particular tribe-county nature of the local political system acted to place extraordinary power in the hands of Bukedi chiefs at every level. For example there had long existed in Bukedi generally, and in Pallisa and West Budama particularly, strong anti-chief—in fact anti-authority—attitudes which, given the opportunity provided by the riots, quickly dominated the situation. Early in January, 1960, large crowds, often numbering more than 10,000, armed with spears, sticks, and other weapons, gathered throughout Bukedi (except for Samia Bugwe). Chiefs were attacked, some were killed and nearly all were chased from their homes, political authority was effectively destroyed throughout most of the country, and near anarchy reigned for nearly three weeks. On numerous occasions the Uganda police detachments were required to fire upon the crowds to save themselves from attack or to protect chiefs and European district officers from being engulfed and mobbed. In Pallisa, for example, on January 19, twenty or more chiefs had taken refuge from the mob in the local police posts. The police, in order to protect these chiefs, had no choice but to fire on the mob, killing two and wounding many more.[64]

Two sub-county chiefs in Pallisa were in fact killed and many others fled their posts and subsequently resigned their positions. In

West Budama the Nyapolo-Catholic faction took advantage of the chaos and confusion to renew its struggle against the Protestant non-Nyapolo chiefs. The chiefs were attacked, their homes burned, and gardens destroyed. Along the border with Tororo the state of anarchy provided an opportunity for renewed conflict between the Iteso and the Padhola.

There is some evidence that partisan party leadership was responsible for the emergence of the tax assessment issue to the point of violence. However, the rioting was surprisingly spontaneous and without over-all direction or leadership. It reflected the pent-up factionalism and latent conflict of multiple varying interests that are so pronounced in this region. It is evident that the imported local government system to date has not successfully coped with these complex and emotion-charged problems. After order had been restored the central government levied a special tax on every Bakedi taxpayer to compensate for the destruction of property. But indicative of the prevailing attitude toward the riots was a late 1962 District Council resolution that those imprisoned for rioting but released as part of the independence amnesty be exempted from 1963 taxation, on the basis that because they were unavoidably detained they could not work.[65]

Local Government Finance in Bukedi

Both revenue and expenditure are influenced by the tribal heterogeneity which characterizes Bukedi District. The assessment of the graduated tax, for example, is affected by variations in the tribal social systems. Assessment is carried out by a committee at the sub-county level composed of the chief plus a parish chief and a member of the sub-county council. In each parish, however, this committee was assisted by the chief of that parish, the parish councillors and the village chief. The village chiefs were also charged with the responsibility of preparing a census list showing relative wealth and liabilities.[66]

Although the rate of tax is established by the District Council by ordinance, the peasants, even if aware of the decisional source, do not interpret District Council action as indicative of their consent to be taxed. The rate of tax is determined largely by the Finance Committee and its chairman. That the rate of tax is, in effect, somewhat arbitrarily arrived at, and only slightly dependent upon the wish of the citizenry, is a fact that cannot be denied. The 1960 riots in part reflected the frustration of the peasants with this state of affairs. The education tax when first initiated in 1955 was only five shillings but was raised to ten in 1957 and doubled to twenty in 1959. At twenty shillings it was exceeded in only one other district in Uganda.

Although each taxpayer was theoretically to be assessed according to his assets and liabilities, an informal quota system existed which required each chief in the hierarchy to collect an established amount of money. Thus assessment and collection reflected not only capacity to pay but the requirements of the quota as well.

Where the organized procurement of public resources is closely associated with differing tribal custom, a great deal of variation ensues. In Teso, for example, the District Council on occasion has passed bylaws establishing maximum dowries in cattle and cash equivalents applicable throughout the district. In multitribal Bukedi, however, it has been necessary to refer the question of cash equivalency to the respective tribal-county councils for information and advice. For not only does the amount of bride price vary by tribe, but the kinship distribution of the bride price is also different. A limitation upon bride price in a tribe where the distribution of bride price does not loom large in the local economic system may only slightly affect local integration. Where this distribution is critical to the local economy, as it is in many tribes, the consequences are apt to be severe. Bukedi tribal variations in dowry are shown in Table 15.

TABLE 15

VARIATIONS IN BRIDE PRICE BY TRIBE AND COUNTY, BUKEDI DISTRICT, 1959

Tribe and County	Head of Cattle*	Goats*	Cash (Shs.)*
Pallisa (Teso)	9	10	30
Bugwere (Bagwere)	5	5	20
Bunyuli (Banyole)	4	4	20
W. Budama (Padhola)	7	8	18
Tororo (Teso)	12	8	30
Samia	13	6	50
Bugwe	—	—	1000

* Maximum amounts indicated.
SOURCE: Bukedi Local Government Files.

Development programs, which necessitate the placement of skilled personnel within the counties, are often viewed with disfavor by the Bukedi local government. The possibility of an Iteso veterinary scout or forest ranger being posted in Bugwere is sufficient reason to suspect the assignment. Teachers posted in the schools in a county of a tribe different from their own have been denied land for a house and garden. Needless to say, the difficulty of securing qualified teachers for the lower grades is further magnified by the existence of five different languages.

A similar situation arises with respect to health and medical facilities. The difficulty of providing local government services in a multitribal community is illustrated well by the problem of caring for lepers. Bukedi District possesses one of the highest leper populations in Uganda and it is estimated that nearly 15 per cent of the country's 70,000 lepers are in Bukedi. However, only about 3,000 of the 9,000 lepers were thought to have been receiving treatment in 1959. A major problem in providing such treatment in Bukedi is the reluctance of the leper to leave his tribal area and admit himself to a leper camp in the territory of a foreign tribe. Often the cure is thought to be more dangerous than the disease. For example, the Padhola leper will not eat a steady diet of matoke (plantain), the Iteso leper will not eat eggs, while the Banyuli will eat no fish.

The British have not been any more successful in implementing a sense of public service and civic responsibility in Bukedi than they were in Teso or Bunyoro. The average councillor feels little obligation to his constituents. The councillors, aware that the chiefs receive a salary for exercising authority, are inclined to feel that if they have been selected to meet periodically to decide matters relevant to a comparable area, they too should be reimbursed for their efforts. The money that councillors receive for attending meetings is considered by the British administration to be "subsistence allowance" but the councillors regard it as income-earned. The District Council periodically votes itself an increase in its attendance allowance which in turn is generally disallowed by the British administrators. This infuriates the councillors who cannot understand why they are not permitted to pay themselves for their own services. "If a carpenter builds a bed for us we must pay him. If we are to make rules for the people we too should be paid."[67]

British administration has attempted, in Bukedi, to develop a heterogeneous complex territory and people into a unified local government area, patterned on the British model. Outwardly the local political system resembles that of the kingdom of Bunyoro and of tribally homogeneous Teso. But local government and politics in Bukedi have also been shaped by the welter of traditional cultures and social systems which characterize this problematically complex district. In Bukedi the crucial variables are those associated with the multiple, traditional tribal-kinship systems, with authority and solidarity clustering at levels lower than the district. The exact locus of authority in each case is a reflection of the unique characteristics of the respective tribal-county political system.

CHAPTER SEVEN

Conclusions

THE PROPOSITIONS RESTATED

In the first chapter it was hypothesized that government at the local level consists of a number of organized procedures and roles designed to solve problems which obstruct local order and integration. It was further stated that the way in which the local political system seeks to approximate these ends is conditioned, in part, by the nature of the problems, which in turn are largely a product of the locality's physical environment and its social system. It was then concluded that there exists a crucial relationship between the structures of the local political system and its environment and social system.

From this postulate an additional proposition more directly relevant to the problem of developing a uniform system of local government based upon the English model in multitribal Uganda, was advanced.

1. If the structures of a local political system are rapidly altered without corresponding changes in the problems with which the structures are designed to cope, some problems may exist without means of adequate solution; the implications being either local disorder and/or local malintegration.

2. If the problems with which a local political system is required to cope change, or new problems arise as a consequence of changes in the social system or environment, and the structures fail to change so as to bring the new problems within the system, a state of disorder or malintegration is liable to exist.

Possibly the single most striking phenomenon of contemporary Africa, south of the Sahara, is the scale and rapidity of "change" and surely the richness of the literature treating with the subject is indicative of an acute awareness of the importance of transition. For the purpose of this work the significance of "change" is to be seen in its impact upon local social and political organization and upon the maintenance of a minimum level of social order and integration.

Folkways and Ordinances

Traditional and transitional decisional structures in the centralized kingdom of Bunyoro, in tribally homogeneous, but decentralized Teso, and in multitribal Bukedi are intricately interrelated. In Bunyoro, decisions affecting many people over a large area were made traditionally by a hierarchy of chiefs responsible ultimately to a divine-right king. In Teso District, order and integration were the collective responsibility of a combination of age-grades, small territorial units and extended families. Bukedi District was characterized by a bewildering variety of traditional organization, reflecting the respective cultures of the many tribes inhabiting that area. Authoritative decisions in the case of the Bantu Banyuli, for example, were made by a hierarchically organized clan system, while among the Nilotic Padhola decisions were made by a combination of relatively autonomous segmented clans and, more recently, by an embryonic royal clan.

Over this mosaic of traditional decisional mechanisms the British superimposed a system of local government based upon the English model. Prior to World War II the British generally sought to rule through existing institutions; but where sufficiently large-scale and specialized political organizations did not exist, they imported the hierarchical chief system indigenous to the centralized kingdoms. Shortly after the war, a process of developing both the indirectly ruled kingdoms and the directly ruled small-scale societies into local government units was begun. Because of its large size, relatively high state of development, and the peculiar nature of its treaty relationships with Great Britain, the kingdom of Buganda was largely excluded from this process.[1]

Briefly, the British model called for a central government grant of detailed authority to the local governments to undertake a wide range of local services. Authority to make binding decisions, within the limitations posed by the legal delegation of authority from the central government, is exercised by large, predominantly popularly elected councils which are responsible for the execution as well as the formulation of policy. The large councils deliberate and execute policy through the agency of a number of functional committees. The local authorities employ a variety of technical officials to carry out their executive decisions and to advise them on policy. Ideally the role of councillor and official are sharply differentiated. The council may make only those authoritative decisions expressly authorized in its delegation of authority from the central government.

Although the subject is not treated in detail, local government in England itself has undergone considerable change through the years which might usefully be analyzed in terms of the approach employed here. For example, parish government has ceased to command the respect and interest of the residents in much of rural England. Nonetheless, uniquely local problems of order and integration continue to exist in the rural villages and, as in Uganda, organized (though un-official) means for coping with these problems have evolved.[2] In some regions the village pub is the institution within which certain aspects of community conflict are reconciled. Many rural English pubs have a regular clientele and an organized structure of decision-making which acts to protect the members from external threats to their well-being. This unofficial aspect of the modern local political system has assumed partial guardianship of many community norms and is capable of applying effective sanctions. For example, one member of a local community studied in considerable detail, who failed to care for his aged mother according to local custom, after due deliberation, was effectively snubbed and otherwise ostracized until he conformed. Outsiders who might pose a threat to locality integration are required to undergo a lengthy process of "socialization" before being accepted into the community.[3]

The critical role of environment as a conditioner of social forms and functions has long been recognized. Upon the basis of an extensive study of a number of tribes in Southern Africa, Monica Wilson, for example, was particularly impressed by the correlation between scale of political organization and environment. Where the landscape permitted easy navigation in healthy open country, the resultant societies tended to be large. Wilson contrasts the small-scale nature of African society with that of Europe and notes that "in Africa physical conditions have tended towards isolation."[4] Nevertheless, the natural environment is but one factor conditioning the problems a locality must face and therefore the decisional structures that evolve to cope with such problems. As the political system becomes more extensive, the relative influence of geography and other natural physical features becomes less important, for an increase in scale tends to be accompanied by an increased capacity to cope with the environment.

The culture of selected regions in Uganda was treated in some detail in the foregoing. With respect to variations in decisional structures it was concluded that the prevailing characteristic of the Nilotic and Nilo-Hamitic peoples is the clustering of authority in the clan and lineage heads. This pattern has rendered the evolution of an effective authority system, based upon shared territory, more difficult than has been the case in the former Bantu kingdom-states. The official court of the Omukama of Bunyoro-Kitara for example, was relatively large and involved many people carrying out a wide range of specialized duties. In the case of the Padhola, transition was noted from a less to a more complex political system following upon their migration into what is now Bukedi District. It would appear that the political requirements of living in relatively concentrated units is related to a change in their decisional organization from one based upon small-scale diffuse kinship units to a larger-scale, more specialized, territorially based, system. Sidney and Beatrice Webb have observed a similar variation between the rural and more concentrated settlement areas in eighteenth-century England;

Wherever changes occur the new developments are always in the same direction. From out of the Court of Justice there emerged two other organs of government, a County Executive, itself administering public services, and . . . a County Legislature formulating new policies.[5]

The superordinate-subordinate status pattern which is characteristic of aristocratic Bantu Banyoro, in contrast to the equalitarian nature of the Iteso, has made it more difficult to approach the British model with respect to developing a tier of all-purpose local authorities in the former than in the latter area. The lower councils in Bunyoro are relatively impotent. A related observation was made with respect to northern Nigeria by Margery Perham, who noted that the Emir "shrinks from delegating his powers except to those members of his family whom he feels he can trust. . . ."[6]

The evolution of new roles in the wake of the introduction of Western political, social, and economic institutions has given rise to corresponding alterations in local authority structures. In Teso District, where the scale of the decisional structure has been most noticeably expanded, authority is being transferred generally from lineage heads to a bureaucratic civil service composed of government chiefs, party leaders and local government officials. The parochialism of the extended family organization and small-scale solidarity pattern of the Iteso contrasts with the national orientation of the Banyoro and the tribal affiliation of the small Bukedi tribes. An analogous distinction, contrasting the difference between solidarity patterns in the United States and England in the early 1900's and the implications for the autonomy of local government institutions, was made by Ernest Griffith.[7] He observed that the relative absence of class-oriented solidarity in the United States acted to make the composition of central and local governments relatively similar, with the result that central government in the United States has been more inclined to delegate authority to local units than has been the case in England.[8]

A major problem encountered in implementing large-scale specialized local government in Uganda has been the parochial and often nonrational nature of the patterns of communication and expression. Transition is less characterized by instances of disorder and malintegration in those areas where traditional patterns do not unduly conflict with the acceptance of new ideas and behavior. The Iteso, for example, have been able to accommodate to perceptual and value changes more rapidly than have the Banyoro.

Analyzing the manner in which some rural English villages have accommodated to changes in the decisional structure of parish government, Duncan Mitchell observed that the rural villages which had more readily adapted themselves to the new structure imposed upon them were those in which there existed few impediments to communication with nearby market towns.[9] There is little doubt but that the relatively uniform patterns of communication and expression in the West have enabled a more universalistic development of local government than has been the case in East Africa, where considerable local uniqueness and isolation persist.

Both the substance and procedures of traditional values, as they condition authoritative decision-making, vary significantly among the tribal groups studied, and these variations are reflected in the respective governmental systems. Griffith contends that the differential evolution of local government in the United States and England is also, in part, a consequence of a difference in value pattern. As conditions changed, local governments in both countries, in response to new problems, assumed new duties and altered their structures accordingly. However, while the English, for reasons peculiar to conditions in their country, emphasized health and municipal trading, the Americans concentrated on education and public works.[10]

Old and New Roles

The major positions within the local government system are similar throughout Uganda, even though the titles and symbols differ considerably. This uniformity has required considerable alteration in the respective traditional systems of Uganda's many parochial and vastly different cultures. For example, the Omukama of Bunyoro has been deprived of his many powers and is now responsible to a democratic constitution; the Iteso have been amalgamated into a district and for the first time perceive of themselves as a single people. Nevertheless, the shoe pinches differently in Teso than in Bunyoro. A major problem in Bunyoro has been the tendency for authority to cluster at the center, while in Bukedi considerable difficulty has been experienced in aggregating sufficient authority at the center. Traditional authority figures in both regions continue to play important roles in the respective local political systems. In Teso District, a traditionally fragmented small-scale political system hindered the gradual evolution of specialized political roles. Confronted with this problem, the recruitment and function of Teso clan leaders were modified so as to correspond more closely to the requirements of a more specialized and inclusive modern local government system. The restyled clan system, now termed the Teso Elders and Parents Association, currently rivals the District Council and political parties. In 1963, combining modern and traditional influences, the Teso Elders and Parents Association sought to claim for itself authority to designate a constitutional head (Ekaraban) for Teso.

In multitribal Bukedi District, role recruitment has had to take into account the maintenance of a delicate tribal balance of power. The coincidence of tribe and county there has rendered the role of the chief and the district and county councils considerably different from either Bunyoro or Teso.

Social and environmental transition has introduced a number of new authority roles into the local political system. The significance of these new roles varies from one society to another, but in all areas the traditional role carriers continue to exercise considerable, though often altered authority. On occasion when it appears that decisions are made by the official local government, in reality the local government is but giving effect to decisions already arrived at by the traditional authority figures. The trend, however, is for the assumption of more and more authority by the local government officials and councils, and a decline in the authority and responsibility of traditional offices. In Bunyoro many of the traditional authority figures have been incorporated into the modern system, with the result that the distinction between traditional and modern is not so sharply posed as it is in Teso where problems of scale, as well as a variety of other factors, have precluded a similar synthesis. Thus, in Bunyoro, the chief, whose legal authority is almost identical to that of his counterpart in Teso, actually possesses considerably more influence. It will be recalled that a chiefly hierarchy is not indigenous to the Iteso and that the chiefs, though now generally accepted, are nonetheless perceived in a different fashion than they are in Bunyoro.

Qualifications for filling authority positions have changed throughout Uganda, with a higher premium today being placed upon universal criteria generally and particularly upon education. . . . In Bunyoro, however, traditional criteria continue to play a relatively important role, for customary differentiation on the basis of wealth and status in that former kingdom has enabled the traditional authority figures to secure modern leadership criteria for their sons, and in this fashion perpetuate elements of the traditional system.[11]

Obligation and Consent

It is paradoxical that, in one respect, local identification with the modern local governments has been so intense as to delay the emergence of an independent unified Uganda. It is understandable that the kingdom of Bunyoro would continue to regard itself as a more or less independent entity. It is surprising, however, that the Iteso, who until they came under British rule early in the 1900's never perceived of themselves as a nation, subsequently developed a high degree of district nationalism, which in its intensity is no less than that of the Banyoro. The British model requires that the local governments be subordinate creatures of the central government. However, not a few representatives to Uganda's National Assembly are inclined to regard themselves (and, just as important, are regarded by their fellow tribesmen) as district-tribal ambassadors.

Ideally, the British model also calls for the local authority wielders to be accountable to the adult population through the agency of a hierarchy of democratically elected councils.[12] Mass support for the exercise of districtwide authority by the local government was relatively easily achieved in Bunyoro where there has long existed a tradition of districtwide legitimacy centered about the king. In Bukedi District, however, consent to the district local authority has been granted only grudgingly. The loci of legitimacy for the exercise of authority vary in Bukedi and depend upon the differing social systems of the respective tribes, while in Teso District parochialism, despite a newly discovered tribal homogeneity, persists.

It was noted above that the composition of the democratically elected Bunyoro District Council did not approximate the general occupational and social distribution of the country. We attributed this deviation, in large part, to the persistence of traditional legitimacy sufficient to render kinship-based status a requisite to modern council eligibility. Duncan Mitchell has observed a similar pattern in the recruitment of parish councillors in England:

> There is a very small number of skilled and manual workers prepared to stand for election due almost entirely to the problem of traditional legitimacy, which also affects the small farmers as well; *i.e.*, that despite the legal right there is no belief in the social right to stand for election and no recognition of the present machinery of local government.[13]

The tenacity with which the people of the multitribal districts cling to their traditional parochial units of authority and responsibility is one of the major problems facing the development of modern local government in Uganda. Many of the lower tier local government areas are inefficient and incapable of evolving into viable units of local authority along the lines required by the British model. Nevertheless, these administrative areas often coincide with traditionally legitimate political units, and attempts to deprive them of their collective identity have failed.[14]

Although conditions are changing in a direction conducive to an enlarged area of consent, it would appear that the scale of modern local government in Uganda, at the moment, is considerably in advance of the existing level of local consensus. This is especially true in the diffuse, small-scale, segmented societies. However, as communication improves, as people move about in search of work in a diversified economy, and as multiple loyalties based upon specialized roles and associations evolve, it is probable that local parochialism, as reflected in the legitimacy awarded the multiple of traditional units of authority, will gradually decline. In the meantime, the role of the formal local government authority figures, who must secure the consent of the local people to rule effectively but who are also accountable to larger-scale relatively alien units, continues to be a difficult one. In order to render their positions tolerable they frequently are required to obstruct the development of local democratic procedures or to ignore their obligations to the larger-scale bureaucracy.

New solidarity patterns have led to the evolution of local institutions in Uganda that often compete with traditional as well as with modern-day institutions for the support of the local community. In those instances where traditional leadership also is associated with modern institutions, the locus of accountability tends to be particularly diffuse. For example, some chiefs are not only accountable to the central and local governments and to their kinship units, but also to a political party and to influential leaders in the Catholic or Protestant church.

Political parties also have interjected an additional divisive force. The proper relationship of political parties to local government in England remains controversial with party government and party accountability generally confined to the urban areas.[15] In Uganda the tendency of parties to coincide and overlap with other and sometimes traditional solidarity units, has further complicated the problem of pinpointing accountability.

Local government in Uganda has developed in the shadow of the Buganda Agreement. The quasi-sovereign status of this large kingdom encouraged the smaller and less powerful monarchies to acquire a similar status. The prestige, ceremony, and special privileges surrounding the kingdom governments, in turn, colored the development of local government throughout the remainder of the country. Not only were British administrators accustomed to thinking in terms of special agreements, prior consultation, and hereditary deference, but the leaders of the newly emergent, nonmonarchical districts were quick to emulate the kingdoms and to demand similar prerogatives for themselves. Thus, in contrast to Kenya and Tanganyika, local government in Uganda evolved in a quasi-federal milieu.

An independent Uganda has inherited this legacy and the integration of the federal kingdom of Buganda, the three western kingdoms (also possessed of some federal characteristics) of Toro, Ankole, and Bunyoro; the "federal territory" of Busoga; ten districts and the territory of Mbale, into a unified viable nation-state is problematically complicated by this confusion of special status and privilege.

The UPC-dominated central government, within the limitations dictated by its dependence upon Kabaka Yekka, is seeking to bring some semblance of order to the local government scene. Although nowhere stated as government policy, there would appear to be a determined effort to narrow the difference between the kingdoms and district local governments. While the special privileges of the former are gradually being circumscribed, the districts are being permitted to adopt the monarchical and parliamentary trappings and symbols of the kingdoms. Teso's long, but not yet completely successful, campaign for an Ekaraban was noted in Chapter Five. A comparable tale could be related for nearly every district. Kigezi, for example, which is beset by problems of multitribalism only slightly less intense than Bukedi, has also demanded that it be permitted to have a ceremonial ruler (Rutakirwa Engabu). Although the Minister for Regional Administrations has not opposed the provision of "heads of state" for Uganda's local governments, he has refused either on partisan political grounds or on the basis of fiscal prudence to authorize the wholesale appointment of ceremonial rulers.

Another manifestation of this legacy of tribalism and separatism as it affects the development of local government in Uganda is the tendency toward continued political and administrative fragmentation. A strong sense of local self-determination fed by a history of "negotiation" with the British Colonial administration plus the promise of a host of prestigious and lucrative offices, in conjunction with political party and religious factionalism, have inclined ethnic and regional minorities to demand secession and the establishment of separate districts. Incidents of this nature in Bukedi and Teso were dealt with at some length in the preceding pages. In May 1963 the East Acholi Region of the UPC called for a division of Acholi into two districts. The intense factionalism which characterizes Uganda politics, together with a legacy of autonomy, inclines minority councillors to frustrate local government deliberation and decision by boycotting or withdrawing from meetings. Fearful that majority power will be employed primarily to harass and destroy the opposition rather than to pursue policies to which the minority might be opposed, the leaders of the dissident factions are inclined to retaliate by obstructing the system of local government. In Bugishu in 1962 and 1963 the struggle between the UPC majority and the DP minority bordered upon violence and there have been repeated petitions by the minority that the council be dissolved. In March and again in May 1963 DP members walked out of the Bugishu District Council. Almost identical demands have been made by the Lango branch of the Democratic Party. In West Nile District in September 1962 the minority Democratic Party walked out of the newly elected District Council in protest against the composition of committees. When the new Busoga District Council met for the first time, also in September 1962, eighteen opposition members staged a walkout over the selection of the council's six specially elected members.

The most serious instance of intertribal hostility that not only affected local government but which also threatened the peace of the fledgling nation of Uganda, were the disturbances in the kingdom of Toro. The state of emergency in Toro in 1962-63 deserves lengthy comment for two reasons: not only have the disturbances drastically affected the local political system in Toro but the scope and special nature of the crisis raise a serious threat to the stability of a newly independent Uganda, and pose international implications as well. Furthermore, the Toro crisis sharply illustrates the interaction of the crucial political forces and institutions, as well as the pattern of reconciliation, which the central government appears to be developing to cope with this all too common situation.

The kingdom of Toro, it will be recalled, was once a principality of the Empire of Bunyoro-Kitara. However, through a series of administrative decisions the kingdom of Toro and subsequently Toro District came to include a large territory in the region of the Ruwenzori Mountains inhabited by Baamba and Bakonjo tribesmen. These Bantu mountain people never have accepted Batoro hegemony and have smarted under a half-century of humiliation as being inferior, backward, and apelike. Long memories harken back to a time when the Batoro sold them as slaves to the Arabs. Despite the fact that the Baamba and Bakonjo number 136,000—only fifty thousand less than the Batoro, they have had almost no role in the government and political life of the district. However, direct elections to the District Council in 1962 for the first time enabled this large minority to exercise its influence and to give voice to its many complaints. The newly elected Rukurato (District Council), with a Baamba-Bakonjo minority of 21 of the 72 elected members, selected a constitutional committee to work out the details of a new Toro Agreement that was required as a part of the pre-independence arrangements. The Baamba and Bakonjo demanded that the new agreement not only be made with reference to Toro and its Omukama, but explicitly include the Bakonjo and Baamba as well. The Batoro majority which had long ignored the wishes of the Bakonjo and Baamba did not look with favor on this request.[16]

As early as February 1962 Mr. Mukirane, Chairman of the unofficial Bakonjo-Baamba and Toro Constitutional Committee, requested separate district status for the two tribes, complaining that seventy years of being ruled as slaves by an alien and arrogant people should be ended.[17] At a subsequent meeting of the Rukurato the twenty-one Baamba and Bakonjo staged a walkout. The leaders of the delegation were arrested by Toro police, charged, convicted, and sentenced to eight-month imprisonment (under customary law) for insulting the Omukama. The Toro government then declared seven Rukurato seats in the Ruwenzori area vacant because of the refusal of Baamba and Bakonjo representatives to attend meetings; by-elections were scheduled to fill the vacancies. In March Mr. Mukirane, in a letter to the Katikiro of Toro, demanded that Batoro chiefs be removed from the Bakonjo-Baamba areas; he further declared June first as self-government day for the Ruwenzori region. On the eve of the day on which nominations were to be made for the vacant seats, a Batoro sub-county chief was attacked and forced to flee for his life.[18]

On August 28, 1962, the police opened fire on a large crowd rioting in protest against the by-elections, killing one person and triggering a series of violent incidents. Baamba County, bordering on the Congo (Leopoldville) was declared a "disturbed area"; the central government dispatched a detachment of Uganda Rifles to Toro. The possibility that the disturbances would cause an international incident was nervously appreciated by Prime Minister Obote. In the spring of 1962 Mukirane informed the central government that "if the Government is opposed to the issue of granting a separate district, we are prepared to join the Province of Kivu in the Congo where we have the backing of twelve members of our tribes in the Congo National Assembly."[19]

The opposition of the Baamba and Bakonjo became more intense and violent in proportion to the increasingly repressive measures of the Batoro police, chiefs, and courts. Crowds of two thousand or more Bakonjo and Baamba attacked Batoro farms, public buildings, chiefs, and police. The situation was rapidly moving beyond the control of the joint capability of the Batoro and central government police. There was also considerable evidence that numerous Congolese brethren of the Baamba were crossing the border at night to join their fellow tribesmen in firing poisoned arrows at the Batoro. In September 1962 —one month before Uganda's independence—the central government appointed a commission to inquire into the reasons for the disturbance and to make appropriate recommendations for the reconciliation of the conflict.[20] The leaders of the secessionist movement demanded that the Commission report its findings and that the issue be resolved before independence for, as with the Banyoro and their lost counties, it was evident that partisan politics in an independent Uganda would render a solution most unlikely. The report released the day after independence strongly supported the Bakonjo-Baamba position, blamed the Toro government for the conditions leading up to the disturbances, but did not advise separate district status for the Ruwenzori region. Instead the Commission recommended that new Rukurato elections be held and that the leaders of the movement be permitted to return to public life. Other recommendations provided for the allocation of educational expenditures and Toro government bursaries for the Bakonjo and Baamba. The Commission also suggested that two county chiefs be selected from among the minority tribes to serve, initially, in predominantly Toro counties. The recommendation that another commission be appointed to inquire into the efficiency and operation of the Toro government, as shall be seen, was to have farreaching effects.[21]

One month after independence, the new nation of Uganda was threatened by civil war. The leaders of the Bakonjo and Baamba Secessionist Movement appointed their own chiefs, printed their own tax receipts, and generally set about establishing a separate region in the near impenetrable foothills of the fabled Mountains of the Moon. Prime Minister Obote reluctantly agreed that all four counties should be designated disturbed areas. Isaya Mukirane, the erratic leader of the movement, from his headquarters hidden deep in the mountain forests wrote the Prime Minister declaring the Ruwenzori counties independent from Uganda; copies of this declaration were sent to the United Nations Secretary-General. By February, 1963, matters had deteriorated to the point that a state of emergency was declared and the Uganda army was ordered to move into the region in force.

Considerable drama was interjected into the situation by the kidnapping and brutal assault of a Toro member of the National Assembly and by the arrival in Uganda of Tom Stacey—a British journalist whose intimate knowledge of the dissident mountain people hopefully would enable him miraculously to bring peace where the combined efforts of the Toro and central government had failed.

The Uganda government's first White Paper of 1963 on "The Report of the Commission of Inquiry into the Disturbances Amongst the Baamba and Bakonjo People of Toro" advised against the establishment of a separate district, but did not support the more radical position of the Commission which called for new Rukurato elections. The White Paper also proposed the immediate appointment of two

Bakonjo-Baamba chiefs to serve in Batoro counties, and charged the Toro government with responsibility for the disturbances. The White Paper urged that county councils with their own taxing powers be established and that this, in effect, would grant considerable local government to the disaffected counties.

In March the central government appointed a commission to investigate the administration of the Toro government. The Lubowa Commission concluded that as the Toro government was unable to provide adequate administration and services in much of the district, the central government should assume responsibility for education, roads, and tax collection, and should replace the Batoro courts and chiefs in Baamba and Busongora counties with central government administrators. This action by the central government met with the emotional opposition of the Batoro who feared the dismemberment of their kingdom and an end to their quasi-federal status. In a dramatic ceremony the Lubowa Report was burned before a crowd of more than two thousand Batoro assembled at the capital. Batoro leaders appealed to their fellow monarchists in the neighboring kingdoms for support, warning that the heavy-handed action of the central government would be directed next against them.

As for the Baamba and Bakonjo, they demanded that the central government implement the recommendations of the Lubowa Report immediately for they anticipated that central government administration would be but the first step to complete separation and the eventual establishment of their own district. In April 1963, the Uganda cabinet confirmed the Report and declared its intention to implement it immediately. The following month the Toro Rukurato passed a resolution opposing the central government's decision.

Uganda celebrated its first anniversary as an independent state on October 9, 1963, still plagued by this incipient revolt. Though the state of emergency has been withdrawn, much of the area is still designated a disturbed area and as 1963 came to a close, the Uganda Rifles were still trying to enforce a curfew in the Ruwenzori region. During the day an uneasy peace reigns, while at night Baamba and Bakonjo rebels effectively control much of the hinterland. "King" Mukirane still holds sway over the Ruwenzori valleys near the Congo border. At the insistence of the central government, the Toro government established a Ministry of Local Government and awarded this portfolio along with a second to the dissident faction. But unfortunately the portfolios were awarded to tribesmen regarded as quislings by their fellow nationals. Instead of reconciliation, the appointment brought renewed violence including the burning of the home of one of the newly appointed ministers. Sporadic and swift attacks in the dead of night upon uneasy Batoro farmers continues. The rebels grew so bold in November of 1963 as to stage an attack on a Batoro village only a few miles from Fort Portal—the capital and major town of the kingdom. More than forty homes were destroyed and at least three Batoro killed before the security forces arrived at the scene and dispersed the rebels.

Uganda can ill afford the extraordinary cost that this continual security problem poses. The issue is a constant source of partisan politics and a ready indicator to other dissident ethnic minorities and factions that rebellion is possible. Only the future can tell what the consequences of this and the lost counties controversies will be for central-local relations and for the future of the new nation.

Sanctions and Coercion

The judicial system in Bunyoro and in other Bantu kingdom states more closely approximates the British model than any other single aspect of the traditional local political system. Sanctioned behavior amongst the Banyoro was explicit, and the norms, though unwritten, were well known, as were the degree and form of coercion arising from deviation. The style and degree of coercion were clearly related to, and measured by, the nature of the deviation. In the diffuse social and political system of the Iteso, however, adjudication more closely resembled simple arbitration, for the extended Iteso family heads, unlike the king and chiefs of Bunyoro, possessed neither the capacity nor the authority to apply public coercion. Remedial action depended more upon the relationship of the litigants and the peculiar nature of the situation than upon explicit and universal laws.

The profusion of tribes in Bukedi and the parochialism of the Iteso local political units has precluded the evolution of a uniform code of customary law. The development of a districtwide judicial system paralleling the local government hierarchy, plus the interjection of Uganda law and specialized district council bylaws, has tended to render the structure of sanctions and coercion problematically diffuse. Because of the emergence of new norms and the presence of conflicting traditional customary laws, local judges are in possession of a wide range of alternative definitions of what is sanctioned behavior. As might be expected, this situation has given rise to frequent cases of judicial irresponsibility. On the other hand, the Ugandan has adapted more quickly to a modern judiciary than he has to other aspects of the modern local government. The relatively close resemblance of traditional judicial systems to the British model and an apparent capacity for rapid assimilation of the techniques of Western adjudication have rendered transition in this area less difficult.

Under certain conditions traditional problems persist, but have lost their uniquely local character and have become districtwide, while the traditional structures, with respect to such problems, often remain parochial. However, the Western-based judicial system cannot cope with a number of these traditional problems. In response to situations of this nature, an unofficial structure of sanction and coercion often emerges to cope with problems that are neither completely traditional nor modern.

Resource Procurement and Allocation

In Western local political systems, a money economy is taken for granted; resources designed to enable persons in positions of authority to cope with local problems of order and integration are obtained primarily from a levy on the members of the political community, from charges for services rendered, and from grants-in-aid received from a more inclusive political system. The resources thus procured are allocated according to the decisions reached by the constituted local decision-makers within the limitations posed by the delegation of authority from the center, and with reference to their assessment of local problems and needs.

The traditional structure of resource procurement and allocation in the kingdom of Bunyoro, was not based upon monetary exchange. However, the bureaucratic manner in which taxes in the form of cattle, beer, and labor were levied and collected resembled the Western model more closely than did the system in Teso or Bukedi. In Bunyoro, local resources were collected by specialists responsible to the king; specified amounts were retained at each level in the hierarchy and a considerable portion of the procured resources were allocated to the monarch. As in the Western model, a portion of the resources were expended to support the bureaucracy while the remainder was allocated in the public interest as determined by the authority hierarchy and its specialist advisors.

Resource procurement and allocation among the Iteso, however, was largely a family affair and existed as an integral part of diffusely defined kinship and age-grade obligations. Authority was exercised on such a small scale and over so few people, that the authority role carriers did not require special compensation for the exercise of their duties over and above the informal sharing of food and drink. But among the slightly more highly organized Padhola there were exact rules for the allocation to clan leaders and to ad hoc specialists of portions of wild game, crops, and booty.[22]

The British model, based upon a money economy and the concept that the provision of social services is the primary purpose of local government, has been superimposed alike over the kingdom of Bunyoro and the districts of Teso and Bukedi. Where a heritage of organized resource procurement on a large scale did not exist, the African has only reluctantly accepted the necessity of parting with a portion of his new-found wealth for purposes that often are perceived only dimly or that seem relatively far removed.

A subsistence economy places a high premium upon the land, and the allocation of land was a most important responsibility of all traditional local political systems. In Bunyoro, this allocation and the political authority which accompanied it bear a striking resemblance to the classical institutions of feudalism. The land belonged, in theory, to the king and it was his to allocate as he saw fit. This allocation carried with it a grant of authority over the cultivators residing on the land.

In Teso District, however, the land was perceived to belong to the members of the extended family, both living and dead. A consequence of British rule and the adoption of a cash economy has been a change in the use of the land. Cash crops have been introduced and were encouraged initially as a means of introducing a monetary exchange capable of facilitating the collection of revenue. Population pressures arising from a lowered mortality rate, the preclusion of large-scale migration, and the increased values accruing to productive cropland, have tended to strain traditional concepts of land procurement, allocation, and usage.[23] In order to render land usage and tenure more appropriate to the necessities of a cash crop economy and a rising population, the British sought to introduce Western principles of land usage and ownership. In Bunyoro, where authority over the land traditionally rested with the king, this proposed change has met with relatively little opposition. In Teso and Bukedi, however, where the land is more densely settled and where tradition assumes that land is a birthright and cannot be bought or sold, the proposals were received with antagonism bordering upon violence.

The relationship of land allocation to resource procurement can be seen in a contrast of American and English local revenue systems as well. In England individual ownership is exceptional, while leasehold interests in the land, and tenant occupation are more common. As the role of occupant and owner is more likely to coincide in the United States, the value of property has come to be an important measure of the individual's liability for local taxes. In England, on the other hand, the occupant, as contrasted to the owner, is generally liable for a levy based not upon the market value of the property, but rather upon its rental worth.

An Approach to a Typology of Local Political Systems

In the material presented above a number of environmental and social factors have been examined with the view that there exists a correlation between these factors and the structures of a given local political system. It has been suggested that when certain conditions prevail the local political system, with respect to the five structures employed in this study, will tend to assume a distinctive pattern. The typology of local political systems which has grown out of these observations is presented below. It should be regarded as experimental and indicative of the directions that future research and analysis might take.

In a recent publication the noted British anthropologist, I. Schapera, developed a typology and transitional thesis based primarily upon changes in the method of food production.[24] Certainly alterations in the pattern of food production are important to an understanding of structural change in primitive societies. An explanation of organizational variation in the political system on the basis of changes in the manner of food production subsumes a number of other important variables while overemphasizing a single factor.

Gabriel Almond, by proposing a matrix composed of three sets of factors, e.g., functions, structures, and styles of performance, has proposed a more sophisticated typology.[25] It is quite evident, however, that much more sufficient data is needed to develop a matrix of this sort; but it is possible, by lowering the level of generalization, to seek to apply the data at hand to formulate a typology of local political systems. The typology advanced here rests upon a combination of the three major sets of variables employed in this approach: functions, structures, and conditioning factors.

Findings, to this point, suggest the feasibility of identifying types of local political systems, with each style tending to correlate with a rather distinctive patterning of the noted conditioning factors. The three types of local political systems to which it is thought all empirical systems more or less approximate are: predominantly segmented local political systems; predominantly spatial local political systems; and predominantly functional local political systems.

The Predominantly Segmented Local Political System

Kinship, as a form of social organization, is not without importance, even in the local political systems of relatively highly developed Western societies. However, it is both more pervasive and more significant in primitive cultures. Societies organized primarily on kinship, or on the basis of other small-scale social segments, tend to exist in relatively inaccessible regions which are often geographically isolated from societies politically organized primarily in terms of space or function. The members of a segmented local political system are inclined toward a mixed or a subsistence hunting and herding economy. The rigors of migratory warfare, hunting, and the preservation of the herd encourage little role differentiation other than that based upon generation. Small-scale kinship association (generally in the form of localized lineages or extended families), in conjunction with age-grade organization, predominate over other solidarity forms. As the roles to be assigned are few and unspecialized, authority and responsibility are diffusely allocated.

The decisional mechanism, whereby authority and responsibility are allocated over the members of the community, is organized, in the first instance, in terms of biological (real or fictional) relatedness. The territorial unit which, along with kinship, establishes the boundaries within which authority and responsibility are allocated is not precisely defined. Authority is exercised diffusely over relatively few people by kinship, age-grade and other segment leaders. Little if any social status distinctions exist. However, social mobility is inflexible and determined by customary law. Law is not rationally legislated but is derived from custom which in turn is related to the supernatural.

Predominantly political roles are not specified and authority wielders are recruited on the basis of age and kinship. Membership in the system similarly depends upon real or fictional biological relatedness, and on other small-scale segments such as age-grades and secret cults.

The segmented local political system is not formally accountable to larger-scale territorially based units although localized kinship and other segments may be accountable to somewhat more inclusive groupings of a related nature.

Member obligation is diffusely owed to a wide range of individuals, both living and dead, and little distinction is made between office and office holder. The little differential allocation of authority and responsibility that exists in this relatively equalitarian society is legitimatized in terms of nonrational criteria.

There is a predominance of norms directly related (though not necessarily rationally perceived as to the relationship of means to ends) to the physical maintenance of the members and their livestock and to the continued integration of the kinship unit. Sanctions are diffuse and are designed to compensate rather than to award or deprive, while forms of coercion are flexible, informal, and situational.

The limited and diffuse authority does not require specialized means for procuring and allocating local resources either to compensate the authority figures or to provide a wide range of local services. Inheritance, marriage, and warfare account for the greater part of the limited procurement and allocation of resources for the purposes of maintaining local integration and order.

The Predominantly Spatial Local Political System

The allocation of authority and responsibility over a group of people primarily on the basis that they share a common territory is a more universal phenomenon in the twentieth century than that depending primarily on association in terms of social segment. Although kinship, and to a lesser extent age-grade organization, continue to play a significant role, it is apparent that the trend in Africa is toward spatially oriented political organization. In traditional Uganda, the Banyoro and other kingdom-state peoples were politically organized on a predominantly territorial basis, while in Teso and in many other non-Bantu areas, kinship and age-grade organization prevailed.

As the community becomes stabilized, it tends to increase in population. The significance of kinship to the maintenance of local order and integration recedes as the population becomes larger and more diversified through the incorporation of biologically unrelated members, or as Tonnies has noted:

> A common relation to the soil tends to associate people who may be kinsfolk or believe themselves to be such. Neighborhood, the fact that they live together, is the basis of their union . . . the bond of field and soil and living together first takes its place along with, and later more and more supplants, the bond of common ancestry.[26]

A spatial local political system is more likely to exist in rural as opposed to urban areas, but the density of population is somewhat higher than in the regions characterized by the segmented type. More important is the factor of population stability and occupation. With a climate and topography relatively conducive to a subsistence sedentary agriculture, the members of a spatial local political system are permanently settled on relatively precisely demarcated and institutionally allocated land.

Human interaction within the community occurs primarily in terms of residential proximity and solidarity tends to cluster more about "neighborhood" than it is associated with either kinship or specialized function. Most interpersonal relationships continue to be of an intimate and relatively intense nature. However, there begins to evolve relatively large-scale non-face-to-face associations such as representative assemblies and bureaucracies. Such traditional institutions as the tribe are adapted to conform to increased spatial mobility and employed to maintain order and integration in regions far removed from tribal place of origin. A relative profusion of predominantly economic and political roles is accompanied by correspondingly large-scale organization. In contrast to the segmented variety, roles are precisely defined and tend relatively to be allocated on the basis of more universal standards of achievement. The more complex spatial system extends over a larger area or over more people than the segmented variety, and is characterized by a relative specialization of political roles while institutionalized political positions, independent of the person occupying the office, predominate. The increased scope of the economy contributes to migration in search of employment which is both required and enhanced by the fiscal requirements of the spatially defined political system.

Political institutions deliberate and make binding decisions in the first instance over a clearly demarcated territory to which most members of the community attach certain values and symbols.

The constitution of a predominantly spatial local political system is relatively explicit and the government operates within limitations posed both by precise internally and externally derived rules. The allocation of authority over an extended area generally implies a hierarchy of lesser regional authorities, while the considerable psychological and material resources accruing to the numerous territorially responsible authority-role carriers accentuate competition for official positions of influence.

The problems of maintaining local integration and order require a relatively large expenditure of human and physical resources. This, in turn, necessitates a precise system of procuring and allocating resources in such a way as to cope effectively with problems that are of a relatively technical nature. Furthermore, it is necessary that wealth and deference commensurate with their specialized responsibility and authority be allocated to the governing element of the community.

As government, in contrast to other social institutions, assumes more authority over the lives of the members of the community, the structure of consent and accountability becomes correspondingly more elaborate and formally ascertained. Membership is determined by voluntary residence, in contrast to involuntary kinship or other social segment. The relatively large-scale nature of the predominantly spatial local political system precludes the possibility of a single authority figure possessing knowledge and skills sufficient to the effective functioning of the system. Specialists to provide technical information and skills, plus a representative agency to assist in deliberation and to aggregate consensus, are required. The voluntary nature of membership in conjunction with relatively mobile social status endows the individual with considerably more autonomy than he had in a segmented system. A spatial political system is more likely to be legally accountable to progressively larger and more inclusive territorially based polities than is a predominantly segmented system. The accumulation of hoardable wealth, which is more likely to occur in a nonmigrant community, acts to emphasize values associated with material possessions and with the rights of land occupation and use. This in turn provides a base for a relatively sophisticated system of taxation which is required to accumulate the resources necessary to safeguard life and property as competition and conflict for scarce valuables increases.

The Predominantly Functional Local Political System

This study has not dealt with predominantly functional local political systems for two reasons. The nature of political transition in Africa is primarily away from segmented to spatial association, although this is not to say that there do not exist illustrations of the evolution of predominantly functional local political systems. Secondly this work deliberately has concentrated on political transition in the rural areas of Uganda while the predominantly functional style of local government and politics tends to be found in an urban and more highly developed milieu. However, a brief description of the major conditions and corresponding structures of the functional variety are presented in order to complete the model and also to raise some questions about the nature of future developments.

Functional local political systems tend to be located in densely populated metropolitan areas, in highly developed Western cultures as well as in the less developed regions of the world. This is not to suggest that the allocation of authority and responsibility in such cities as Lagos, Nigeria and Birmingham, England is identical. However, it is suggested that the local political system of Lagos resembles more closely that of Birmingham than it does, for example, that of the Padhola village of Senda described in Chapter Six.

A functional local political system coincides with a society characterized by a mobile population engaged in a highly inter-dependent system of production and consumption. Whereas member interaction in a spatially oriented system was said to take place primarily in terms of shared locality, the human interaction requiring the exercise of authority and responsibility in the functional local political system occurs largely in terms of specialized roles, associations, occupational obligations, and shared interests. Solidarity is fragmented and is oriented about a variety of associations reflective of the members' multiple roles and interests.[27] Smaller scale segmented and spatial local political systems combine to provide scope for functional interests and values. Interaction on the basis of shared locality in a functional local political system is characterized by formal, impersonal, and predominantly avoidant behavior. The members of this system, in common with those in a predominantly segmented system, are not inclined to attach emotional values and symbols to a territorially defined local community. Whereas the former emphasize kinship association, the latter are more inclined to identify symbolically either on the basis of specific function or with a more inclusive spatial unit, such as the nation-state.

A functional local political system is characterized by a complex shifting social stratification which coincides with the highly differentiated assignment of roles. Communication and expression, in a segmented local political system, are diffusely associated with the community defined in spatial terms. However, in a functional local political system, expression and communication are not circumscribed by the territorial community, for the interaction and interests of the members are largely in terms of specific functions such as specialized occupation, recreation, and religion that cut across frontiers and boundaries.

All local political systems reflect the general characteristics of the society and culture within which they operate. Authority and responsibility in a predominantly functional local political system are specifically allocated, primarily through a multitude of specialized institutions including local government. The proliferation of associations, not in the first instance concerned with the problems of governing a given locality, has served to establish a web of specialized loci of community influence which, along with local government institutions, constitute the local political system.[28]

The standardization of values, the extra-locality nature of the system of communication and expression, and the dependence of a community's economy on a more extensive system, together serve to circumscribe narrowly the authority exercised by local government and by any other single local institution in a predominantly functional local political system. Not only is responsibility for aspects of local order and integration assumed by predominantly nonpolitical agencies, but more inclusive political systems such as the nation-state and the political party have assumed relatively more responsibility and exercise considerable authority with reference to local problems.[29]

The highly technical nature of the operations which must be

performed to ensure local order where a multitude of roles and institutions compete for limited resources and where culture and population density require the provision of an extensive range of integrative
services, necessitates an elaborate classification of political roles and a
complex system of recruitment.

An analytical typology of local political systems, as briefly outlined above, raises some pertinent questions concerning the nature
of political transition at the local level in highly developed nations as
well as in countries such as Uganda. In the preceding pages concentration has been on the problems of transition from a predominantly
segmented to a predominantly spatial local political system. In the
process of this analysis an attempt was made to determine the relationship between the structures of a local political system at a given
moment to rapidly changing problems of community order and
integration.

Rarely have men everywhere in the world been so uncertain about
the excellence of their existing political systems as they are today.
The search for improved political institutions increases in intensity as
the problems threatening the order and integration of men pile one
upon the other. At the international level, mankind is coming to
recognize the limitations of the "state" as a set of institutionalized
structures capable of coping with nuclear threats to health and bodily
violence—or with the supranational forms of intergroup conflict that
have emerged in the wake of World War II. Within the United States,
for example, there is a growing realization that existing forms of local
government are inadequate, and that the threats to health, welfare, and
safety, as well as to that sense of security deriving from "community,"
are disproportionate to existing, out-moded political structures.
Throughout the emergent two-thirds of the world, the search for
governance—for order and integration—is even more intense and
critical because there the existing forms are even less appropriate; for
the problems with which these forms must cope are changing even
more rapidly than in the West.

This continual process of seeking for those organized means capable
of coping with constantly changing social problems cannot be separated
from the institution of the nation-state. However, it would appear to be
more and more evident that problems of order and integration are
clustering at levels other than the nation-state. The simultaneous
trend toward international organization on the one hand, and regional
and communal organization on the other, may be a preview of the
demise of one style of political organization and the emergence of
another. As to what form that other style might take, it is, of course,
too early to tell. But if the transition is to be as painless as possible, it

is important that to the extent possible a knowledge of the dimensions and directions of the process be obtained.

Africa, which has so often been accused of having contributed nothing to civilization as it experiments simultaneously with new styles of local governance and novel forms of transnational association, may contribute to mankind some desperately needed concepts of political organization which may contribute significantly to the solution of those peculiar problems of order and integration characterizing the latter half of the twentieth century.

APPENDIX:

Methodology

This study was designed to achieve two distinct but interrelated goals: first, to construct a systematic method of comparative local government analysis and research that might contribute to the comparative study in this field; secondly, to analyze the development of local governments and politics in Uganda within this frame of reference.

The greater part of existing methodologies in the field of local government is subjectively oriented toward local government institutions emphasizing their legal relationship to the nation-state system. To devise an approach which might encompass politics and government at the local level, regardless of institutional form, recourse has been had to a structural-functional method.[1]

To employ an explicit method is of itself no guarantee of sound research, but is simply a recognition that a careful selection of tools plus a preliminary survey of the work to be done, more likely than not, will ensure the successful completion of the task as originally conceived. But to clutter the completed structure with the methodological scaffolding requisite to its construction not only serves to detract from its aesthetic qualities, but also is likely to lead the observer to confuse the scaffolding with the completed structure.

There is not evidence that man ever lived in a Hobbesian state of nature, while history testifies to his predilection to collect into groups and establish for himself and his fellows specific and enforceable rules of behavior capable of regulating his inevitable interrelationships. Therefore, it would seem to require little daring to suppose that this tendency for human interaction as well as the necessity to organize and regularize (institutionalize) that interaction is universal in time and space. That some form of organization is required to secure the advantages of association is rarely denied, while generations of political philosophy and controversy have been concerned with the virtues of one form of organization over another.

The postulated universal existence of any phenomena accompanied by an awareness of time and space variation suggests the utility of comparative analysis as a technique conducive to explaining the variation. Comparison, as a method of analysis, is here understood to mean the application of a type of logical inquiry which is devised to draw attention to those elements of the phenomena that are held in common by all of its manifestations, and to identify and explain variations in time and space. A comparative method is used in this work to prove or to disprove propositions about the universal characteristics of cer-

247

tain environmental and social factors with the intent of making worthwhile generalizations about aspects of organized social behavior.

This study, in the first instance then, is concerned with a certain aspect of social organization to which we have attached the label "local political system." A local political system for our purposes is the totality of organized human activity which through the allocation of authority and responsibility is directed toward, or serves to maintain order and integration amongst a people on the basis of their sharing a common spatial locality. Viewed in this manner, the local political system can be regarded as an "agent" of a people of a given locality in so far as it acts in the name of the members of the locality as a corporate unit and is assigned the task of ultimately ensuring that order be kept and that a level of integration be maintained sufficient to ensure the continued existence of the system. By concentrating on one aspect of social action rather than on a particular political institution, political analysis is not limited to the legal corporation but can extend to areas delimited on the basis of a sense of shared community as well. This flexibility is important in treating with those regions where significant political organization and activity does not always coincide with legally constituted local government areas.

The most general objective of any local political system, as developed for the purposes of this study, is termed the maintenance of locality order and locality integration.[2] It is important at the outset to note that the maintenance of order and integration within a given locality may not initially be achieved as a direct consequence of organized political activity; a distinctive feature of political organization as contrasted to other systems of social action is important in this respect. A political system is a latent system of action. Whereas nonpolitical systems of social action seek to achieve specific goals relative to the purposes for which they are organized, the range of involvement of a local political system is more diffuse for it takes its cue to action from the effect of the activity of other organizations, individuals, and systems upon locality order and integration.

A desirable state of affairs in any area organized on the basis of shared locality is the maintenance of the security of the lives and property of the members of that locality. It is with this fundamental assumption in mind that the maintenance of "order" is postulated as one of the two most basic functions of any local political system.[3]

The second general function postulated is that of "locality integration." A fundamental distinction between problems of control or order and those of integration or conciliation is not novel and has been made by a number of pioneering scholars who in the process inspired much of the subsequent scholarship in this area. Ferdinand Tonnies, for example, contrasts the elements of material advantage and assistance to the element of binding social will which works on and controls the individual will.[4] Talcott Parsons contrasts negative problems which define the limits of individual behavior to institutionalization of positively integrative functions of the social system treated as a collectivity.[5]

The function of integration as employed here refers to those territorially organized activities controlling the incidence of individual and group deviation from locality norms. The general concept is broken down into two aspects—socialization and conflict resolution. The assumption underlying this distinction is that local political organization and activity serve to inculcate the new members of a locality (youth and immigrants) with the values and norms of that locality. This, of course, is the reverse side of the Weberian coin of compulsion. A locality wherein the members are unaware or indifferent to the community values and norms would be malintegrated, and subsequent deviation from the norms would necessitate the exercise of compulsion. But to concentrate analysis upon compulsion and coercion to the exclusion of socialization is to view but one side of the coin. Legally constituted local governments are everywhere concerned with the provision of education. Other local institutions are also involved in instructing the youth in the do's and don't's of the locality.

Conflict is inherent in society and though the philosophical explanations of why this is so are interesting and even potentially relevant to the study, the issue is but rather, simply to work from the assumption that conflict—latent and manifest—is a universal characteristic of society and that social organization generally, and political organization in particular, exist, in part, to control this human tendency.

Thus, it is assumed that those activities of the local political system directed (consciously or unconsciously) toward reconciling interpersonal and intergroup conflict in the locality are an important part of the function of locality integration. Parsons' view of this requirement supports this position: a "fundamental problem of integration concerns the mutual adjustment of these units or sub-systems from the point of view of their contribution to effective functioning of the system as a whole."[6]

A functional approach to local political systems is also useful to mark the boundaries of the inquiry. Max Weber set the tone for treating political organization as means: "It is not possible to define a political corporate group including the state, in terms of the end to which its corporate action is devoted. . . . Thus it is possible to define the 'political' character of a corporate group only in terms of the means peculiar to it. . . ."[7] The "means" of political action which sets it off from other types of activity according to Weber, is the "use of force." The state, he maintained, is the corporate entity possessed of a monopoly over the instruments and legitimate use of physical violence and compulsion in society. In contrast to this relative emphasis on the exercise of power and compulsion, other scholars have sought to further circumscribe the phenomena by regarding as political, only the *territorially* based legitimate exercise of power or compulsion. This distinction is important for it bears upon the controversy as to whether some traditional African societies are organized on the basis of shared territory or alternatively on the principle of kinship or other form of nonspatial association. However, we proceed from the assumption that the exercise of authority, even when it is carried out primarily in the name of, or as a consequence of, kinship or other segmental association, in some degree is related to territoriality. And though this assumption complicates analysis of tribal political organization, this difficulty is more than compensated for by its delineation of fairly precise lines of inquiry.

The related assumption which postulates functions toward which organized local political activity is directed also requires some preliminary elaboration if not justification. Earlier generations of political scientists were not adverse to postulating ends or purposes toward which political organization was ultimately directed; and even though this "purposeful" approach tended to interject a subjective element of what "ought" to be rather than what in fact was, it nonetheless did contribute to systematic and comparative studies of delineated sets of political means—e.g., those employed with reference to gaining the a priori postulated ends or purposes. It is sometimes useful for analytical purposes to treat certain highly generalized states of affairs as functions toward which political organization and behavior is directed. This is not meant to infer that the generalized "end" or "purpose" as the concept is employed here must be regarded as either desirable or concrete, nor does it require that political organizations be judged on how and to what extent they achieve these ends.

The major purpose, however, is not a concentration on comparison of functions. The functional approach is employed as a tool analytically to manipulate political systems to assist in the identification of concrete locality problems of order and integration and to contrast the political cultures of Uganda's constituent localities.

Having postulated the generalized functions of any local political system toward which the inquiry is directed, it is possible to systematically and comparatively examine the political life and political evolution of selected Uganda localities. A local political system, if it is to attempt to cope with problems of locality order and integration, must provide for organization directed toward the solution of such problems whenever they arise or whenever they cease to be adequately provided for by the "nonpolitical" elements of the social system. There exist, of necessity, organized forms of ultimate authority over and responsibility for the regulation of disintegrative or disorderly behavior within the locality—however it may be defined. Institutions whose primary purposes are not political in a certain place or time may serve as the concrete context within which those aspects of social activity here labeled political, take place. It is important to bear in mind that the aspect of organized social activity with which we are concerned, irrespective of the institutional units within which that activity is exercised, is the allocation of authority and responsibility in the name of the locality. For example, if in a certain locality the ultimate responsibility for maintaining certain aspects of locality integration or order is undertaken by a clan or a lineage, then the task is to seek to establish the manner in which those persons responsible for this activity in the clan or lineage, go about their jobs.

The phenomena we are seeking to compare are variations from time to time and from place to place in the organized way in which various local political systems seek to accomplish or to maintain locality order and integration. So as to ensure that comparison is objective and not a captive of one's subjective culture or training, it is necessary to abstract the most general means or structures which are thought to be applicable to all local political systems. Structures are used as objective guides; for though functions direct attention to analytical problem areas, it is the structures that direct attention to the political activity that is undertaken with reference to those problems.

The five structures (forms of organized activity) which are employed to analyze the local political systems in selected regions of Uganda are: 1) structure of authoritative decision-making, 2) structure of recruitment and role definition, 3) structure of accountability and consent, 4) structure of sanction and coercion, 5) structure of resource procurement and allocation.[8]

If comparison is to yield more than ad hoc contrasts, it is necessary that it be employed to detect patterns of variation. For example, it is thought that certain social and environmental factors tend to condition the style of a given local political system and therefore affect the manner and extent to which it contributes to national development and unity. The effect of geography, topography, climate and demography upon the nature of the problems that the residents of a given locality must collectively cope with, of course, are readily recognized.

As man's capacity to control his human environment improves, these conditions are relatively less significant—while such factors as history and culture, differentiation and assignment of roles, varying economic systems, differing patterns of solidarity and communication, values and authority assume proportionately greater importance.

Notes

NOTES TO CHAPTER ONE

INTRODUCTION

1. Great Britain, *Colonial Office Dispatch from the Secretary of State for the Colonies to the Governors of the African Territories*, February 25, 1947.
2. A few works directly concerned with local government have appeared in recent years and have helped to fill this need. However, studies of local political systems have tended to be primarily anthropological, treating only incidentally with modern local government and politics, or primarily structural with a corresponding emphasis on legal description of local government institutions. Only a few have sought to combine these approaches. Among the best are Lloyd A. Fallers, *Bantu Bureaucracy* (Cambridge: W. Heffer and Sons, 1956) and Henry Fosbrooke and Roland Young, *Smoke in the Hills* (Evanston: Northwestern University Press, 1960); while Isaac Schapera, *Government and Politics in Tribal Societies* (London: Watts, 1956) deals primarily with traditional tribal political systems. Both L. Gray Cowan's *Local Government in West Africa* (New York: Columbia University Press, 1958) and N. U. Akpan's *Epitaph to Indirect Rule* (London: Cassell, 1956) are primarily descriptive of the legal and institutional changes in African local government.

NOTES TO CHAPTER TWO

BACKGROUND TO UGANDA

1. George Homans, *English Villagers of the Thirteenth Century* (Cambridge: Harvard University Press, 1941), p. 12.
2. For more comprehensive data on the physical features of Uganda see H. B. Thomas and Robert Scott, *Uganda* (London: Oxford University Press, 1935) and E. W. Russell (ed.), *The Natural Resources of East Africa* (Nairobi: East African Literature Bureau, 1962).
3. Homans, *op. cit.*, p. 27.
4. Aidan W. Southall and P. C. W. Gutkind, *Townsmen in the Making* (East African Studies No. 9, Kampala: East African Institute of Social Research, 1956), p. 8.
5. Interview with a Madi university student, Moyo, West Nile, December 20, 1956.
6. Both Fallers and Southall approach the ethnographic question in this light. Fallers, *op. cit.*, pp. 23-26. Aidan W. Southall, *Alur Society* (Cambridge, England: W. Heffer and Sons, Ltd., 1956). Also see J. D. Middleton (ed.), *Tribes Without Rulers* (London: Routledge and Kegan Paul, 1955).
7. Fallers, *op. cit.*, p. 23. Fallers uses this criteria as distinction between Bantu and non-Bantu.
8. For an excellent and analytical treatment of the political system of Buganda and its response to changing conditions, the Protectorate government and other regions of Uganda, see David E. Apter, *The Political Kingdom in Uganda* (Princeton: Princeton University Press, 1961).
9. Uganda Protectorate, *The Laws of the Uganda Protectorate*, 1936, Vol. VI, pp. 1373-1411.

10. At the turn of the century, it even appeared as if the large kingdom of Ankole would also be placed under the suzerainty of the Kabaka of Buganda. See D. A. Low, "Establishment of British Administration: Two Examples from Uganda 1900-1901," (A paper read at the Conference of the East African Institute of Social Research, Kampala, July 7, 1956), p. 2.

For an excellent account of the development of the relationship between the Colonial government and Buganda see D. A. Low and R. Cranford Pratt, *Buganda and British Overrule 1900-1955* (London: Oxford University Press, 1960).

11. D. A. Low, *Political Parties in Uganda 1949-62* (University of London, London: The Athlone Press, 1962), p. 29. Also see Apter, *The Political Kingdom in Uganda, op. cit.*, especially chap. 14.

12. For a thorough and excellent study of Buganda government and politics, see Apter, *The Political Kingdom in Uganda, op. cit.*

13. In February 1960, for example, a large meeting was called in Kampala to discuss ways of modernizing the clan system of Buganda. *Uganda Argus*, February 5, 1960, p. 1.

14. Max Weber, *Essays in Sociology*, H. H. Gerth and C. Wright Mills, trans. (London: Kegan Paul, Trench, Trubner and Co., 1947), p. 204.

15. International Bank for Reconstruction and Development, *The Economic Development of Uganda* (World Bank Report) (Baltimore: Johns Hopkins Press, 1962), p. 15.

16. *Ibid.*, p. 80.

17. Although Uganda's per capita gross domestic cash product is slightly lower than Kenya's, the cash return to the African is probably higher. See H. W. Ord, "The Growth of Money Incomes in East Africa," *East African Economics Review* (June 1962), pp. 41-47.

18. Government of Uganda, *Uganda the Background to Investment* (Entebbe: Government Printer, 1962), p. 9.

19. 1960/61 was a year of unusually heavy rainfall with disastrous effects on agriculture. Nonetheless the 1962/63 production amounted to only 353,000 bales.

20. *Uganda the Background to Investment, op. cit.*, p. 55.

21. T. G. Watson, "Progress in Agriculture," Supplement to the *London Times* (Winter, 1956), p. 27.

22. World Bank Report, *op. cit.*, p. 231.

23. Walter Elkan, *An African Labor Force* (East African Studies No. 7, Kampala: East African Institute of Social Research, 1956), p. 16.

24. *Uganda Argus*, April 12, 1961, p. 1.

25. *Report of the Constitutional Committee 1959* (Wild Report) (Entebbe: Government Printer); *Report of the Uganda Relationships Commission 1961* (Munster Report) (Entebbe: Government Printer).

26. Uganda Constitution, chap. 1, par. 2.

27. Thomas and Scott, *op. cit.*, p. 67.

28. Uganda Protectorate, Bunyoro District Native Government Estimates, 1961/62.

29. For an excellent study of this aspect of the Colonial Service see Robert Heussler, *Yesterday's Rulers* (Syracuse: Syracuse University Press, 1963).

NOTES TO CHAPTER THREE
EVOLUTION OF LOCAL GOVERNMENT AND POLITICS

1. See Lord Lugard, *The Dual Mandate in British Tropical Africa* (Edinburgh: William Blackwood and Sons, 1922).

2. Donald Cameron, *The Principles of Native Administration and their Application* (Lagos, Nigeria: Government Printer, 1934), p. 1.

3. Uganda Protectorate, *An Ordinance to Make Provision for the Powers and Duties of African Chiefs and for the Enforcement of African Authority* (Native Authority Ordinance), chap. 72, Laws of Uganda.

4. *Ibid.*, par. 3.

5. *Ibid.*, par. 7.

6. *Ibid.*, par. 7, sec. A.

7. Uganda Protectorate, *The Uganda Agreement—1900*, Vol. VI (1936), pp. 1373-1411, Laws of Uganda.

8. Uganda Protectorate, Native Authority Ordinance, par. 7.

9. Lukiko is a Luganda term and refers to a council of advisors.

10. In Buganda the batongole possessed authority because of their ownership or control of land. In the Eastern Province there existed no landed squirocracy. Thus, in Buganda today the lowest level of official chief is the miruka chief while in the Eastern Province (except Busoga) the batongole chief is an official and salaried chief.

11. Uganda Protectorate, *An Ordinance Relating to the Amendment of Native Law*, Legal Notice No. 613 of 1919, *Uganda Official Gazette.*

12. Great Britain, *Colonial Office Dispatch from the Secretary of State for the Colonies to the Governors of the African Territories, op. cit.*

13. *Ibid.*

14. Uganda Protectorate, *An Ordinance to Define the Composition of African Local Governments and to Make Provisions for the Reconstitution of African Councils Throughout the Protectorate* (Local Government Ordinance of 1949), chap. 74, Laws of Uganda.

15. *Ibid.*, par. 4, art. 1. This refers to the delegation of appointive power to the Provincial and District Commissioners and in certain cases to the native rulers of the kingdom states.

16. *Ibid.*, par. 4, art. 2.

17. C. A. G. Wallis, *Report of an Inquiry into African Local Government in the Protectorate of Uganda* (Wallis Report) (Entebbe: Government Printer, 1953).

18. Uganda Protectorate, *District Administration (District Councils) Ordinance of 1955.* This ordinance does not apply to Buganda.

19. Uganda Protectorate, *Local Government Ordinance of 1949*, par. 3.

20. Uganda Protectorate, *District Administration (District Councils) Ordinance of 1955*, par. 3, sec. 1.

21. Uganda Protectorate, *District Administration (District Councils) Ordinance of 1955*, part IX, par. 44.

22. *Ibid.*, part II, sec. 22, par. 1.

23. See the *Report of the Uganda Relationships Commission 1961; Report of the Constitutional Committee 1959; Report of the Uganda Constitutional Conference 1961; Uganda (Constitution) Order and Council, 1962; Uganda (Independence) Order and Council, 1962.*

24. Constitution of Uganda 1962, chap. 8, part I, par. 75.

25. Par. 79, sec. 1, 2, 3 of the Constitution of Uganda. The Constitution stipulates that a commission of inquiry must first investigate and recommend any unilateral action by the central government.

26. Uganda Constitution, chap. 8, par. 88, sec. 1.

27. Chap. 12, sec. 5.

28. The Administrations (Western Kingdoms and Busoga) Act, 1963, part 10, chap. 74.

29. *Ibid.*, chap. 74.

30. *Ibid.*, chap. 74 (no. 4).

31. Unless otherwise dissolved the Kingdom Assemblies sit for five years whereas the District Councils sit for four years.

32. This is particularly true in the case of farm schools, rural trade schools and home craft centers under the first eight years of education.

33. This estimate must be qualified by the fact that many Africans are members of more than one council.

34. The only exception to this provision is legislation on those few ceremonial and customary matters falling within the exclusive powers of the federal states.

35. Local Administration Ordinance 1962, act VII, par. 41, sec. 6; Administrations (Western Kingdoms and Busoga) Act, part VII, par. 34, sec. 6.

36. The resolutions derived from lower councils are theoretically passed on up and acted upon by the respective higher councils, the assumption being that the will and wants of the people thus find their way to the District Council and assume the form of bylaws and policy. If it is recalled that it is the chief who must administer local government policy, his interests in the content of such resolutions is obvious.

37. In practice, officials in English local government often do assume the role of local authority executives but in the name of and with prior approval of the council.

38. W. J. M. MacKenzie, "The Conventions of Local Government," *Public Administration* (Winter, 1951), pp. 348-49.

39. Uganda Protectorate, *African Local Government Ordinance, 1949; District Administration Ordinance, 1955* (District Councils).

40. Whereas earlier legislation prohibited the election of central government civil servants, eligibility for local councils is based upon that of the national assembly as specified in the Uganda Constitution and does not preclude the civil servants from standing.

41. Sidney and Beatrice Webb, *The Parish and the County* (Vol. I, *English Local Government from the Revolution to the Municipal Corporations Act,* London: Longmans, 1908), pp. 218 and 419.

42. Uganda Protectorate, Native Court's Ordinance, Legal Notice No. 3 of 1940, chap. 76, par. 10.

43. *Ibid.*, chap. 76, par. 11. (It is this provision that empowers the chief to adjudicate violations of rules previously laid down and executed by himself under the terms of the Native Authority Ordinance.)

44. The local and national courts currently are undergoing a process of amalgamation.

45. Supplement to the *Uganda Official Gazette*, LX, February 15, 1962, LN 12 of 1962.

46. Uganda Protectorate, *An Ordinance to Make Better Provision for the Constitution of African Courts and for the Administration of Justice by Such Courts* (African Courts Ordinance, 1956).

47. *Ibid.*, par. 12.

48. Uganda Protectorate, Teso District Annual Report, 1919, (District Archives).

49. Uganda Protectorate, *Native Administrations Tax Ordinance 1938,* Legal Notice No. 16 of 1938, *Uganda Official Gazette.*

50. Uganda Protectorate, District Annual Report, 1940, 1955, 1956.

51. Local graduation may take one of two forms. In the simple form, which is used in Uganda, the rich are assessed more than the poor but on an arithmetical as opposed to geometrical progression. In 1960 African local governments collected nearly 2.4 million pounds from the graduated tax—only a million less than the central government derived from the income tax.

NOTES TO CHAPTER FOUR

BUNYORO-KITARA: FROM EMPIRE TO DISTRICT

1. Bunyoro is the state, Munyoro (singular) and Banyoro (plural) the people, and Runyoro the language.

2. John H. M. Beattie, "The Banyoro—a Social Study of an Interlacustrine Bantu People" (unpublished doctoral dissertation, Oxford University, 1956), p. 29. Also see John H. M. Beattie, *Bunyoro, an African Kingdom* (New York: Holt, Rinehart and Winston, 1960).

3. There are about 11,000 Lugbara and 4,000 Congo tribesmen living in Bunyoro.

4. Beattie, "The Banyoro—a Social Study of an Interlacustrine Bantu People," *op. cit.*, p. 30.

5. John Roscoe, *The Bakitara* (Cambridge: Cambridge University Press, 1923), p. 22.

6. Roscoe, *op. cit.*, p. 23.

7. *Ibid.*, pp. 87-88.

8. The history which follows is derived from a variety of sources. Much of the data was provided verbally by the present Omukama.

9. It was customary among the interlacustrine kingdoms that the sons of the deceased king, in alliance with their respective factions, would fight for the succession. During this period near anarchy would prevail which posed an ideal time for alert enemies to invade the kingdom.

10. The sequence of events which follows is largely taken from material prepared by the present Omukama of Bunyoro, Sir Tito Winyi, IV. Some of it is included in his pamphlet, *The Bunyoro's Claim of Their Lost Land* (Hoima: March 8, 1948).

11. Letter from the Omukama of Bunyoro-Kitara to the Honorable Minister of Local Government, January 19, 1957, p. 1.

12. Winyi, *op. cit.*, p. 15.

13. *Report of the Commission of Privy Councillors on a Dispute Between Buganda and Bunyoro* (CMND. 1717), May, 1962, p. 7.

14. Uganda Government Secretariat, "The Lost Counties of Bunyoro," no date shown.

15. *Report of the Uganda Relationships Committee, 1961* (Entebbe: Government Printer), p. 89.

16. *Ibid.*, p. 90.

17. *Report of the Commission of Privy Councillors on a Dispute Between Buganda and Bunyoro, op. cit.*, p. 9.

18. *Ibid.*, p. 21.

19. *Ibid.,* p. 20.

20. *Report of the Uganda Independence Conference, 1962* (Entebbe: Government Printer, 1962), p. 17.

21. *Ibid.*

22. *Kenya Daily Nation,* August 14, 1962.

23. Uganda (Independence) Order in Council, 1962, sec. 26.

24. He was subsequently released.

25. District Annual Report, 1955 and 1961.

26. Beattie, "The Banyoro—a Social Study of an Interlacustrine Bantu People," *op. cit.,* p. 64.

27. "Bunyoro District Book" Headquarters District Administration, Bunyoro District.

28. Uganda Protectorate, 1961 Statistical Abstract.

29. Roscoe, *op. cit.,* p. 13.

30. William Hart, *Introduction to the Law of Local Government and Administration* (5th ed., London: Butterworth, 1952), p. 610.

31. The data on blood brotherhood was largely provided by the first woman district councillor in Bunyoro, Sara (Nyendwoha) Ntiro.

32. Winyi, *op. cit.,* p. 4.

33. Roscoe, *op. cit.,* pp. 52-53.

34. See K. W. (Omukama of Bunyoro) "The Procedure in Accession to the Throne of a Nominated King in the Kingdom of Bunyoro-Kitara," *The Uganda Journal* (May 1937), pp. 289-99.

35. *Ibid.*

36. *Ibid.,* p. 292.

37. A new palace was completed in 1963.

38. Roscoe, *op. cit.,* p. 61.

39. Lord Hailey, *Native Administration in the British African Territories,* (London, 1950), part I, p. 46.

40. Uganda Protectorate, *Bunyoro Agreement, 1955* (Entebbe: Government Printer), p. 1.

41. Uganda Protectorate, *The Bunyoro Agreement, 1933,* Legal Notice No. 150 of 1933, Laws of Uganda, 1933, par. 12.

42. Uganda Protectorate, Bunyoro District File, Adm. 20, II, par. 14.

43. Lord Hailey, *op. cit.,* p. 52.

44. Uganda Protectorate, *An Ordinance to Define the Composition of African Local Governments and to Make Provisions for the Reconstitution of African Councils Throughout the Protectorate,* Legal Notice 2 of 1949, Laws of Uganda. Also see *The Bunyoro Rukurato Regulations 1955,* Legal Notice 167 of 1959, Laws of Uganda.

45. Uganda Protectorate, Bunyoro District File, Adm. 20, II, par. 14.

46. If this is an example of Colonial Office inefficiency, we should not conclude that it is capable of nothing more for shortly after the Omukama signed the new agreement he journeyed to England where Queen Elizabeth conferred a knighthood upon him.

47. The Omukama is entitled to appoint the following members of his official household: Owekitinisa Nyina Omukana—the Mother of the Omukama; Owekitinisa Kalyata—the official sister of the Omukama; Owekitinisa Okwiri—the head of the Babito; Mugema—Keeper of the Royal Tombs; the Nyakakuma—official custodian of the Royal Regalia; and twelve monarchical heads of the Bikwato or hereditary keepers of the regalia. Schedule Three to the Uganda Constitution, part 1.

48. Except for judicial affairs and policies Bunyoro is divided into four counties (sazas), twenty sub-counties (gombololas), sixty-nine parishes (miruka), and 169 villages (bakunyu), presided over by a corresponding hierarchy of chiefs.

49. Meetings, ideally, must be held every second month. The purpose of a meeting is generally to: (a) meet the District Commissioner when he tours the gombolola; (b) meet with and listen to central government departmental officers, encourage agricultural productivity, etc.; (c) meet with reference to the graduated tax; (d) greet visitors to the district; (e) on occasion, at the decision of the sub-county chief, to consider local problems either initiated by the chief or referred from higher councils.

50. Letter from the Assistant Katikiro to the county chiefs of Bunyoro, November 22, 1949. Also miscellaneous unclassified papers from the Bunyoro District Archives.

51. It is worth noting that the federal kingdom of Buganda has its own Ministry of Local Government.

52. Western Kingdoms and Busoga Act, 1963, part VI, par. 31. Similar powers were granted in the 1956 Bunyoro-Kitara Regulations.

53. Uganda Protectorate, Bunyoro District, Rukurato Agenda, June 25, 1951, Bunyoro District Files, Item 15, File Adm. 21.

54. Letter from three women of Bunyoro District to the District Commissioner. Bunyoro, January 26, 1955, File "Bujenje Complaints and Petitions," Bunyoro District Files.

55. Uganda Protectorate, Bunyoro District Annual Report, 1933, Bunyoro District Archives.

56. The description is with reference to a village chief prior to independence. However, there have been only minor changes in this respect.

57. By 1963 this had risen to £35.

58. By 1963 this had risen to £77.

59. After 1963 the chiefs will be precluded from membership.

60. The description is based primarily on research conducted in 1956. However, there has been little change.

61. In 1956, for example, 241 elephants providing the people with one and one-half million pounds of meat valued at £80,000 were shot. In 1961 the number was 611 providing meat valued at approximately £190,000, an amount greater than total recurrent local revenue. District Commissioner's speech to the Rukurato, February 1957, District Annual Report 1961.

62. As translated by a council member.

63. Before the announcement of self-government for Tanganyika and the recent turn of events in Kenya, there was a dominant fear throughout Uganda of forced union based on a number of earlier attempts at federation. Some Uganda Africans still fear that federation would threaten the traditional monarchies and anti-federation sentiment is particularly strong in Buganda.

64. The head of the Princes and the keeper of the royal tombs.

65. The clan categories are based upon Roscoe's delineation, *op. cit.*, p. 23. The data was obtained through interviews and a survey of Rukurato members.

66. The relatives include father, brother, grandfather, father-in-law, and brother-in-law.

67. Bunyoro District File Misc.

68. Letter from E. Kiburabugizi to the District Commissioner, Bunyoro District, June 22, 1953. Bunyoro District File Misc. Kibanda Petitions and Complaints.

69. Letter from the Omukama of Bunyoro to the District Commissioner, August 8, 1953. Bunyoro District File Misc.

70. Rukurato Central Court, Civil Case 96/55.

71. Letter to the District Commissioner, Bunyoro, July 29, 1954, Bunyoro District File Misc., Petitions and Complaints.

72. Uganda Protectorate, *Native Courts Ordinance of 1940*, Legal Notice 3 of 1940, *Uganda Official Gazette*.

73. Clan leaders did play a part in distributing the land, but only with the sufferance of the Omukama ruling through his hierarchy of chiefs.

74. In 1962 there were about 120 cooperative societies with a membership of approximately 13,000.

75. *Bunyoro District Local Government Estimates*, 1953 to 1962, Bunyoro Local Government Files.

76. For example, in 1932 the income received from crops in Bunyoro was estimated at about 402,000 shillings. Total taxation in Bunyoro in 1932 amounted to 327,000 shillings. See also World Bank Report, *op. cit.*, p. 442.

77. Not including expenditure for teachers' salaries which is met by an equivalent grant-in-aid. Total expenditure in 1962 less teachers' salaries estimated to be about £150,000. Total salaries plus transport and other personnel allowances totals approximately £107,000.

NOTES TO CHAPTER FIVE

TESO: CHANGE AND PROGRESS

1. Teso is the country, Itesot (singular) and Iteso (plural) the people, and Iteso the language.

2. Much of Teso was unexplored as late as 1908, the year that the first missionaries arrived. The district was not formally gazetted until late in 1912.

3. The term clan leader (apolon ka ateker) should not be regarded as synonymous with clan leader in reference to the Banyoro or other Bantu peoples. This important distinction is developed in detail below.

4. This scene was observed by the author in Usuku sub-county headquarters on May 26, 1956.

5. The average altitude in Teso District is 3,500 feet above sea level as contrasted to 4,186 feet at Entebbe on Lake Victoria.

6. A letter from the District Commissioner, Teso District, to the Provincial Commissioner, Eastern Province, April 22, 1914, Teso District Files.

7. *Ibid.*

8. The author's community survey of two villages in Usuku parish, Usuku sub-county, Usuku County, from May, 1956 to July, 1956.

9. Teso District Administration Estimates, 1962/63.

10. Although the Teso tribe is the second largest in Uganda, very little written information of either a historical or anthropological nature exists. J. C. D. Lawrance, a former District Commissioner in Teso, combining the traits of scholar and administrator, has done much to fill this gap. J. C. D. Lawrance, *The Iteso: Forty Years of Change in a Nilo-Hamitic Tribe of Uganda* (London: Oxford University Press, 1957). The account of Teso history is taken in part from Lawrance's work and from verbal statements of a number of Iteso.

11. For the contemporary history which follows, the author is indebted to J. C. D.

Lawrance, "A History of Teso to 1937," *Uganda Journal,* IXX (March, 1955), p. 22.

12. Lawrance, *The Iteso, op. cit.,* pp. 21-22.

13. *Ibid.,* p. 22.

14. Today etem also refers to the sub-county local government area. In the 1930's when Teso nationalism emerged, the imported Luganda terms for the hierarchy of administrative areas and chiefs were rejected in favor of Iteso terms. Thus, the county (saza) became ebuku, the sub-county (gombolola) became etem (not to be confused with traditional reference to a slightly smaller area) and the parish (muruka) became eitela. The Iteso village, the lowest official administrative level is termed "irony."

15. The data on the largely defunct Teso age-grade or age-set system is derived from personal interviews and from Lawrance, *The Iteso, op. cit.,* p. 72-83.

16. Lawrance, *The Iteso, op. cit.,* p. 79.

17. A. C. A. Wright, "Notes on Iteso Social Organization," *Uganda Journal,* 9 (1941-42), 57ff.

18. *Ibid.,* author's emphasis.

19. Indicative is the fact that only 26 of Usuku's nearly 12,000 people according to the 1960 census were neither Iteso nor neighboring Karamajong.

20. Uganda General Census 1959, Tribal Analysis Vol. II (part 3), East African Statistical Department 1960, p. 448.

21. A letter from a Roman Catholic priest to the District Commissioner of Teso, 1912 (exact date unknown), Teso Archives, Missions and Missionaries.

22. Essays were written by junior secondary students at the Teso Local Government Junior Secondary School at Aloet in 1955. They were assigned upon the author's request and then prepared in conjunction with English instruction.

23. This excerpt vividly points up the conditioning significance of environment and social system upon perception. The perception, in turn, makes for difficult cross-cultural communication and tends to increase the likelihood of misunderstanding and suspicion.

24. Uganda Protectorate, Teso District Annual Report, 1917, Teso District Archives.

25. Uganda Protectorate, Teso District Annual Report, 1920, Teso District Archives.

26. Uganda Protectorate, Teso District Annual Report, 1930, Teso District Archives, p. 19.

27. Uganda Protectorate, Teso District Annual Report, 1912-13, Teso District Archives, p. 21.

28. Uganda Protectorate, Teso District Annual Report, 1918, Teso District Archives.

29. In 1919 the second districtwide meeting of Iteso chiefs operating under the terms of the Native Authority Ordinance, decided to abolish child-marriages throughout Teso. A convention of local nontraditional quislings and foreigners altering Teso customs is an interesting reflection on the application of Indirect Rule in Teso. The resemblance of this chiefs' Lukiko to the early English Quarter Session is striking. The Lukiko met weekly as a court of justice and semi-annually in order to pronounce on the welfare of the district.

30. Uganda Protectorate, Teso District Annual Report, 1933, Teso District Archives.

31. Uganda Protectorate, Lango District Annual Report, 1934 (Special supplement), Lango District Archives, p. 17.

32. Uganda Protectorate, Teso District Annual Report, 1937, Teso District Archives, p. 3.

33. Data on the modern organization of the Elders and Parents Association was obtained in a series of interviews with the secretary and other officers of the Association in March, 1963.

34. Senior Officials and County Chiefs Conference, Minute 35, February 18, 1963.

35. *Ibid.*, Minute 36.

36. Uganda Protectorate, *District Administration (District Councils Ordinance,* Legal Notice No. 1 of 1955, *Uganda Official Gazette.*

37. Uganda Protectorate, *African Authority Ordinance,* 1919, chap. 72, par. 3, Laws of Uganda.

38. Uganda Protectorate, Teso District Files (District Council), 1949.

39. *Report of the Commission of Inquiry into Disturbances in the Eastern Province, 1960* (Entebbe: Government Printer, 1961).

40. Teso District Council, Minutes 127 and 143 of 1962.

41. Teso District Council Resolution, September 26, 1962.

42. This, however, is not an atypical situation for Ministers in the central government continue to be involved in politics within their home districts.

43. Teso is divided into five parliamentary constituencies. Teso North, consisting of Kaberamaido and part of Amuria; Teso West, made up of Soroti and Serere Counties; Teso Northeast, made up of Usuku and part of Amuria; Teso South, consisting largely of Ngora; and Teso Southeast, comprised largely of Bukedea and Kumi. Four constituencies including Obwangor's Teso Northeast are held by UPC members and only one—Teso Southeast—by the Democratic Party.

44. The Minister also disallowed the appointment made by the previous board.

45. Although a northerner and UPC, Mr. Obwangor is himself a Catholic.

46. Referred to as "Lukiko cows" by the Iteso.

47. For a more complete description of the role of Emurwon, see Brother K. Luger, "Control of Crime in a Primitive Society: an Example from Teso," *Uganda Journal,* XVI (January, 1952), p. 130.

48. Teso District Council, Minute 6 of 1959.

49. The biographical data on the Teso local government official is derived primarily from personal interviews.

50. "Elected members" here refers to those councillors elected up from lower councils.

51. Uganda Protectorate, *District Administration Ordinance,* 1955, Legal Notice of 1955, *Uganda Official Gazette.*

52. Uganda Protectorate, Teso District Annual Report, 1926, p. 11.

53. *Ibid.*

54. Relations between Council Members and Chiefs, Minute 24/58.

55. Teso District Files, 1962.

56. Uganda Protectorate, Teso District Annual Report, 1955, Teso District Archives, p. 7.

57. Local Government Files, Ministry of Regional Administrations, LGC 219-1.

58. Teso District Council, General Purposes Committee Minute No. 6 of 1959.

59. A letter (translated) to the Secretary-General, Teso Local Government, June 18, 1948, Teso Local Government Files (Petitioners, 1948).

60. Great Britain, Secretary of State to the Colonies, *East African Royal Commission, 1953-1955 Report* (London: CMD 9475, 1955) pp. 290-377. Uganda Protectorate, Land Tenure Proposals (Entebbe: Government Printer, 1955).

61. One cannot help but be impressed by the absence of violence in the relation-

ship of the British Administrator and the Africans. Violence, when it does arise, is therefore, most significant. Early in 1955 a British District Officer, attempting to outline the land tenure proposal to the Iteso in Pallisa County, was severely beaten.

62. Teso District Council Minutes, May 28, 1962.

63. This in contrast to Kenya where delegates to the Lancaster House Conference were largely determined on the basis of party.

64. Teso District Council Minutes, June 1962.

65. Uganda Constitution, chap. VIII, par. 89.

66. Mr. Obwangor, the dynamic Teso Minister of Regional Administrations, in common with other UPC Ministers is aware of the implications of the threatened Kabaka Yekka–Democratic Party merger that would destroy the UPC-KY coalition and lead to the collapse of the present government.

67. Water Committee and Hospital Committee.

68. At a two-day meeting between the Teso and Karamoja Blood Money Committee in December 1962, it was decided that the Karamoja District Council should pay 147,000 shillings to Teso for forty-nine Iteso killed by Karamajong during their raids into Teso District.

69. Unofficial clan court observed by the author on June 12, 1956. Usuku subcounty, Teso District.

70. Based on discussions with Teso Chief Judge, March 1963.

71. Uganda Protectorate, Teso District Annual Report, 1949, Teso District Files, pp. 6-7.

72. Teso District Files (District Council, 1949).

73. Uganda Protectorate, Teso District Annual Report, 1949, Teso District Files, p. 48.

74. In 1961 there were 13,392 court cases reported. The adult male population in the same year was about 139,000.

75. This estimate is based upon the opinion of district officers, chiefs, clan leaders, and other Iteso.

76. Local Administration Ordinance 1962, part VII, par. 41, sec. 5.

77. Uganda Constitution, chap. XII, par. 118.

78. The elaborate revenue system of traditional Bunyoro is described in Chapter Four.

79. Uganda Protectorate, Native Authority Ordinance, 1919, Laws of Uganda, chap. 72, par. 3.

80. Uganda Protectorate, Teso District Annual Report, 1936. Teso District Archives.

81. Communal Work Bylaws of 1962.

82. Bunyoro District Council Estimates.

83. Teso District Administration Estimates 1962/63.

NOTES TO CHAPTER SIX

BUKEDI: FROM TRIBES TO COUNTIES

1. Space and time preclude a detailed study of each Bukedi tribe. In many respects the traditional political system of the Bagwere is similar to that of their southern Bantu neighbors, the Banyuli, which is more thoroughly analyzed below.

2. The history and customs of the Banyuli are derived largely from interviews (recorded and translated) with leaders and elders of the tribe in November, 1956.

3. "Senda, a village in W. Budama, is another name for a clan leader (Baki-wondo). Paya means a bull—our warrior there was brave like a bull." *Ibid.*

4. It should be recalled that the Iteso apolon ka ateker, as an area-based author-ity figure, only recently came into being, whereas the Bunyole pattern is firmly rooted in the traditional political system.

5. See Father J. T. Crozzolara, The Lwoo (Part 1: *Lwoo Migrations,* Verona: Museum Combonianum, 1950), pp. 315-316.

6. The early history and customs of the Lwoo are taken in part from Crozzolara and from the private papers of a district officer in Bukedi, Mr. C. R. Clegg. Addi-tional and often conflicting data was gathered from a number of local Padhola informants. The history which follows is that which seemed to most nearly coincide with a majority of Padhola respondents.

7. As reported by an individual accepted as a local authority on tribal lore, November 18, 1956, West Budama, Bukedi.

8. Author's survey of the villages of Senda and Kisoko, West Budama, Bukedi District, Uganda, 1956. Carried out jointly with Professor Aidan Southall, then Director of the East African Institute of Social Research.

9. Interview with an elderly Japadhola, Kisoko Village, November 10, 1956.

10. A clan cluster here refers to an area inhabited by a number of homesteads, the heads of whom are members of the same kinship group.

11. Author's survey of Senda Village.

12. A survey of all West Budama sub-county councillors was completed by the author in December, 1956. This survey included a recording of the councillor's clan association and genealogy. The identity of West Budama clans is based pri-marily upon this councillor survey.

13. As in Teso, the Padhola chiefs were supervised and responsible to Baganda agents.

14. *Report of the Commission of Inquiry into Disturbances in the Eastern Prov-ince, 1960, op. cit.*

15. Author's survey of all West Budama sub-county and parish chiefs and a sample of village chiefs.

16. A statement made by a number of Padhola respondents while recounting this incident.

17. *Report of the Commission of Inquiry into Disturbances in the Eastern Province, 1960, op. cit.,* p. 34.

18. Of its total population of approximately nine and one-half thousand, more than two and one-half thousand are Iteso and nearly one thousand members of miscellaneous other tribes.

19. Resolutions passed by lower councils are theoretically passed upwards and acted upon by the respective higher council, the assumption being that the will and wants of the people thus find their way to the District Council and emerge in the form of bylaws and policy. If it is recalled that it is the chief who must admin-ister local government policy, his interest in the content of lower council resolutions can be better appreciated.

20. Uganda Protectorate, *The District Administration (District Councils) Or-dinance, 1955,* Legal Notice No. 11 of 1956, *Uganda Official Gazette.*

21. Uganda Protectorate, *An Ordinance to Define the Composition of African Local Governments and to Make Provisions for the Reconstitution of African Councils Throughout the Protectorate,* par. 3, chap. 74, Laws of Uganda.

22. *Report of the Commission to Review the Boundary Between the Districts of Bugishu and Bukedi* (O'Conner Report) (Entebbe: Government Printer, 1962), p. 6.

23. A letter to the Provincial Commissioner, Eastern Province from the District Commissioner Bugwere, February 17, 1936, Bukedi District Archives.

24. Combined archives of Bukedi and Bugishu Districts (Mbale District), miscellaneous papers, 1936.

25. *Ibid.*

26. The recent administrative history of the Eastern Province is most complex and often confusing. The frequent reorganizations, amalgamations, etc., reflect the efforts of the British administrators to accommodate the political system to the complex local social system and environment and, at the same time, to retain efficient administrative areas. The description of the changes is drawn from a careful review of the combined Bukedi–Bugishu District Archives now located at Mbale.

27. Unable to achieve a solution to the emotional question of whether Mbale town belonged to Bugishu or Bukedi, the British, beginning in 1941, sought to resolve the issue by granting separate status to the town. In 1939 the Bugishu Native Authority constructed its headquarters in Mbale. This building subsequently became the headquarters for Bukedi district which included Bugishu and then the joint property of Bukedi and Bugishu when they became separate districts.

28. Uganda Protectorate, *Bukedi District Annual Report,* 1944, Combined Bukedi–Bugishu District Archives (Mbale District).

29. *Ibid.,* 1945.

30. Uganda Protectorate, *Mbale District Annual Report 1953,* Bukedi District Files.

31. In 1962 the northern portion of Bugishu was designated the separate district of Sebei.

32. The history of the controversy over Mbale is documented in the O'Conner Report, *op. cit.* Our account, based upon records and interviews, coincides in most instances with that of the 1962 Commission.

33. *Report of the Uganda Relationships Commission in 1961* (Entebbe: Government Printer), p. 173.

34. Uganda Constitution, section 2, sub-section 1-3.

35. O'Conner Report, *op. cit.,* p. 26-29.

36. *Ibid.*

37. At the time of writing neither the cause nor the implications of Mr. Kirya's death are known.

38. Mbale District Council Meeting, June 1954, District Commissioner's address. Bukedi District Files (District Council, 1954).

39. *Report of the Commission of Inquiry into Disturbances in the Eastern Province, 1960, op. cit.,* p. 29.

40. For example in 1963 an Itesot from Pallisa was chairman of the Appointments Board; a Munyuli Chief Judge; a Mugwere Secretary-General and a Japadhola Deputy Secretary-General.

41. Bukedi is divided into five National Assembly constituencies which tend to cut across county lines. The two northern constituencies are represented by UPC members from Pallisa and Bugwere. The remaining three are represented by DP members from Bunyole, West Budama and Samia Bugwe.

42. Minutes of the 40th Session, 5th Meeting of the Bukedi District Council, December 24, 1954, Bukedi District Files.

43. Uganda Protectorate, *Local Government Ordinance,* 1949, par. 16.

44. Wallis, *op. cit.,* p. 47.

45. Minutes of the Bukedi District Council, June 12, 1954, Agenda item No. 1, Bukedi District Files.

46. Wallis, *op. cit.*, p. 54. Minutes of the Bukedi District Council 14/54, Bukedi District Files.

47. *Ibid.*, Minute 15/54.

48. Letter from Secretary-General to Bukedi District Commissioner, March 20, 1962.

49. *Ibid.*

50. The remaining five came from Pallisa 3, Budaka Bugwere 1, and Samia Bugwe 1.

51. This movement is led by a Padhola Catholic who is chairman of the DP in Bukedi. The strength of the movement has been weakened by a separate move on the part of the Basamia for their own district to incorporate their fellow tribesmen in Busoga District and ideally those in Kenya as well.

52. Minute of a meeting of the Bukedi District Council, 39th Session, 4th Meeting, Minute 6/54, Bukedi District Files.

53. Bukedi District Council Minute 48 of 1962.

54. Bukedi District Council, Minute 116/62.

55. *Uganda Argus*, December 7, 1962.

56. Minute 91 and 95, 1962.

57. *Ibid.*

58. *Uganda Argus*, December 7, 1962.

59. *Ibid.*, Minute 26/54, October 14, 1954.

60. *Ibid.*, Minute 5/55 January 6, 1955.

61. *Ibid.*, Minute 62/61.

62. Letter from the Provincial Commissioner Eastern Province to the District Commissioner Bukedi District, March 17, 1931, Combined Bukedi–Bugishu District Archives (Mbale District).

63. Uganda Protectorate, Bukedi District Annual Report, 1953, 1961 (court case returns) Bukedi District Files 1940-1962.

64. *Report of the Commission of Inquiry into Disturbances in the Eastern Province, 1960, op. cit.*

65. Minute 115/62.

66. Wealth is approximated on the basis of possessions and occupation, the more important being ploughs, livestock, houses, and nature of employment. Liabilities are measured in terms of wives, children, and school fees.

67. This statement was made to the author by a sub-county councillor in West Budama. However, this concept of earned income was heard many times.

NOTES TO CHAPTER SEVEN

CONCLUSIONS

1. See Apter, *The Political Kingdom in Uganda, op. cit.*

2. The author spent six months in the village of Appleton in Berkshire County, England. Considerable time was spent in analyzing the community in terms of the approach employed here.

3. The breakdown of the traditional parish structure in the eighteenth century is illustrative of the tendency for structural change to fail to coincide exactly with changes in local conditions. The old forms failed to handle new problems efficiently and, as the Webbs noted, corruption and bribery ensued. See Sidney and Beatrice Webb, *op. cit.*, p. 171. A comprehensive study of English local political

systems would as much require a consideration of the pub and related institutions as our analysis of local government in Uganda has necessitated a concern with the clan and the tribe.

4. Monica Wilson, *et al.*, *Social Structure* (Pietermaritzburg: Schuter and Shooter, 1962), p. 42.

5. *Ibid.*, p. 481.

6. Margery Perham, *Native Administration in Northern Nigeria* (Oxford: Oxford University Press, 1937), p. 118.

7. For a contrast in the development pattern of American and English local government with respect to economic transition, see Ernest Griffith, *Modern Development of City Government in the United Kingdom and the United States,* Vol. 1 (London, Oxford University Press, 1927), pp. 22-23.

8. *Ibid.*, p. 84.

9. Duncan Mitchell, "The Parish Council and the Rural Community," *Journal of the Royal Institute of Public Administration,* XXIV (Winter, 1951), p. 393. Also see Mackenzie, *op. cit.*, p. 245.

10. Griffith, *op. cit.*, p. 249.

11. For a contrast of roles within nearly identical legal structures in a Western local political system, see V. D. Lipman, "Some Contrasts Between English and Scottish Local Government," *Journal of the Royal Institute of Public Administration,* XXVII (Autumn, 1949), pp. 168-180. The definition of representative roles in the new local governmental system of Japan which reflects the impact of certain conditioning factors is well stated by Kurt Steiner, "Local Government Institutions in Japan with Comparison to Their French Counterparts," a paper read before a conference on the comparative method in the study of politics, the Social Science Research Council, Princeton University, June, 1955, p. 24.

12. In some districts the hierarchy of councils serves as an electoral college for the succeedingly higher councils whereas in other districts, *the* local authority (district level) council is directly elected. By the end of 1964 direct elections for all councils (except Buganda) will be likely.

13. Mitchell, *op. cit.*, p. 398.

14. A native of Nigeria writing on transitional problems in his country remarked that "in some areas of the Ibos these age-grades are the real local authorities in the village." See Ntieyong U. Akpan, *Epitaph to Indirect Rule* (London: Cassell and Co. Ltd., 1956), p. 37. This problem of the level of authority and consensus of meaningful political units is not unique to primitive societies. A concern with this problem is revealed, for example, in the planning of the English "new towns." See Peter Collison, "Planning and the Neighborhood Unit Concept," *The Journal of the Royal Institute of Public Administration,* XXXII (Winter, 1954), pp. 463-467.

15. See James E. MacColl, "The Party System in English Local Government," *The Journal of the Royal Institute of Public Administration,* XXVII (Summer, 1949), pp. 69-72.

16. The 1900 Agreement, interestingly enough, did not include as part of Toro, the area inhabited by the Bakonjo and Baamba.

17. Central Government Files, Ministry for Regional Administrations, LGC 1599.

18. One of the major complaints of the Baamba and Bakonjo is that of the 38 sub-county chieftaincies in Toro all were filled by Batoro except 6, and that no Baamba-Bakonjo had ever been appointed a county chief. Other complaints concerned discrimination in the provision of services, particularly education, unfair tax assessment and collection, and forced labor; but the most significant issue was

psychological—that is, the long-standing tendency of the Batoro to look down upon and ridicule the Bakonjo and Baamba.

19. Uganda Government Files, LGC 1599.

20. *Report of the Commission of Inquiry into the Recent Disturbances Amongst the Baamba and Bakonjo People of Toro* (Entebbe: Government Printer, October 10, 1962).

21. Because the federal kingdom of Toro falls under the terms of the Western Kingdoms and Busoga Act, the central government may not step in and remove chiefs. However, clause 80 of the Act permits the central government to take over the services of a local government after a commission of inquiry has shown that services are not being adequately provided. Obviously it was impossible for the Toro government to provide services and administration in the Bakonjo-Baamba counties, thus the proposed commission was in effect a bit of constitutional strategy.

22. Among the Nilotic Padhola, and to a lesser extent among the Nilo-Hamitic Iteso, specialist roles did exist but not on a permanent basis as was the case among the Banyoro.

23. The introduction of cocoa led to a change in the allocation of land in the Gold Coast from lineage to individual ownership. There is a tendency today to distribute the proceeds of a cocoa farm, and to provide for its inheritance, to the immediate children. This conflicts with traditional lineage obligations which require that property be inherited through the matrilineal line. "There is a tension in the social structure which is a counterpart to the economic tension about property and inheritance," writes Dr. K. A. Busia, *The Position of the Chief in the Modern Political System of the Ashanti* (London: Oxford University Press, 1951), p. 127.

24. Schapera, *op. cit.*, pp. 201-221.

25. Gabriel Almond and James S. Coleman (eds.), *Politics of the Developing Areas* (Princeton: Princeton University Press, 1960), p. 62.

26. Ferdinand Tonnies, *Community and Association,* translated by G. P. Loomis (London: Routledge and Kegan Paul, 1955), p. 26.

27. Aidan W. Southall, in a paper entitled "A Theory of Urban Sociology," presented at a conference of the East African Institute of Social Research, January, 1957, has suggested an interesting approach to urban research that is neither culturally nor institutionally bound. He rejects both territorial and cultural criteria and concludes that the relationship between "role texture" and density is the crucial variable for fruitful research (p. 6). He poses a continuum, not unlike that developed here, along which he arranges empirical communities from the most urban to the most rural. "The most urban communities we assume to be the modern metropolitan cities and industrial towns, while less extreme urban forms are widely scattered in time and space . . . [and include the] embryonic towns of illiterate tribal societies, past or present. . . . Rural communities may be the farming areas of highly industrialized states, peasant communities, past or present; tribal societies now or until recently non-literate, with or without towns in their midst, including both agricultural and pastoral peoples and, for completeness, the few surviving groups of hunters and food gatherers" (p. 6).

28. Institutionally oriented local government research often fails to take note of the relationship between the "formal" and "informal" structures. A functional approach does not emphasize this distinction. In his evaluation of local government research Allan Richards concluded that: "Deficiencies in local government research result largely from a failure to be concerned sufficiently about relationships . . . relationships between legal norms and government practices, between forms of government and voter participation, between units of government, between com-

munity structures and government policy, between strength and practices of political parties and government organizations, between community growth and changes in governmental policy, and between many other governmental and social phenomena. Through a broader and more intensive study of relationships, it may be possible to predict more accurately governmental and political behavior. . . ." Allan Richards, "Local Government Research: A Partial Evaluation," *Public Administration Review,* 14 (Autumn, 1954), p. 277.

29. The distinction between predominantly spatial and functional local political systems resembles somewhat Tonnies' analysis of *Gemeinschaft.* Tonnies notes three types of *Gemeinschaft,* which resemble our typology and suggests a similar transitional process. "*Gemeinschaft* of blood, denoting unity and being, is developed and differentiated into *Gemeinschaft* of locality, which is based on common habitat. A further differentiation leads to the *Gemeinschaft* of mind . . . [which is independent] of kinships and neighborhood being conditioned by and resulting from similarity of work and intellectual attitude" (pp. 48-49).

NOTES TO APPENDIX
METHODOLOGY

1. The reader will note the similarity in part to the comparative method outlined by Almond and Coleman, *op. cit.,* and the scheme summarized below. The approach employed in this study was first developed in 1957 and is basically identical to that included in the author's 1958 Ph.D. dissertation. There are important differences between the method employed here and Almond's excellent scheme. Almond's input and output functions are essentially what we term structures. What Almond treats as structures (p. 21 and 28) are regarded by us as institutions, e.g., family, church, peer group, school, voluntary associations, political party, and governmental institutions.

2. The argument of whether political organization "establishes," "maintains," or "restores" order is avoided here. The distinction is not important to this study.

3. For most purposes it is both proper and useful, in this study, to regard "function" as being synonymous with "problem." This is particularly appropriate in the study of local political systems which are required to act upon the existence of problems (undesirable states of locality affairs).

4. Tonnies, *op. cit.*

5. Talcott Parsons, *The Social System* (London: Taviseock Publications, Ltd., 1952), pp. 134-35.

6. Talcott Parsons, *et al.* (eds.), *Theories of Society* (New York: The Free Press of Glencoe, Inc.), Vol. I, p. 40.

7. Max Weber, "Theory of Social and Economic Organization," in Parsons, *Theories of Society, op. cit.,* p. 228.

8. The analytical structures are generally the same as those developed by David Apter. We are indebted to David Apter for the general outline of the structures employed as well as for many valuable insights he shared with the author in Uganda in 1956. Professor Apter has further developed these concepts. See "A Comparative Method For The Study of Politics," *American Journal of Sociology,* LXIV (November, 1958).

Index